Resilience
& Melancholy

Pop Music, Feminism
Neoliberalism

Resilience
& Melancholy

Pop Music, Feminism
Neoliberalism

Robin James

Winchester, UK
Washington, USA

First published by Zero Books, 2015
Zero Books is an imprint of John Hunt Publishing Ltd., Laurel House, Station Approach,
Alresford, Hants, SO24 9JH, UK
office1@jhpbooks.net
www.johnhuntpublishing.com
www.zero-books.net

For distributor details and how to order please visit the 'Ordering' section on our website.

Text copyright: Robin James 2014

ISBN: 978 1 78279 598 8
Library of Congress Control Number: 2014948080

A CIP catalogue record for this book is available from the British Library.

Design: Stuart Davies

Printed and bound by CPI Group (UK) Ltd, Croydon, CR0 4YY

We operate a distinctive and ethical publishing philosophy in all
areas of our business, from our global network of authors to
production and worldwide distribution.

CONTENTS

Acknowledgements

Thinking is hard and writing is even harder. I couldn't have finished this book without the intellectual, moral, and material support of more people than I can name here.

First, some parts of this book are reworked versions of writing that was previously published elsewhere. The discussion of the soar in chapter one follows form my "Loving the Alien" article in The New Inquiry. Rob Horning invited me to write on Attali, and his brilliant editorial work on that piece shaped my thinking in that article and in this book. He also edited my May 2013 TNI piece on Rihanna, which was the foundation for chapter four. Chapter two is a reworked version of my December 2013 article in The Journal of Popular Music Studies Trans/Queer Special Issue; I'd like to thank both the guest editors, Tavia Noyng'o and Francesca Royster, as well as my anonymous reviewer, for their positive influence on my work.

Other parts of the book began as lectures. I delivered parts of chapters three and four as invited talks at Luther College (Holly Moore organized this talk), Rhodes College (thanks Sarah Hansen & Leigh Johnson), Colby College (at Rick Elmore's invitation), and Wayne State (thanks Steve Shaviro). Parts of the introduction and conclusion formed my talk at philoSOPHIA 2014; I'm extremely grateful to my co-panelists Sina Kramer and Jana McAuliffe, as well as my interlocutors at the session for their feedback.

I've talked a lot about resilience in my feminist theory classes. I have some super smart students, and our conversations have significantly shaped my thinking in this book. Thanks to Ashley Williams, Jason Rines, Desi Self, and Chad Glenn, among others. Thanks too to Chad for his work helping to prepare this book for publication.

Almost everything in this book started out as a blog post on

Its Her Factory. My readers, and those of you who talk with me on Twitter, y'all have been one of the biggest positive influences on my thinking. Musicology Twitter has been especially helpful (and fun, and generous, and one of the rare parts of academia that isn't just not horrible, but is actually positively great.) I'm also grateful for the support of colleagues at XCPhilosophy, Cyborgology, SPEP, and in the philosophy department at UNC Charlotte. I'm also thankful for the support of similarly progressive-minded philosophers, including Tina Chanter, Emily Zakin, Elaine Miller, Bill Martin, and Darrell Moore, who taught me everything I know, as well as colleagues at the XCP Collective and at Cyborgology.

More than anyone else, my partner and sound art collaborator christian.ryan made this book possible. He listens to the first version of every single idea I have, and provides invaluable feedback. He puts up with ignored chores while I rush to meet writing deadlines. He keeps me from underselling myself and underestimating my abilities. Without his intellectual and personal support, I couldn't do any of this.

Atari Teenage Riot lyrics are used with the kind permission of Digital Hardcore Music. I am both excited and grateful that Digital Hardcore Music recognizes the importance of fair use. It is simply impossible for me, a humanities professor, to pay for all the lyrics I'd wanted to cite in this book; thus, I've had to delete and either paraphrase or work around lyrics from artists whose rights are owned by more profit-oriented companies. This means I can't treat their work with the same detail and rigor as I can ATR's.

Introduction

1. Sweet Nothing

A number one hit in the UK and a top ten hit in the US, Calvin Harris's "Sweet Nothing" seemed to catch on because it, like his 2011 hit with Rihanna, "We Found Love," evoked the zeitgeist in a particularly apt and compelling way. Featuring vocals by Florence Welch (of Florence & the Machine), it sets the story of a woman overcoming her emotionally and physically abusive relationship to Harris's trademark EDM soars. The lyrics tell us of a woman who is exhausted, hollowed out to a shell of her former self; she's running on fumes, living on, as the title says, "nothing." Nothing is all she's got, so Welch's character has to figure out some way to capitalize on it. Welch's character doesn't just dialectically turning nothing into something (as in the first few sections of Hegel's *Science of Logic*), she resiliently recycles "nothing" into the fuel she needs for living.

Instead of becoming some *thing*, "nothing" fuels a metabolic process, an explosive reaction that generates energy and momentum. The song's lyrics depict Welch's character as she undergoes this process. More interestingly, its musical composition *performs* the process the lyrics merely describe. If we listen closely to the song and how it works, we can hear how this metabolic process distills energy from nothing. In the same way that Welch's character has found the sweet spot at which nothing alchemically transforms into life force, the song, as I will explain more fully below, is composed so that "nothing" intensifies and augments sonic and affective energies. This is a song, not so much *about* nothing as *made of and with nothing*.

The first big musical climax—the "soar," to use a term popularized by Dan Barrow—arrives at the end of the first chorus.[1] As I will explain in more depth in the first chapter, the soar works by building rhythmic and often also timbral intensity up to a climax; this tension is then released with a "hit" on the downbeat of the next measure. In the first soar, the repetition of the phrase "sweet nothing" initiates the soar. Dividing the song's phrases into shorter, more closely-spaced events, this repetition prepares us for the soar's main thrust, which happens in the last eight beats of the chorus's first half as Welch sings the song's titular phrase, "sweet nothing." Here, the snare goes from a 16th-note ostinato to a roll, which it holds for 7 beats as the bass drops out, and the pitch of a windy, "swoosh"-like synth ascends as its timbre sounds more constrained. The song is closing in on the upper limits of ability to hear speed and pitch—that is, the point at which we would hear *nothing*. The song builds its climax out of "nothing"—both literally, with the word itself, and metaphorically, by blowing our ears. On the 7th beat, the soar peaks; the snare roll spills over, on the eighth beat, into a less intense two-sixteenth-eighth-note motive that echoes the rhythm of the song's main treble synth, and which replaces Florence's vocals as the primary melodic voice in the second half of the chorus. We land relatively hard on the downbeat of the bridge. The soar-hit structure works like a weak harmonic cadence in a more traditional, tonal song. Instead of resolving dissonance, "Sweet Nothing's" soar-hit compresses nothing so intensely it explodes into an energetic burst—here, the "bubbly," energetic bridge. *Nothing* isn't resolved into some *thing*, but metabolized into the energy that fuels an explosive climax of musical pleasure.

But this soar, and its repetition later in the song, aren't' the song's main climax; they're just intermediary steps up to it. This climax happens at the end of the chorus's first repetition, about ⅔ of the way through the song. Here, the percussion and bass initially drop out, bringing us down to our lowest low so the subsequent high will seem all the more intense. Welch sings over string synths for four bars, at which point the soar begins. The instrumentals are basically the same as in the choruses, but her vocals intensify the affective energy of this soar by, perhaps

2

paradoxically, cutting their rate of repetition. Instead of repeating "nothing" more rapidly, Welch sings it only twice, holding it for several bars, once as the soar builds, and then, significantly, right at the peak of the soar and on into the bubbly, dancy section. For added oomph, this bubbly section is repeated with the addition of vocals. The vocals, however, say nothing; Welch utters either unintelligible syllabifications (she's not saying anything) or the phrase "sweet nothing" ("nothing" is the thing she's saying). The song builds itself out of nothing, intensifying both literal and figurative nothingness into musical and affective energy.

Diplo and Grandtheft use a similar strategy in their remix of Harris and Welch's original. The original's accompaniment is cut and replaced with some trapstep percussion. The very rapidly repeating hi-hat 808s echo the percussion in the very peak of the original's soars. What was once excess is now a baseline norm. If you're already maxed out from the beginning, it seems like there's no room left to build a soar. How, then, do you make the song *more* intense? You do this by actually crossing over into the sonic "nothing" that Harris's soar only suggests. Harris's soar maxes out by pushing up against the threshold of our rhythmic perception. The only way to squeeze more out of it was to cross this threshold into noise and/or silence. And that's what Diplo and Grandtheft do. They takes Harris's soar, extend it by four measures, and instead of spilling over into a peak, drop the bottom out (In Chapter 1 I talk more extensively about this technique, common in dubstep and trapstep, which I call a pause-drop). In the last measure of the first half of the chorus, the remix cuts all instrumentals and inserts a male-sounding voice in place of Welch's natural voice. This male voice says "sweet," but doesn't complete the titular hook; instead of saying "nothing," he doesn't say anything. If the original soars up to a bubbly plateau, this remix falls of cliff, landing hard on the downbeat of the next measure. Eviscerating and hollowing out the soar only makes it more powerful—sort of like how Obi-Wan Kenobi warns Darth Vader "If you strike me down, I shall become more powerful than you can possibly imagine."[2] The remix had to "sweeten" the musical pleasure of the original, and because Harris's mix already hit the "sweet spot" (it was already maxed out), the only way Diplo could further sweeten that sweet spot is to pass over into "nothing," into a dubby-pause-drop.

"Sweet Nothing" was a very popular song. This concept of "sweet nothing"—both as an abstract idea, and as a process you undergo (as either Florence's character in the song, or someone listening to the song unfold)—must strongly resonate with audiences across the globe. But why? Why does this song—this story, this style of composition—seem to really speak to people now, in this sociohistorical moment? Why do people find nothing so sweet? What's aesthetically pleasing about the process of metabolizing energy from nothing?

Sweeting nothing is more than just a neat musical gimmick or a bittersweet story. "Sweet Nothing"'s narrative and its musical composition are examples of resilience discourse. Resilience is neoliberalism's upgrade on modernist notions of coherence and deconstruction—the underlying value or ideal that determines how we organize artworks, political and social institutions, the economy, concepts of selfhood, and so on. Resilience is the hegemonic or "common sense" ideology that everything is to be measured, not by its overall systematicity (coherence) or its critical, revolutionary potential (deconstruction), but by its *health*. This "health" is maintained by bouncing back from injury and crisis in a way that capitalizes on deficits so that you end up ahead of where you initially started (one step back, two steps forward) (Neocleous). If resilience is the new means of production, this means that crisis and trauma are actually necessary, desirable phenomena—you can't bounce back without first falling. When you can't expand your market any further because you're already globalized, the only way to increase

4

profits is by intensifying your current processes, recycling waste into resources (Naomi Klein calls this disaster capitalism, David Harvey calls this "neoliberalism as creative destruction). In fact, resilience discourse often treats crisis and injury as the only ways of getting ahead. So, for example, investors bet *against* stocks, turning what is traditionally a loss (poor performance) into a net win. "Sweet Nothing" exemplifies resilience, both musically, in its transformation of "nothing" into surplus aesthetic value, and narratively, in Welch's performance in the video. People find musical gestures like EDM soars pleasurable because *they perform the resilience we seek to embody.* [3]

The video fleshes out the story told in the lyrics. Welch plays a singer in a hostess club; she (intentionally or unintentionally, this isn't clear) convinces Harris, a club patron, to hire someone to beat up her abusive boyfriend. As of this writing, the song's Wikipedia entry interprets the video as the story of a woman "pouring the pain and frustration of her unfulfilled life and abusive relationship into every revealing and explosive performance." This "explosive performance" happens at two levels: first, there's the on-stage performance-within-a-performance of the song; second, there's her overcoming of her victimization by her partner. She fights back, both by verbally confronting him, and by having him beat up. The epitome of resilience, Welch's character takes her personal damage and transforms it into aesthetic surplus value for others, both within the video and beyond the fourth wall, to consume. Our pleasure isn't just in her character's musical performance in the club, but in her "bouncing back" from domestic abuse.

Even though Welch's character fights back against a man, she's still the victim of the Man, of patriarchy. As the video cuts back and forth between scenes of Welch's character's onstage breakdown and her partner's alley beatdown, it depicts them in parallel positions. Both are shown thrashing about on the ground, pushed up against walls, and throwing things (punches in his case, props in hers). Cutting directly from a shot of her partner's assailant stomping or kicking his victim to a shot of Welch's character writhing in pain on the stage floor, the video makes it seem like *she's* the one being beaten up. So, instead of reversing the dynamics of her abusive relationship, making her male partner the victim of male violence, this visual resonance suggests that Welch's character is still the victim of patriarchal violence. Her change in wardrobe reinforces this point. Unlike the waitresses, who were wearing lingerie, Welch was fully clothed in a suit and tie. However, by the song's main soar, she has stripped down to her bra. Now she is more intensely sexualized than the waitresses, because her spectacular performance places her as the object of everyone's gaze; in comparison, the waitresses, as scantily clad as they are, seem mundane. Her resilience doesn't fight back against patriarchy, but feeds it.

2. Resilience

"Sweet Nothing" is a quintessential example of both postmillennial EDM-pop music and neoliberal ideology because it shows how the two are intertwined. Its compositional structure, its lyrical content, its video, and even this Diplo remix all turn damage and deficit into surplus value. The songs incite damage for the purpose of recycling it. Noise isn't disruptive or critical, but a resource or raw material. Noisemaking is the means of musical, cultural, and social production. This economy of noisemaking is what I call "resilience discourse." Connecting the political economy of resilience to more abstract musical structures, "Sweet Nothing" encapsulates the main argument I make in this book: *Resilience discourse is what ties contemporary pop music aesthetics to neoliberal capitalism and racism/sexism.*

But what do I mean by "resilience"? I am using the term in a theoretically and historically specific way to refer to a distinctively neoliberal ethical and aesthetic ideal. Neoliberalism upgrades systems designed to secure against, conquer, or otherwise "cover" (to use James Snead's term) damage; the point of the upgrade is to make these systems more efficient means of social and economic management. Instead of expending resources to *avoid* damage, resilience discourse *recycles damage into more resources*. Resilience discourse thus follows a very specific logic: first, damage is incited and made manifest; second, that damage is spectacularly overcome, and that overcoming is broadcast and/or shared, so that; third, the person who has overcome is rewarded with increased human capital, status, and other forms of recognition and recompense, because: finally, and most importantly, this individual's own resilience boosts society's resilience. The work this individual does to overcome their own damage generates surplus value for hegemonic institutions—this is what distinguishes "resilience" in the narrow sense from other forms of recovery or therapy.

For example, contemporary pop music normalizes and mainstreams the noisy sonic damage of modernity's avant-gardes. As I will argue in chapter one, the pop charts are full of sounds—like glitches, rapid and jarring cuts, overdriven synths, etc.—that, just a few decades ago, were relegated to hip hop, industrial and avant-garde art music. The corporate music industry now profits from subcultural sounds and aesthetics that used to evade and challenge it—what used to kill it now makes it stronger, as Nietzsche would say. Contemporary race/gender/sexuality politics are similarly upgraded. As I will argue in chapter three, resilience discourse normalizes the sexist, racist damage traditional white supremacist patriarchy inflicts on white women and people of color as the ultimately innocuous damage that they are individually responsible for overcoming. This transforms traditional feminist and anti-racist methods of resisting oppression into techniques for reinforcing and augmenting the very oppressive institutions these methods were originally designed to resist. In both cases, noise is recycled into signal, and that signal boosts the overall health of white supremacist capitalist patriarchy (to borrow bell hooks' phrase).[4]

3. Biopolitics

Resilience is a technique for investing in life—life as human capital, or as a measure of individual and/or population-wide "health" and success. Thus, a theory of biopolitics, or what Michel Foucault calls "the power over life" (HSv1 135), is key to understanding resilience, both in itself and as a hinge between neoliberal ideology and music aesthetics.

"Biopolitics" is a trendy concept that gets used in a lot of ways and that can mean any number of things. My understanding of biopolitics draws primarily on Michel Foucault's version (rather than, say, Giorgio Agamben's), mainly because I find it the most productive account of biopolitics for thinking about music.[5] For Foucault, biopolitics is both an ideology of vitality, health, and sustainable flourishing, and a political or governmental method whose medium is "life."

As a method, biopolitics is "a life-administering power" that is "bent on generating forces, optimizing them, making them grow, and ordering them" (Foucault HSv1 136). The object of biopolitical administration is "the population"—it deals with individuals only insofar as they are members of one population or another. So, the "life" it cares about is the population's life. This population could be a nation, a marketing demographic, people with specific conditions, traits, or backgrounds— basically, a population can be sliced in a lot of ways. In this book, I understand "population" to be all the people who count as full or relatively full members of society, the people whose lives contemporary American society is designed to support. Society supports these individual lives because their health contributes to society's overall health—it's a positive feedback loop. Neoliberal biopower incentivizes and rewards people for choosing lifestyles that keep social institutions like capitalism, the patriarchal family, and the white supremacist nation, fit and healthy. It also disincentivizes individual ones that do not contribute to the overall health of society, it renders them "unviable" or, to use Lester Spence's term, as "exception."[6] Biopolitics compels us to invest in "life," to put our time and resources into ventures that maximize social viability (HSv1 139). At the same time, it compels us to actively seek the death of what and whomever diminishes social viability. As Foucault argues, "the procedures of power have not ceased to turn away from death" (HSv1 138). *Hegemony actively incites death and damage; resilient populations recover and even profit from it, while precarious populations exhaust all their resources in their constant struggles to stay barely alive.* Resilience discourse is a biopolitical technology that reinforces the line between those fit to live, and those whose death is necessary for society's ongoing health.

Jodi Dean argues, via a reading of Foucault, that biopolitics is a "byproduct" (Dean 7) of the shift from classical to neo-liberalism. It is the "effect of...the appearance of the market as a site of truth" (Dean 4). This approach to "the market as a site of truth" is the main thing that distinguishes neoliberalism from its predecessors and alternatives. But what does it mean to think of "the market as a site of truth"? It means that everything — biology, psychology, sociality, aesthetics, and so on—works like a competitive, "free" market.[7] Market logic is a site of truth because that's the instrument we use to evaluate and assess everything, to tell us, for example, whether society is healthy or whether an artwork is any good. A good artwork will perform in the "marketplace of ideas" just like a hot stock will on the NASDAQ or the FTSE.

But to frame everything as a free market, you have to translate biology, society and whatever else into something quantifiable in a certain way—they have to be *statistical*. Biopolitics grabs hold of "life" by modeling it statistically and "effect[ing] distributions around the norm" (HSv1 144).[8] For example, "big data" is a biopolitical enterprise; it seeks to statistically model and predict any and everything, from my health risks to what YouTube video I'd like to watch next to who poses the most serious threat to national security. Basically, if neoliberalism views everything as a deregulated, "free" market, biopolitics is the name for the application of this view to "life"; *biopolitics understands life as a deregulated, "free" market*.

If life is modeled statistically, like the market, then individual people's lives are measured as human capital. As Dean argues, "American neoliberalism was particularly effective in extending biopolitics via its theory of human capital" (Dean 10). Human capital, briefly, is the idea that individuals are stockpiles of wealth (i.e., capital), and that everything one does generates "a return on investment, a return on capital" (Dilts 136). Human capital is the interest and resources invested in you, the quality or intensity of "life" deposited in you, by yourself and by others; it's a biopolitical theory of subjectivity that views the "self" like a neoliberal market. [9]

So, biopolitics wants to quantify everything so it can model it statistically, like the supposedly "free" market. This is why we see an explosion of data-gathering and modeling everything, from consumer behavior, to ongoing "health" and "risk" assessments by medical insurance providers, to NSA-style surveillance of our electronic communications. "Oh my, what big data you have!" we might say; "the better to manage you with, my dear," biopolitics responds.

Statistics owes a hefty conceptual debt to acoustics. For example, statisticians such as Nate Silver use the terms "signal" and "noise" to refer to accurate, useful data and corrupt, misleading data, and the term "stochastic resonance" refers to cases in which adding noise to a statistical model improves its ability to process signal.[10] These terms were likely borrowed from acoustics and audio engineering: noise is whatever extraneous sounds interfere with the clear transmission of the primary sound, the signal.[11] Similarly, visual representations of both sonic pressure waves and many of the most commonly-used probability function algorithms take the same general shape—that is, of a sine wave. Big data algorithms and sound waves have *a lot* in common. Statistics, sine waves and signal/noise ratios are the common denominators that make it easy to translate between (bio)politics and music.

If you're interested in pop music, biopolitics is a particularly productive way of approaching the broader discourse of neoliberalism because biopolitical practices and norms are already translated into sonic terms. Also, because many musicians use the idea of *death* to push back against neoliberal hegemony and resilience discourse, biopolitics brings these critiques easily into focus. When power demands that you *live*, that you resiliently make more life for yourself, and, in turn, for society/capital, *death* seems like the obvious way to fight back. Or, alternatively, if power banks on your death, if it abandons you to die, what happens if you don't die *in the right way, at the right time*, if you don't decay *at the rate it anticipated*? If resilience is a biopolitical technique for investing in life, *melancholy* is a dysfunctional, queerly biopolitical method of investing in and intensifying "death" (i.e., hegemonically unviable practices). *If resilience is the norm, is melancholy the way to disrupt it?*

But, before I talk more about disrupting the norm, I want to further clarify my account of neoliberal normalization—specifically, how neoliberalism upgrades classical white supremacist capitalist patriarchy (to use bell hooks's term) into multi-racial white supremacist patriarchy, or MRWaSP for short. MRWaSP retools both what the norms (e.g., whiteness, masculinity) are and how normalization works. Because neoliberal ideology conceives of *everything* in economic terms, its upgrade of the means of capitalist production (from commodity to finance capitalism) also changed how gender and race work. Instead of using binaries to regulate, objectify, and exclude, MRWaSP uses resilience to deregulate the work and the effects of racialization, gendering, sexualization, and so on.

4. Multi-Racial White Supremacist Patriarchy, or MRWaSP

Multi-Racial White Supremacist Patriarchy, or MRWaSP, is my term for early 21st-century globalized Western race/gender/sexuality/capitalist hegemony. I put a lower-case "a" in the acronym to both make the acronym something pronounceable to English speakers, and to echo the older acronym WASP (White Anglo-Saxon Protestant). You say it like "Mr. Wasp"—emphasis on the "mister" shows that this is not just about white supremacy, it's also about patriarchy.

MRWaSP is an upgrade on WASP. As critical theorists of race have been arguing, white supremacy has retooled itself to work more efficiently in and for globalized, neoliberal hegemonies. Instead of explicitly *excluding* those with minority identities, MRWaSP purports to be *all-inclusive*: "diversity" and "multiculturalism" are now widespread norms, for example. Not only are exclusion and border-patrolling resource-intensive, they're also not the most efficient ways of promoting white supremacist, capitalist, patriarchal interests. As Jared Sexton argues, contemporary multiculturalism/multiracialism is a "protest less against the genocidal objectives of Anglo white supremacy than the inefficiency of unrestrained violence as the *means* of its accomplishment" (Sexton 200). You can extend this argument to patriarchy and other institutionalized forms of identity-based oppression. It is more cost-effective to include *some* formerly excluded/abjected groups in racial/gender/sexual supremacy, because *this inclusion further reinforces both the supremacy of the hyperelites and the precarity of those who pose the greatest threat to* MRWaSP hegemony. As the always-brilliant philosopher Falguni Sheth explains,

more and more men and women of color have been invited

into the offices of White Supremacy to share in the destruction of other men and women of color who are vulnerable, disfranchised, and rapidly being eviscerated through the policies of a multi-racial white supremacy...A multiracial white supremacy is a system of power that has invited in—or exploited wherever it could—people of color in order to wage institutional, legal, political assaults on other black, brown, and poor people—at "home" and internationally.

Sheth cites numerous recent examples, including African-American former Secretary of State/National Security Advisor Condoleza Rice's central role in establishing and maintaining the US prison facility at Guantanamo Bay. Though installing people of color in positions of real political, economic, and social power may not seem to benefit white supremacy, it actually does. Putting otherwise privileged people of color at the center of white supremacist institutions obscures the white supremacy (and the imperialism/coloniality), thus allowing it to run all the more efficiently. [12](The efficiency comes as reductions in anti-racist protest and pushback—there's less resistance to police.)*This inclusion is always conditional and always instrumental*—this can't be emphasized enough. People of color are admitted into white supremacy only insofar as this augments white supremacy; the moment this becomes a bad deal for white supremacy, it ends.

Though I've used Sheth's account of race to demonstrate MRWaSP's characteristic method of domination, this method applies equally to gender, sexuality, disability, and all other social identities. Homonationalism, an idea developed by Jasbir Puar, is another example of this method.[13] The nominal inclusion of formerly abjected groups—here, gays and lesbians—is used to distinguish between successful, resilient nations and those nations in need of (white) savoirist intervention. "Good" societies recognize that gays and lesbians are normal people, too; "bad" societies cling to primitive homophobic views and traditions. Similar discursive moves also distinguish "good" post-feminist societies and "bad" traditional societies that still overtly oppress women (e.g., through veiling, genital cutting, child marriage, sex work, etc.).

Supposedly liberated attitudes about gender, sexuality, and often also race distinguish resilient societies from primitive ones. Sometimes this distinction is used to disaggregate whiteness, generally along the lines of social class. For example, in 2013 World Wrestling Entertainment (WWE) featured a bad guy character (a "heel," in industry parlance), Jack Swagger, who expressed anti-immigrant, nationalist, and sometimes overtly white supremacist views. The schtick is that these racist views are what qualify him to be a heel: they're obviously odious to fans, evidence of the character's villainy. "Good guys" should not harbor the racist, anti-immigrant views espoused by Swagger, and should instead be fully comfortable cheering on Swagger's Mexican-American nemesis, Alberto del Rio. As neoliberal capitalism restructures the economy and leaves working-class and rural whites in the lurch, framing them as backwards and uneducated makes their increasingly marginal socioeconomic status seem like the result of their individual failings, not the result of broad economic forces. Just as it conditionally and instrumentally includes otherwise privileged people of color within white supremacy, MRWaSP conditionally and instrumentally excludes otherwise underprivileged whites from the privileges to which they are accustomed as white. Similarly, just as it conditionally and instrumentally includes otherwise privileged women, gays and lesbians, and people with disabilities (think about pre-murder-trial Oscar Pistorious, or Temple Grandin's recent fame), MRWaSP conditionally and instrumentally excludes otherwise underprivileged women, queers, and people with disabilities.

Another way of saying that is: *MRWaSP uses resilience* to cut the color line—and the gender binary, the line between homonormative and queer, and to differentiate between mainstreamable and non-mainstreamable people with disabilities. (And, to clarify again, by "resilience" I mean a specific neoliberal ideology, not the general sense of surviving in the face of hardship and oppression.) Resilient populations who can overcome their race/class/gender/ sexual/immigrant/religious/ damage *in socially profitable ways* move closer to the center of white supremacist privilege, whereas less resilient, precarious populations move further and further from this center. Resilience *deregulates* the work of racialization, gendering, sexualization, bodily normalization, and so on; it treats racialization/ gendering/sexualization/etc. like a deregulated marketplace.

Tradtionally, race and gender are *regulatory* mechanisms: they determine to whom and to what extent specific laws apply. They do so explicitly (e.g., the ⅗ rule in the US Constitution), and implicitly (e.g., racial profiling). Deregulation, on the other hand, "displace[s] fordist mechanisms of social control," like social identities, with "market incentives and disincentives" (Fraser 168). In our post-identity world, we don't directly prescribe what particular individuals can and can't do (e.g., employment and housing opportunities must be open to anyone regardless of race or cis-gender identity). Rather, people are given nominally free reign to be "actively responsible agent[s]" (Fraser 168), free agents who play the (supposedly neutral) market for themselves. With deregulatory techniques like resilience, "the color line becomes etched more deeply even as it is, in some quarters, dissolved" into matters of individual choice" (Sexton 244). Rather than tying race status directly and primarily to phenotype (visible race), and then regulating on the basis of racial identity (e.g., Jim Crow, apartheid, etc.), *resilience frames race or gender as an effect or outcome* of one's response to underlying, background conditions.

At the surface level, individual "choice" isn't regulated... because, at a deeper level, the game is rigged. Instead of writing rules for the game (that would be directly regulatory), deregulation dispenses with rules and regulates the playing field, the equipment, players' access to training and practice—what Foucault calls "the conditions of the existence of the market" (BoB 140), its "material, cultural, technical, and legal bases" (141). A deregulatory institution carefully monitors and adjusts the conditions in which the game (i.e., the "market") can be played so that no matter what happens, the outcome will always be one that hegemony has already bet on. It's a way of fixing the match by managing background conditions rather than foreground activity. Background conditions are not equal, and they're definitely controlled by histories of racial exploitation, patriarchy, and so on. It's harder to bounce back if you're starting from behind. Hegemony can regulate without appearing to or feeling like it's regulating—that's deregulation.

MRWaSP is deregulated, but it is also dynamic. Your social/political status in MRWaSP—is thus not taken as an immutable given (like a "born this way" social identity), but as the effect of an ongoing process—the process, as Lester Spence puts it, of being "formed according to market logic" (Spence 15). MRWaSP doesn't care so much who you are, but what happens through you: that investing in you furthers the aims of MRWaSP, and that these aims are not better accomplished by divesting your human capital. If the color line and the gender binary cut inside from outside, human from sub/non-human, MRWaSP *doesn't so much cut a line as create a feedback process*, one that's flexible, tuneable, and tweakable so that the white always get whiter and the black always get blacker, so to speak. Racialization, gendering, etc., these aren't lines that cut but processes that distribute.[14] The process of resilience *compounds* past successes and past failures, creating a probabilistic distribution of success and failure. Your ability to bounce back from a crisis depends on the resources at your disposal; these resources (i.e., your material and social situation) is the result of your response, or your family's response, to past crises. So, the more resilient you and your family have been, the more resilient you are likely to be now and in the future. Because white supremacy, sexism, ableism, and so on all shape the background material and ideological conditions in which we all work, those who have the best odds of successfully demonstrating their resilience are the ones who have the most heavily stacked decks. Moreover, bourgeois, cis-gendered, able-bodied people of color are generally the most resilient ones...in no small part because MRWaSP has to make fewer material and ideological compromises to let them in. Thus, though MRWaSP's methods are dynamic, the overall distribution of power, bodies, domination, resources, and so on, that remains relatively consistent.

The second half of the book discusses the relationship between resilience discourse, MRWaSP, and pop music in much greater detail; it focuses especially on the role of anti-blackness in ideals of resilient femininity. There I will argue that resilient femininity plays a very specific and central role in producing African Americans" as "the exceptions unable to be re-formed" by neoliberal market logic" (Spence 15).

MRWaSP is absolutely anti-black, anti-queer, ableist, and misogynist. It is a strategy for producing blackness, queerness, disability, and femininity as mutually-intensifying feedback loops of precariousness.[15] Just think about the most vulnerable populations in the US: it's usually queer people of color, people whose situations actively deny them the opportunities and resources necessary to profit from their own resilience. People in precarious situations are constantly bouncing back from adversity, but they don't get to re-invest the surplus value they generate back into their own human capital. Femininity, blackness, queerness, disability, class—these have always been technologies for extracting unpaid surplus value (e.g., slavery, housework, commodified labor). MRWaSP just updates them to work in neoliberalism's preferred mode: deregulation.

If MRWaSP hegemony actively encourages you to break rules, to innovate, and to "disrupt," to use a trendy Silicon Valley term, how do you fight MRWaSP hegemony? Conventional white supremacist capitalist patriarchy excludes people; the way to resist this exclusion was by making a disruptive demand for inclusion. If "the human" constitutively excludes black men, then Frantz Fanon's claim to a new humanism reconfigures the very category of "humanity" itself. However, because MRWaSP includes and incites difference, it is immune to the old methods of opposition and resistance (in fact, as I will argue later in the book, MRWaSP has appropriated these very methods of noisy disruption as the means of value-production and normalization). How, then, do we critique and challenge biopolitical MRWaSP? One answer, I think, is by practicing *melancholy* rather than resilience. Instead of intensifying and investing in life, *melancholics go into the death.*

5. Melancholy

Just as the peak of a sine wave turns back toward a valley, "biopolitics," as Jodi Dean argues, "turns into an intensified politics of death" (JDean Krisis 5-6). Too much life is, after all, cancerous. Death is an inevitable byproduct of life-investment. Just as a stereo system needs an equalizer, so biopolitics needs "equalizers" to filter the noise—the excess life, the death—away from privileged populations and towards minoritarian ones. MRWaSP racism is one example of this; resilience discourse is, as I will argue in the second half of the book, another. In resilience discourse, femininity is the filter or, in more electrical terms, the resistor, that manages the signal and its transmission. Feminine subjects (who include but are not limited to or coextensive with "women") are responsible for reproducing "life"...just like they've always been. Except now their charge isn't limited to sexual reproduction (and all the notions of fidelity wrapped up in its politics), but extends to caring for biopolitics' ability to consistently reproduce multi-racial white supremacist society, for the fidelity of its signal to hegemonic institutions. If "good girls" resiliently generate life, might "bad girls" melancholically invest in death?

Resilience, like biopolitics generally, capitalizes on death. The death of some intensifies the lives of others. As I will discuss in the second half of the book, resilience actively produces "exceptions"—people whose damage is too expensive or inefficient to rehabilitate. Killing in the name of "health," biopolitics *says* "life" but *does* death. Going "into the death"—investing in (rather than divesting) exceptional groups and individuals, upsetting the delicate balance of death/life—may be a tactic of counter-resilience. I call this tactic "melancholy." My concept of melancholy upgrades Freud's classic formulation in a way that parallels neoliberalism's upgrade of commodity capitalism and contractarian liberalism. As Jeffery Nealon argues, neoliberal capitalism creates value "not by conquering or assimilating new territory, but rather by intensifying new versions of familiar things" (Nealon 81). In industrial/Fordist capitalism, commodity form (understanding products as monetary values, e.g., X amount of pork belly for Y dollars) assimilated different use-values to the common denominator of exchange value. [16] Similarly, for Freud, mourning was the acceptance and assimilation of a loss into one's psyche. Melancholia was the failure to conquer and thus resolve this lack.[17] Resilience is the contemporary update of mourning; instead of conquering damage we recycle it. Damage isn't a bug to eliminate, but a feature to exploit. In this context, melancholia is not the failure to *resolve* a lack but *a misfired resilience,* the failure to bounce back *enough* and/or in the *right direction.* If properly executed resilience produces specific populations as exception, melancholy misfires because it does not produce these exceptions.

Similarly, *melancholia can also manifest as the failure to die in the right way, at the right time, or at the right pace.* Biopolitics banks on death—the health of some requires the death of others. However, if you don't die in precisely the way hegemony has bet you will, then it won't make the returns it anticipates and counts on. For example, if a banker bets against a stock, and that stock drops too soon or too late, or if it drops too much or not quite enough, then that bet is lost. Even if the banker still makes some money, they might not break even. *Misfired resilience and queered death, melancholia bends biopolitical techniques so that its positive feedback loops work instead like homeostatic holding patterns or vicious circles.*

Melancholy isn't opposed to or outside resilience.[18] At the level of individual choice and intention, melancholy is not the rejection or refusal of resilience...because resilience is not just something one chooses to perform, but also a means of judging other people's "choices." *Because resilience discourse is hegemonic, your "choices" will be judged against an ideal of resilience way whether you like it or not.* Melancholic behaviors are ones that are judged to be insufficiently resilient. Intentionally melancholic practices count on others to judge them and find them lacking; they treat resilience discourse as an inevitability. At the level of technique, melancholy is often more or less identical to resilience. Melancholy takes the "turning-a-bug-into-a-feature" routine, but it applies it to material that can't generate fully-functional features—that is, to the exception. So instead of producing dysfunction, as accelerationism does, melancholy produces *suboptimal functionality*, functionality that just doesn't feel like it's profitable enough.[19] Melancholy invests in enterprises whose profits don't register in MRWaSP's leger—enterprises that are *too* "exceptional," too femme, too black, too queer to "count," that is, to boost the vitality of MRWaSP in general.

Queerly intensifying resilience discourse, melancholy is a method of going *into the death.* If biopolitics incites everyone to live at a precisely-managed level of resilience or precarity, going into the death incites and intensifies individual-level phenomena so they produce an unviable, unhealthy mix or balance. The "death" we're going into here is not necessarily or even primarily about individuals—it's about biopolitical death, the unviability of a *population* tuned to optimize MRWaSP. In fact, one of the main ways to go into the death, to practice melancholic subversion, is to take care of yourself in non-resilient ways—for example, getting a regular, full night's sleep rather than constantly pushing the edge of burnout and exhaustion. *"Into the death" isn't about killing ourselves, it's about upsetting the balance of factors that contribute to the production of multi-racial white supremacist patriarchy and neoliberal capitalism,* making them unviable projects, bad investments, dead ends.

Melancholic sirens seduce us to make choices that send MRWaSP hegemony and neoliberal capitalism off course and into death spirals. They do this by making bad investments, investments that don't help them perform the cultural work they've been assigned by resilience discourse (that is, the work of making exceptions). Often, as I will show in chapters 3 and 4, these investments manifest as commitments to non-bourgeois black men and masculinity.

5. Siren Songs

(a) On Method, or philosophy through music

In this book, I analyze some pop songs and videos, and from this analysis I build theories and arguments about politics and aesthetics. This is both philosophy *of* music and philosophy *through* music. The two types of inquiry are, I think, complementary. The former type asks: What philosophical assumptions and ideas are embedded in musical works, performances, and aesthetics? And the latter asks: How do specific pieces of music articulate, revise, and critique philosophical concepts? The musical works I discuss do more than just *reflect* dominant concepts, ideals, and structures. They also respond to, critique, and rework them, just as any philosophical text would.

My aim is not to provide an exhaustive, unbiased account of the music. I'm trying to think with and through musical works, performances, practices, and aesthetics. To do so, I have to interpret these musical phenomena. I'm not attempting to give an historical, ethnographic, or journalistic account of what "really" happened; I'm interpreting songs to offer a theory of how they work, why they work that way, and what it all means. This interpretative work is different from more conventionally historical or ethnographic studies of music, which aim to present a more objective account of the music. I am certainly interested in the objective properties of musical works, and their historical and cultural contexts; they're the building blocks of my interpretive argument, the evidence I use to construct a compelling theory. However, as any good historian or ethnographer would tell you, the facts never speak entirely for themselves—they require, to greater and lesser degrees, interpretation. Artworks amplify this fuzziness, refusing didacticism and explicitly demanding interpretation. Often, building a coherent interpretation means privileging some "facts" about the work and its context over others. My interpretive bent is one huge bias that determines which facts I focus on and which ones I ignore. I will show how a work supports an interpretation, but I am not at all interested in making definitive claims about, for example, the intentions of its creators. Artworks support more interpretations than the ones explicitly intended by their authors. And the theoretical lenses I use to bring my interpretations into focus have their own biases and will shape the results of my analysis. What are these lenses? Critical-race feminism, continental philosophy (especially Foucault, Attali, Marx, & Rancière), and critical musicology and film studies.

(b) Overview of the book

Through these lenses, I philosophically examine musical practices and values aesthetics of contemporary pop are connected to broader and more fundamental shifts in epistemology, capitalism, and politics. I've broken my analysis into four parts: norms and resistance, on the one hand, and resilience and melancholy, on the other. These two pairs of terms are roughly analogous. Resilience is the "norm" to which melancholy responds or, in a very loose sense, "resists."

Chapter 1 is about the norm. How does biopolitics manifest as a music aesthetic? How are specific techniques of biopolitical administration applied in musical contexts (that is, in compositional and performance practices)? How, specifically, does contemporary Anglo-American pop "upgrade" 20th century pop aesthetics and compositional strategies to make them compatible with neoliberal upgrades to capitalism and to ideology? EDM-pop, the genre of electronic-dance-music inspired Top-40 hits by artists from David Guetta to Calvin Harris to Psy, has some answers. It upgrades classic rock and R&B techniques and aesthetics, integrating them more fully into contemporary neoliberalism.

Chapter 2 is about what might commonly if clumsily be called resistance. As many theorists have noted, traditional concepts and practices of "resistance" have been so successfully co-opted by neoliberal hegemonies that they no longer have any counter-hegemonic punch. If you can't "resist" neoliberalism, what do you do? How can you critique or subvert the power over life? Is "death" the answer? I think it is. However, just as resilience discourse is fueled by "nothing," biopolitics runs on death. So, some kinds of death support neoliberal hegemonies. Death has to be made subversive, pushed to the point that, when fed back into biopolitical systems, it queers if not crashes them. Atari Teenage Riot's 1995 song "Into the Death" exemplifies this strategy.

Chapter 3 is about resilience, the imperative to recycle death and damage into life. How does resilience discourse impact gender/race/sexuality, both as structures of subjectivity and as institutional norms? And how does resilience discourse interact with the EDM-pop aesthetics and conventions discussed in Chapter 1? Supposedly post-feminist, post-racial neoliberalism uses resilience discourse to regulate gender, race, and sexuality. It is both a gendered ideal and a technology of racialization. Both aspects are manifest in the "Look, I Overcame!" narrative of feminine subjectivity. Today, you become a "good" Western woman by spectacularly overcoming the damage done to you by the male gaze. As Beyoncé's "Video Phone" demonstrates, this patriarchal damage is often attributed to the figure of the non-bourgeois black male "thug." What women have to overcome is affective and social attachments to unprofitable blackness.

Chapter 4 is about melancholia, a possible way to push MRWaSP resilience *into the death*. How does the "into the death" strategy developed in Chapter Two apply to the specifically gendered, racialized, and sexualized stakes of "Look, I Overcame!" resilience? To answer this question, I distinguish between Lady Gaga's and Rihanna's use of goth damage and monstrosity. Gaga's work ultimately overcomes the damage represented by monstrous masculinities, transforming it into human and social (media) capital; Rihanna's *Unapologetic*, on the other hand remains hung up on precisely the unprofitable black masculinities good women are supposed to overcome. Unapologetic combines both the political critique of resilience with melancholic musical strategies. I examine these musical strategies in some detail, and use them as the basis for thinking feminist responses to resilience. If resilient good girls choose life, melancholic bad girls (like Rihanna's persona) go into the death.

The conclusion returns to the discussion of biopolitics, and considers adaptations in both resilience discourse and pop music aesthetics.

This is a book about how pop music and the politics of gender and race work—both in parallel and in intersection—in the age of biopolitics. It asks: If hegemony compels us to live, what sorts of counter-hegemonic potential is there in going into the death? Pop music has some answers to this question, and that's one main reason why it is important to think carefully about pop music *and* biopolitics. So, to get started, in the first chapter I consider the ways neoliberal ideology and biopolitical techniques have influenced the aesthetics and technical conventions of contemporary EDM-Pop.

1

Hearing Resilience

Neoliberal ideology thinks everything can and should work like a deregulated market, from parenting (as Foucault discusses in *Birth of Biopolitics*), to education (charter schools and standardized tests), to environmental protection (cap and trade) and health care (the recent Affordable Care Act in the US).[20] Biopolitics is, in a way, the application of neoliberal market logic to "life." Biopolitics uses the statistical and probabilistic models we see in big data and finance capital to understand, assess, and promote life and health. But *how do neoliberal market logics influence how music is made, performed, heard, and consumed?* How does resilience discourse, as a value system, shape what people find likeable or pleasurable in music, and how does it, as an epistemology or logic, influence how *pop* songs work or "make sense"? If music always reflects and shapes broader cultural and political ideologies, how does resilience cache out in terms of aesthetics and songwriting?

The answers to these questions can be found in a specific style of EDM-inspired pop that dominated US and UK pop charts in the early part of the 2010s. This genre uses different musical and expressive conventions than the ones common among most 20th century pop genres, from Tin Pan Alley to jazz to blues and rock. 21st century EDM-pop has its own musical lingua franca: it centers rhythm and timbre rather than harmony, is modular rather than teleological, and instead of bridges, breaks, long melismatic flourishes, key changes, and guitar solos, it uses "the [David] Guetta soar," the "dubstep drop," and stuttered vocals to craft meaningful musical expressions.[21] In this chapter, I'll analyze these features of EDM-pop, break down how they work, and explain how they're different from (and similar to) more conventional pop song structures. The musical techniques I discuss in this chapter perform, in music, the broader social and ideological norms we're compelled to endorse and embody. They're sonically and aesthetically *resilient*, and that's why people find them intuitively logical and pleasurable.

EDM-pop illustrates just one way that modernist and post-modernist pop music (e.g., swing and hip hop) have been upgraded so that their logic and aesthetics are compatible with neoliberal norms and ideals. They don't replace older norms and practices so much as *upgrade* them. Often, the techniques I describe below exist together, in the same song, with some version of the older phenomena to which I contrast them.

This chapter is, at a more abstract level, about these upgraded norms: both the impact of broader epistemological and political norms on music, and the rise of compositional conventions and aesthetic values to fit this ideological context. Though I'm talking about "the norm," there are most certainly exceptions to this rule. The trends I'm describing here (both political and musical ones) aren't absolutely universal, they're *hegemonic*—that is, they're widely legible, "common sense" ideals, values, and practices that saturate but do not exhaust their fields of application. I will discuss counter-hegemonic practices in the next chapter; but before talking about how to resist or subvert these norms, I want to get a clear account of what these norms are and how they work.

The first half of the chapter is about composition and songwriting. To begin, I focus on the two most prominent and structurally significant features of EDM-pop: soars and drops. These are both methods of generating musical energy and crafting spectacular climaxes; soars and drops structure a song's gravitational center. Then, I shift focus to what musicologists call a song's "foreground" and consider how rhythmic stuttering and timbral nuance are used to craft melodic variation and interest. Then, returning to the level of structure and background organization, I show that EDM-pop songs, like Manovichian "new media" or "post-cinematic" film, are not integrated or fragmented wholes, but composites of modular parts. The second section of the chapter explains why these compositional techniques work, and why pop audiences like them. To do that, I show how the features I identified in the first half of the chapter correspond to features of resilience discourse and neoliberal ideology more generally: intensification, deregulation, transmission and profiling, and MRWaSP.

1. Soars, Drops, Stutters: some features of EDM-pop

Every musical work has some organizational principle or strategy that holds it together as a meaningful whole. In order to be recognized *as* a song, and then as a *good* song, a work follows and remixes established compositional structures and performance practices. Blues-based pop (R&B, rock, soul, funk, etc.) relies on the same *harmonic* system of chords and key changes that Mozart and Beethoven used; musicologists call this system "tonal harmony" or "tonality."[22] For much of the 20th century, tonality was the main way of organizing (Western) pop songs. EDM-pop, however, works with a musical palette that pushes beyond and outside tonality, but does not exclude it—it's *extra-tonal*.[23] Songs will often include some chord progressions or other elements of traditional harmonic language; however, these are generally ornamental and do not constitute the song's compositional backbone. Tonality is an accessory, not a foundation. What, then, is the compositional backbone or foundation of EDM-pop songs? And how do they create melodies on top of that?

One of many genres of extra-tonal pop (hip hop is another), EDM-pop defined by a family resemblance of common features, including: the soar, the drop, stuttering, and the foregrounding, even centering, of timbre.[24] Looking at examples from David Guetta, Calvin Harris, Flo Rida, and Skrillex, I'll discuss what compositional strategies, performance and production techniques, and aesthetic approaches are common among mainstream EDM-pop songs, and how these work to hold a song together and make it sound interesting.

(a) The Soar

Conventionally (which, of course, means there are exceptions), pop songs have some sort of climax, hit, or other apex of sonic and affective energy. Once built to a crisis point, tension is then released in a big "hit" on the downbeat of a new formal section or module (usually some version of the hook or chorus). This "hit" could take the form of a break (e.g., James Brown's oeuvre), or a key change (the best example of this is Whitney Houston's "And I Will Always Love You").[25] EDM-pop songs score hits by soaring to climaxes or dropping to nadirs. Soars and drops are different tactical approaches to the same underlying strategy of building and exacerbating sonic and affective tension. Here, I'll talk about the Soar; in the next section, I'll turn to the drop.

Dan Barrow popularized the term "Soar" as a description of the sweeping, upward/forward-moving intensificatory gesture that is common in EDM-inspired Top-40 pop. Barrow defines it as

> that surge from a dynamically static mid-tempo 4/4 verse to a ramped-up major-key chorus, topped, in the case of female singers, with fountaining melisma; the moment the producer deploys the riff, the synth-gush, the shouted vocal-hook for which the whole of the rest of the song is a mere appendage, a prologue and epilogue that only the chorus validates.

Barrow's conception of the soar is quite broad; songs can produce the soar affect in any number of ways, combining synth gushes with key changes, cadences, and melismas. Lady Gaga's "Born This Way" soars, Jay-Z and Alicia Keys's "Empire State of

Mind" soars, and The Black Eyed Peas's "I Got A Feeling" soars, but each soar varies the same underlying formula. This underlying formula is, in its most bare-bones form, a combination of timbral modification and rhythmic intensification that builds tension up to a crisis point.

Take, for example, "Empire," which on the surface seems like a combination of rather traditional hip hop and R&B. It soars, albeit in a very muted way. Keys' sung choruses are precipitated by mini-soars in the last measure of each of Jay-Z's rapped verses. In this last measure, Keys' piano drops out and is replaced by a repeatedly strummed guitar chord. On top of this, Keys repeats "c'mon, c'mon, c'mon, c'mon," and after the last "c'mon," there's a percussive stutter that acts as a pickup or lead-in to the downbeat of the chorus. (In the video, this happens first between 0:50 and 1:00).[26] "Empire's" biggest soar happens when break leads back into the chorus (4:00-:05 in the video). Here, the mini-soars are amplified by vocal melismas, both to build tension (the 2 "yeah-eh-eh-eh-ay-ay"s leading up to the hit) and to release it (the non-verbal melismas in the backing vocals at 4:05-:09).

"Empire" was released in 2009. Three or four years later, its soar sounds more anemic than anthemic. More recent EDM-pop has gravitated away from major-key chorus and fountaining melisma toward a distilled soar focused narrowly on rhythmic and timbral intensification. In many songs, we hear these intensificatory soars as "gushes" of activity from the synths and drum machines. This synth-gush is one of contemporary EDM-pop's most common, indeed, formulaic, compositional strategies; it is also, as I will show later, one that is most clearly connected to neoliberalism. But first, let's look more closely at how it works.

This distilled soar is most clearly exemplified in the work of European DJs David Guetta and Calvin Harris, who, in their collaborations with African-American vocalists and rappers (Ludacris, Flo Rida, Rihanna, NeYo, Usher, just to name a few), have scored numerous US Top-40 hits.[27] Guetta and Harris have each developed their own distinctive brands of soars, which seem to function like the Coke and Pepsi of EDM-pop. They dominate the market, inspire many knock-offs, and are generally identical to the untrained ear, though a more discerning palette can easily identify differences.

First, let's look at Guetta's soars. He uses them to build climaxes of differing intensities to mark a song's beginning, middle, and end. In this respect, "Rest of My Life," a late-2012 Ludacris song featuring Usher, is a typical Guetta track. There are three types of soars in this piece: mini-soars that lead from verses into choruses, primary soars in each of the choruses, and a fake-out non-soar at the end (it starts like the other soars, but dissipates rather than intensifies). The mini-soar first appears at the end of Luda's first verse. Here, swooshing synth sounds that mimic blowing wind are added on top of the verse's instrumentals, building timbral intensity and musical energy. Because they often coincide with a rise in pitch, these swooshes impart a sense of upward motion or lift—the Soar's soar, so to speak. This "swoosh" is a typical component of many soars, and isn't unique to Guetta.

The song's main soars happen in the choruses, when Usher sings the titular line "for the rest of my life." Combining rhythmic and timbral intensification, these soars layer increasingly diverse kinds of sounds or voices (i.e., timbres) with increasingly dense rhythmic patterns, building up to an apex of sonic intensity. Let's break them down to see exactly how they do it (all times refer to the official video on Ludacris's VEVO account on YouTube):

First Soar:

1:10-1:18   This is the *baseline*, the nadir from which Guetta soars up to the apex. No percussion, little bass, mainly treble and mid-range vocals and instrumentals create floating effect.

1:18-1:25   *Initial statement of the rhythmic pattern*: sixteenth-eighth-sixteenth (s/e/s) pattern in the drum machine (snare) repeated 8 times; first time Guetta appears in the video.

1:25-1:27   *S/e/s pattern intensified*: Rhythmic events are more dense, and more percussion timbres are introduced. Sixteenths in snare added in penultimate repetition, topped off with a [rest]sixteenth/sixteenth/sixteenth (r/s/s/s) in the kick drum on the last beat of the last repetition.

1:27-1:55   *Peak of the soar*: Song coasts on the momentum just generated. Video shows people living life to the fullest: running, surfing, dancing, etc. Right at 1:27, at the very crest of the soar, the camera focuses on Guetta's face, his hair blowing in the wind. [28]

Second Soar:

2:26-2:33   *Baseline prime*: This soar begins at a level of higher timbral intensity than the first soar. Floaty vocals augmented by interlocking rhythmic patterns in two mid-pitched synths: a higher-pitched one that ping pongs around an octave before doing a full arpeggio of the major chord, and a lower-pitched one that, like a typical alto line, articulates rhythmic patters while staying on the same pitch.

2:34-2:38   *Rhythmic pattern prime*: Interlocking rhythmic synth patterns continue as s/e/s rhythmic pattern enters; handclaps added 2:37ish.

2:38-2:40   *S/e/s pattern uber-intensified:* r/s/s/s in kick drums replaced with dropping mid-pitched synth (descends in pitch, but is also timbrally effected/distorted as pitch descends), topped off with kick drum triplet in last beat of last repetition. The "downward" soar actually builds musical tension, like how free falling accelerates to terminal velocity.

2:40   *Peak prime:* Intensifying the density and frequency of timbral and rhythmic events, these soars create the *effect* of barreling toward a peak of sensory saturation (even if this point is never actually reached). This peak of sensory saturation, or the feeling that one is living one's life to the fullest, is the apex toward which we are soaring.

These two soars are examples of the standard Guetta soar, which ascends to a peak of rhythmic and timbral intensity, stays at this plateau for a while, and then drops off so the song can build again. This formula of increasingly intense percussive repetitions, combined with timbral intensifications (swoops, swooshes, drops, etc.) appears in his two singles with Sia[29], in "Just One Last Time" with Taped Rai[30], and in The Black Eyed Peas' "I Gotta Feeling" (which he produced). It's a basic blueprint that appears, in varied ways, in many other artists' work: it's behind the soar in Flo Rida's "I Cry," will.i.am & Britney Spears's "Scream & Shout," and even Psy's "Gangnam Style."

If Guetta's soar builds up to and maintains a plateau optimized sensory saturation, British DJ/producer Calvin Harris takes Guetta's basic soar formula and pushes rhythmic and timbral intensity past the point of sensory saturation. Harris soars past the plateau and off the cliff. Example's "We'll Be Coming Back" is a particularly clear, um, example of the Harris-style soar. There are two soars, an earlier, basic one, and a later, more intense one. Both are composed of two 2-measure phrases (assuming 4/4 meter). The first soar occurs at the end of the first chorus. From vocals to snares to increasingly high-pitched synths, the timbre becomes more intense as the soar unfolds. It breaks down like this:

First phrase (2 measures): 8 quarter-note repetitions of "back" (one "back" per beat) in the vocals, with eighth-note snare hits. Mid-pitched synth also sounds on quarter notes.

Second phrase (2 measures):

First measure: Double-times first phrase—8 eighth-note repetitions of "back" (two "backs" per beat) in the vocals, and the mid-pitched synth also intensifies to eighth notes. The snare plays sixteenth notes, or four times per beat.

Second measure: The rhythmic intensification is passed off to drums and synths, which continue the sixteenth-note pattern. In the first two beats, the snare is the most prominent rhythmic voice; the mid-pitched synth stays on eighth notes. *In the last two beats, the snare & mid-pitched synth drop out; this implies that we would not be able to perceive faster repetitions as distinct events, in the same way that we perceive still images projected at 24 frames per second as continuous motion.* Attention focused instead on treble synth, which ascends in pitch to a very high note, which is the climax of the soar.

As rhythmic intensity gets exponentially faster, and timbral intensity is exponentially higher, voices (the vocals, the snare) drop out, *implying* that they have intensified past a point perceptible by human ears. The second soar—which happens during the second repetition of the chorus—actualizes what the first soar only implies. It follows the same basic formula as the first soar, but varies it slightly, cutting the vocals and, more importantly, audibly crossing rhythmic and timbral thresholds. Here's how it unfolds:

First phrase (2 measures): This is mostly the same as first soar: snare on eighth-note pattern, mid-pitched synth on quarter notes, but no vocals.

Second phrase: In the first measure, there are sixteenth-notes in snare *and*, new this time, in the treble synth; the mid-pitched synth remains on eighth-note repetitions. In the second measure, the snare goes to thirty-second note roll, which is perceived not as individual notes but one continuous "gush" of uncountably fast drum hits. The treble synths arch in a pitch/timbre flare.

The rhythmic gush actually crosses the threshold of (human) sensory saturation: we hear one continuous gush instead of separate, countable rhythmic events. This literalizes, in music, earlier discussions in the lyrics about drawing lines and transgressing them. Unlike Guetta, who maintains the wave at peak or crest, Harris crashes it, pushing past the asymptotal limit that marks the point of sensory saturation or diminishing returns. Because it both pushes beyond the point of sensory saturation (the rhythmic gush) and crosses rhythmic with timbral intensification (the timbral flare), "We'll Be Coming Back"'s second soar is a particularly distilled and clear example of the Harris-style soar. (It also appears in "Sweet Nothing," which I discussed in the introduction.)

A method of building musical energy, the soar uses rhythmic and timbral intensification to produce a specific *affect*. Soars build musical tension by threatening to transgress the limits of our hearing, to blow out or ears. It's called "the soar" because it makes us *feel* like we're being resilient, cresting at a peak of performance by recycling risk into opportunity. Harris's soars are more typically "resilient" than Guetta's: they bounce back from actual damage, crashed soars making the next downbeat feel even stronger, harder, and more pleasurable.

(b) The Drop

The soar intensifies "up": it ascends to a peak and either plateaus there or gushes past it. The drop, a big "hit" or "climax" of loud, highly distorted (often "wobbly") bass and sub-bass synths, intensifies "down": it rapidly shifts down to bass and sub-bass frequencies and bottoms the song out. Drops de-intensify a song's register—lower pitches are literally less intense frequencies (they oscillate at slower rates than higher pitches). Just as a nosediving plane generates friction and heat, this de-intensificaiton of register feels and functions as an *intensification* of sonic energy. The dubstep drop feels like a "hit" because a combination of the sudden deceleration of frequency and the increased *physical* force of loud bass and sub-sonic vibrations jolts our bodies.[31] It's similar to the experience of thrusting forward into your seatbelt when you suddenly slam on the breaks in your car: the inertia of your body combines with the car's quick deceleration to produce a crash of forces. So it's not a vacuum of intensity, but the building of intensity toward a valley instead of a peak, a nosedive toward a nadir rather than a soar to an apex.

Just as dubstep has grown in popularity and combined with many different genres, the drop has become a generalized type of which there are many individually varying instances, including dubstep bass-drop. As *LA Times* critic Randall Roberts notes, even good-girl tween pop idol Taylor Swift uses a drop in her Max-Martin-Produced track "I Knew You Were Trouble."[32] Here, I want to focus on a style of drop common in EDM-pop, what I call the pause-drop. Compositionally, the pause-drop is a sudden, usually measure-long delay of a big downbeat drop or hit. EDM-pop songs generally soar up and then pause before dropping on the next measure's downbeat. The delay works to exacerbate musical and affective tension, making the drop appear stronger and more gratifying.

There are several ways to craft a pause-drop. Skrillex's "Bangerang," one of the most popular and recognizable dubstep tracks released in 2012, uses a fairly typical one. It soars up to the pause filled with a vocal sample of the song's title, and then does a wobbly bass drop. The post-pause musical material is repeated a bit later in the song; however, this repetition doesn't sounds as powerful as the earlier drop *because it isn't precipitated by a pause*. So, the pause makes the drop sound or feel more intense than it otherwise may be. Intensifying the pause also augments the power of the drop. For example, the pause before the final drop is stretched over sixteen measures (from the first "bang-" at about 2:13 to the drop at 2:47). Even though the actual drop is the same here as everywhere else in the song, it *feels* bigger and more intense because it's been hyped more, so to speak.[33] Skrillex uses this type of pause-drop throughout his oeuvre, e.g., before the first drop in "Scary Monsters and Nice Sprites," before the first big drop in "First of the Year," and in his collaborative remix, with Nero, of Monsta's "Holdin' On" (four whole measures before the first drop about one minute in to the track, *sixteen* measures leading up to the second drop about two minutes in), just to name a few instances.

Some songs, such as Psy's mega-hit "Gangnam Style," punctuate the pause with a catchphrase instead of a proper dubstep wobbly bass drop. "Gangnam Style"'s first soar starts at the beginning of the pre-chorus and culminates in the first line of the chorus itself (about 0:55-1:07 in the official video). In this soar, the rhythmic gush in the snare is accompanied not by an ascending-pitch synth swoosh (as in Guetta's soars), but by one that *descends* in pitch; as I mentioned earlier, a rapid descent can build just as much energy as a rapid ascent—the point isn't the *direction* of the movement, but its *intensity*. The soar culminates in a brief pause. Psy then breaks the silence by speaking the song's title. (This is actually the climax for American listeners— it's the only phrase most non-Korean speakers actually know, so they shout out as the song plays.) This phrase is the drop: speech replaces the wobbly base.

Both the soar and the pause-drop generate noisy transgression so it can be recycled and re-invested in the song's aesthetic, affective, and even ideological payoff. In this way, the soar and the pause-drop are *musical* manifestations of resilience discourse. Transgressed audiological limits are *metaphors for the listener's transgression of their limitations*, which is experienced as a source of pleasure—it amplifies the musical climax, after all. Listening to and enjoying these sorts of songs, we practice the very sort of resilience MRWaSP hegemony and neoliberal capitalism want us to exhibit in all aspects of our lives. In fact, insofar as neoliberal capital has turned leisure and pleasure into forms of work (e.g., even when we use social media for leisure or for fun, that activity is labor from which corporations like Facebook draw their profits), these songs aren't just training exercises for future capital production, they *are* the means of production.[34] If these "resilient" songs are themselves instruments of capitalist production, it makes sense that they work, at the level of form, structure, and logic, just like other instruments of neoliberal capitalism, like financial derivatives and deregulated markets. In the second half of this chapter, I explore the parallels between "resilient" song structures and neoliberal capitalism in more depth.

The soar and the pause-drop are anchor-points in a song's underlying musical form; they're part of what music theorists call a song's background, its basic architectural structure. The next two features I discuss are more foreground phenomena, methods of crafting and embellishing a song's main hook, melody, or voice. Rhythmic stutters and timbral intensification, like the soar and the pause-drop, show that EDM-pop treats rhythm and timbre (and not pitch, as is traditionally the case) as the primary organizational and expressive elements of a song. Though these foreground phenomena don't directly relate to resilience discourse, they do clarify other aspects of EDM-pop's biopoliticization that are relevant to the discussions of resilience and melancholy in the rest of the book. In particular, their foregrounding of timbre and rhythmic intensification clarifies how algorithmic intensification and deregulation have influenced musical practices.

(c) Rhythmic Stutters

In a 2010 *New York Times* article, David Browne posits the end of "the melisma era," which peaked in the 1990s and hung over into early postmillennial pop. While Browne argues that pop became "less frilly, less bombastic," "downsized," and more direct in its vocal delivery, it is now clear that the end of melisma is not necessarily the end of frills or bombast. EDM-pop still ornaments its vocals, but with rhythmic *stutters* instead of pitched melismas.

Melismas and stutters both ornament long vowel sounds; the former runs rapidly through a lot of pitches, melodically outlining scales or arpeggios, while the latter "cuts up" or hesitates the same pitch. As Browne notices, the "eh-eh-eh"s in Lady Gaga's "Telephone" "imitates a busy signal."[35] This is a stutter. There are plenty of other examples. In his 2013 single "My Story," R Kelly uses a similar string of "eh-eh-ehs." Rihanna's "Where Have You Been All My Life" cuts the word "life" up into "li-i-i-i-ife." In both songs, there is no variation in pitch on each articulation of the vowel. Britney Spears's "Till The World Ends" stutters on the "wo-o-o-o-ah-oh"s in the chorus. While she lilts up on the "ah" syllable, her pitch is relatively consistent, and the ornamental effect is achieved, in all three songs, rhythmically rather than melodically or harmonically. These widely popular songs exemplify EDM-pop's tendency to replace the melismatic ornamentation of long vowel sounds with chopped or stuttered vowels sung on the same pitch. Instead of ornamenting pitch relationships, EDM-pop *embellishes temporal patterns* (rhythm). Stuttering is just one way EDM-pop de-centers pitch, here in favor of rhythm. Its melodies reveal another way: they treat timbre as an equal partner to pitch.

(d)Timbre or Affect

Timbre, or a sound's "feel" or "personality," is notoriously difficult to describe. Timbre is related to pitch, and often hard to separate from it. If pitch is a sound wave's frequency, the *quantity* of vibrations per second, timbre is, in part, the *quality* or shape of the sound wave (its "envelope," e.g., attack, decay, sustain, and release). In a way, timbre is a sound wave's outline, its sonic profile. Timbre has *always* been an element in Western musical composition; however, instruments and programs like GarageBand and ProTools make it *very* easy to modify distinct aspects of a signal's timbre.[36] Just as a piano's interface foregrounds pitch (its keys lay out all the chromatic pitches between C1 (32.7 Hz) and C8 (4186 Hz)), contemporary music software and hardware interfaces often foreground *timbre*. Synthesizers, oscillators, delay, reverb, detuning, layering, glide, drive, pan, filter, cutoff, etc., all make specific parameters of that signal's timbre available for manipulation. The interfaces of these electronic instruments make *explicit* and *quantitatively specific* some dimensions of timbre that were generally *implicit, qualitative* features of traditional notation and instruments.[37] The compositional and expressive status of timbre has changed in part because musicians' toolkits have changed.

The increased prominence of timbre is due not just to changes in musicians' toolkits, but also to broader shifts in the culture industry—instrument design is one manifestation of the more general means of ideological and material production, after all. In his late-1980s essay on music in the age of digital reproduction,

Andrew Goodwin argues that the convergence of late capitalism and digital music technology has led pop music to foreground *timbre* in new and distinctive ways. In an interview with Martin Clark (author of the venerable *Pitchfork* column on grime and dubstep), dubstep artist Martyn explains how digital tools allow him to experiment with timbre, which he calls "delay" and "sound color": "When I'm making music I like to *set the equipment free and have it do its own thing, like how a delay machine works*," explains Martyn. "You feed it with a little sound and it makes something else out of it, transforming it until the point where it has a different *sound colour* (emphasis mine). Digital instruments (the delay machine) allow musicians to treat "sound color"— a.k.a. timbre—as a primary compositional medium (and, "set[ting] the equipment free," he uses deregulatory strategies to do so), to put it on an equal footing with pitch, harmony, and rhythm.

In more contemporary terms, we could say pop's timbre-centrism is the effect of the affective or "cognitive" turn in capitalism itself.[38] Just as "new technologies tak[e] affective work practices" and, as Juan Martin-Prada argues, "make them work as an engine for production," new musical technologies take the affective dimensions of musical performance—such as timbral "sound" and "feel"—and make them work as one of the central engines of musical composition and expression.

(e) Compositing & Modularity

While stuttering and timbre-centrism are techniques applied too EDM-pop's musical foreground, compositing is used as both a foreground and a background strategy. I get the term "compositing" from Steven Shaviro's work on contemporary "post-cinematic" film. Compositing, according to Shaviro, "overlays, juxtaposes and restlessly moves between multiple images and sound sources...Images just pop up, without any discernible motivation or point of view" (PCA 71). Unlike both narrative and montage, which are oriented by an overarching goal or perspective, compositing does not synthesize micro-level events into a higher-order logical system.[39] With no end goal or originating point of view, composited media lack the linear temporality—i.e., the sense of "before" and "after"—that makes relations of cause and effect possible. The elements in a composite are not causally implicated, but modular—any part can substitute for any other part. Modules are not fragments, per se, because fragments are pieces of something, whereas modules are atomistic and inert or non-reactive in the chemical sense (like oil and water, they interact but do not combine to form a new substance). Composites are arrangements of modules.

Rihanna's "Where Have You Been All My Life" is an example of this latter type of compositing. Its large-scale organization is a string of six different 15-second long modules. Schematically, the form is: $ABCDEFA^1B^1C^1D^1EFFBCA$. Unlike traditional pop songs, which alternate between verses and choruses and maybe insert a bridge 2/3 of the way through (ABABABCB, for example), "Where Have You Been"'s sections are infrequently repeated (only three modules are repeated more than once) and treated interchangeably.[40] Though the organization of modules in isn't totally random, relations among parts seem more contingent than necessary, more correlational than causal.

Anything can be composited, so long as it can be expressed or (re)produced in terms of a material common denominator(s). That material common denominator is what technologies like mp3s, the internet, VSTs, and Ableton provide. They standardize and regulate the background material media; this allows for superficial randomness, chaos, disjunction, and incoherence. Just as the job of the neoliberal state is to "modify...*facts*" *such* as infrastructure "so that the market economy can come into play" (Foucault BoB 141; emphasis mine), these technologies regulate the medium so it can leave the message deregulated.[41] Compositing is "deregulated" messaging.

So, we know how modular composites work, but this doesn't explain why a composited work is legible as music and not noise. Even though, as Shaviro argues, these works are "entirely incoherent" (PCA 80), they still "make sense" as enjoyable, even meaningful pieces of music. How? Or, more broadly: What is it about the soar, the drop, timbre-centrism, the stutter, and compositing that speaks to contemporary pop audiences? Why are these musical techniques ones that lots of people find especially compelling and pleasurable? Why have these specific techniques and aesthetics gained popularity, and not others? [42] As you can probably guess, the answers have something to do with neoliberalism and resilience discourse.

2. The Resilient Noisiness of Neoliberal Pop

By most traditional standards, soars and drops, stutters, and composites are all quite noisy. However, contemporary Western pop audiences hear them as music, and as enjoyable music, because they follow the same norms that organize listeners' everyday lives. They manifest, in music, the same techniques, practices, and values that neoliberal society uses to manage markets, the state, and subjectivity. In particular, they are organized by many of the same norms and techniques that inform resilience discourse. Neoliberal pop is resiliently noisy.

As I mentioned in the introduction, resilience discourse maintains social order by intensifying damage. Though Western culture traditionally maintains order and security by eliminating and/or assimilating damage through "conquest" (Jeffery Nealon's term) or "exchange" (Michel Foucault's term), both conquest and exchange take a lot of energy—you have to constantly translate the new, different thing into the terms the common denominator. Intensification is an upgrade to these traditional methods of organization and control; it effectively cuts out the middleman—the process of translation—and works directly with the rawest of raw materials.

Liberalism, as Michel Foucault argues, thinks society (and everything else, really) works like a market.[43] Classical, social contract liberalism understands the market in terms of exchanges: for example, we form society by consenting to trade (some) freedom for (some) security.[44] Similarly, "classical" music theory—also called tonal harmony—can be understood as the *exchange of dissonance for consonance*. In both cases, this exchange produces surplus value: social membership has its benefits, just as tonal compositions generate aesthetic pleasure for listeners. Tonal song structures generate musical pleasure by developing *extensively*, that is, by soliciting and overcoming increasingly strong challenges (i.e., dissonances). These challenges are necessary to create interest (just as conflict is necessary in a literary narrative). But, dissonance and difference are pleasurable and not threatening *because* they are assimilated back to a stable, consonant whole. Just as classically liberal societies "eat the other"—assimilate differences into a "melting pot"—tonal musical works ideally bring all excursions away from the primary key back into its terms and territory. For example, in Schenkerian analysis (a school of music theory), all dissonances are nested in and reducible to underlying consonances.[45] As you can see from this brief comparison of social contract theory and tonal harmony, exchange and conquest are techniques of organization and production common to both classical liberalism and "classical" (i.e., 18th & 19th century Western art) music.

As neoliberalism re-imagines markets as systems of free competition (not exchange), conquest and assimilation also get upgraded into intensification or investment. In a truly "free," competitive market, the story goes, everyone is supposedly in competition with everyone else, so we can get ahead only to the extent that we invest in ourselves, individually and collectively.[46] Because competition is so stiff, it is imperative that we capitalize on every resource we have available—we must be *resilient*. Thus, differences and idiosyncrasies become resources to be exploited

44

(e.g., in a YouTube video or snarky social media comment that gets lots of "likes" or "retweets"), not problems to be scuttled behind closed doors. Remember, what doesn't kill you makes you stronger. Intensifying noise also makes signal stronger and more intense. So, investments in challenges (like dissonance, transgression, and noise) are also *investments in your own resilience*. If exchange, conquest, and assimilation are methods for producing security, intensification and investment are methods for producing resilience.

So, instead of *exchanging* dissonance for consonance, EDM-pop *invests in* dissonance, transgression, and noise, "pushing it to the limit" rather than "eating the other."[47] It develops *intensively* rather than extensively, more like Zeno's paradox than Homer's *Odyssey*.[48] It has to develop intensively because there's no "other" to eat. Whereas classical models of musical/political organization assimilate everything to a common denominator or "center" (e.g., in the way we speak of a song's "tonal center," or the metropole as the "center" to which the colonies are the "margins"), neoliberalism tries to grasp and account for the full spectrum of everything. Nothing is excluded or prohibited, so transgression can't be a source of interest and pleasure. Thus, as Nealon puts it, "in a world that contains no 'new' territory—no new experiences, no new markets—any system that seeks to expand must by definition *intensify* its existing resources, modulate them in some way" (Nealon 82). To develop *intensively* is to exploit all the possibilities within a spectrum or "phase space." You modulate frequencies, making them increasingly noisy and irregular. Stuttering and timbral modification are examples of such modulation. The soar and the drop are also methods of intensification. They create tension by building rhythmic and timbral intensity toward, and often past, an upper limit or asymptote.

Courting and transgressing limits, soars churn out sensory and musical damage, damage that *feels* entropic—like the song has or will soon spill over into chaos or noise—but *functionally* generates order. Soars use processes of intensification to produce the kindling that fuels resilience.

Intensification isn't just a way to produce damage for resilience; it's the underlying logic of resilience discourse. Resilience is a feedback loop. Feedback loops literally re-cycle outputs and plug them back in as inputs—like investing profits back in a business rather than paying them out as dividends. When resilience recycles noise into signal, it intensifies this signal both by amplifying it (giving it more fuel) and making it more efficient (all waste is recouped). Processes of intensification both generate damage and feed that damage back into the system.

Resilience runs on political, and economic damage. Noise is recycled into signal, and previously indigestible sonic material is now easily metabolized by mainstream ears. Conventionally, we think of artworks as communicating a *meaning*, a meaning which audiences must interpret in the work. That meaning can be the inner content that is outwardly expressed, represented, or signified by outer form. Or, that meaning can be more abstract, based on something's function rather than its content (what it does rather than what it expresses). According to philosopher Theodor Adorno, the details in an artwork gain their significance by virtue of their relationship to one another, and to an under-lying, coherent whole.[49] In both cases, meaning is something that has to be interpreted—you have to decode the surface to find the inner content, or you have to figure out the large-scale form to understand how all the micro-level details fit together. Interpretation, in other words, gets rid of noise by finding the underlying or hidden signal. Resilience discourse wants us to make *more* noise, not to eliminate it. To overcome damage, we need to generate and recycle it. Trying to find the hidden coherence or meaning behind apparently incoherent phenomena is, in this context, counterproductive—it diminishes noise and gives us less to work with.

In the introduction I argued that resilience and MRWaSP go hand-in-hand: the use of resilience to cut racial/gender/sexual differences is one main thing that distinguishes MRWaSP from regular old WASP patriarchy. MRWaSP has figured out how to exploit racial difference and "diversity" so that they intensify rather than challenge white supremacy. This happens in music, too. In the same way that black *people* get conditionally and instrumentally folded into white privilege, black *aesthetics* gets folded into mainstream pop music aesthetics. For example, in *Black Noise*, Tricia Rose recounts and analyzes an ethnomusicologist colleague's rant about the "unmusicality" of hip hop: its cutting, looping, and pushing "into the red" (i.e., what Rose identifies as the central features of hip hop musical aesthetics) were inassimilable to mainstream musical practices and aesthetics. From the perspective of late-20th-century mainstream American pop music aesthetics, hip hop was literally noisy, just as it was, from the perspective of WASP hegemony, racially noisy. Their disruptive noisiness was what made these aesthetics powerfully critical of established WASP hegemony. That's why, for example, Public Enemy framed their political critique as an attempt to "Bring the Noise."

In the early 21st century, this sonic and racial noise is no longer a disruptive bug, but a profitable feature. The musical techniques and aesthetics I've identified in this chapter both originate in Afro-diasporic musical traditions (like dubstep, hip hop, and techno), and produce noises that continue to be overtly associated with racial blackness. This noisiness is no longer perceived as a disruption of mainstream tastes or MRWaSP hegemony.[50] For example, the drop in Alex Clare's dubstep track "Too Close" was used in advertisements for various Microsoft products (IE 9, Bing)—that is, for the software most corporations and government offices use. "Black noise" no longer needs to be "whitewashed" and assimilated, love-and-theft style; now it can be directly appropriated as sonically noisy and, as I will discuss in chapter two, *as* racially black.

Soars and drops, compositing, the centering of rhythm and timbre—these are musical manifestations of various aspects of resilience discourse. They are, in other words, the norm. But how is this norm contested? If resilience discourse wants you to make noise, if any unrest only makes it stronger, how do you fight it?

The next chapter considers one possible response. If resilience is a biopolitical strategy for investing in, intensifying, and managing *life*, what happens when you invest instead in *death*? Atari Teenage Riot's (ATR) album *1995*, especially the triptych of songs "Into the Death," "Delete Yourself (You Have No Chance to Win)," and "MIDIjunkies," contains several examples of musical and political investments in *biopolitical* death, which they call "riot sounds." Their work suggests that the way to fight resilience isn't anarchic destruction, but intensified regularity and orderliness. Such hyperorganization is insufficiently noisy— it can produce enough of the kinds of noises resilience discourse demands. In this way, it may be a way to create a riot of one's own at the heart of biopolitics.

Into the Death[51]

In the last chapter, I discussed various ways resilience discourse impacts contemporary pop music aesthetics. Here, I consider how it shapes MRWaSP. As a biopolitical strategy, resilience recycles "death" into "life," and treats death or as a means or opportunity for life. Resilience invests in life, but those investments are routed through death. Sometimes, that means overcoming your own failures, transforming past losses into future gains; other times, that means maintaining some portions of the population at or near death in order to maximize elites' quality and quantity of "life." In the same way that capitalism redistributes wealth, resilience is a way of distributing life and death. It invests in the viability of lives who contribute to the overall health and success of hegemonic society by allowing elite groups to receive the benefits from minority groups' struggles to survive. This means that resilience doesn't just produce "life" in general, but specific types or styles of life *and* specific types or styles of death.

For example, MRWaSP makes some queer lives more viable than others.[52] In the US, where employment and marriage are the main means of access to health insurance, laws that permit employment discrimination on the basis of sexual orientation and gender identity, in conjunction with anti-gay-marriage laws, make it more difficult for homosexuals and non-cisgendered people to access employment and marriage, and, by extension, affordable health care. Moreover, in a society where (a) unemployment rates are significantly higher for blacks, Latinos, and other non-white groups, and (b) marriage is increasingly a privilege reserved for the bourgeoisie, it is very difficult for non-bourgeoisie queers of color to access affordable health care, making them much more vulnerable to illness and death than any other group.[53] This method of distributing health care invests in sexually normal lives and divests from queer ones. It maintains the overall balance of power—MRWaSP hegemony—by pushing certain types of queer people to die at specific rates (more than average) and in specific ways (e.g., not of old age).

MRWaSP reproduces itself by divesting and diminishing queer lives; what happens when we invest and intensify them instead? If resilience is dependent on precarity, could "dying" in the wrong way, at the wrong time, at the wrong rate be a way for people to fight back against the resilience discourses that render them precarious in the first place? Here, "dying" means more than just physical death; "dying" means living a supposedly unviable life, a life that isn't profitable for MRWaSP, a life whose support diminishes the resilience of other, more elite groups. What happens when we invest in unviable, unprofitable lives? Can going *into the death* corrupt resilience discourse? If so, how?

"Into the Death" is the title of one of the tracks on Atari Teenage Riot's album *1995*; it's one of a triptych of tracks including "Delete Yourself (You Have No Chance to Win)" and "MIDIjunkies." These tracks elaborate "into the death" as both a musical and a political strategy, a strategy to contest the neoliberal co-optation of punk negation into hipster resilience. As the movie title "1991: The Year That Punk Broke" suggests, 1991 was the year that punk "broke" the US mainstream. And in this break, punk itself was broken. Punk was no longer intolerably noisy or disruptive. Abjection and anarchy fueled the grunge trend in mainstream music and fashion, just as punk's "no future" and DIY ethos provided little critical bite against a cultural milieu premised on "the end of history" and nascent prosumerism. In this chapter, I read ATR's *1995* as a critical response to punk's break/brokenness in "1991." This album transforms co-opted punk negation into what ATR calls "riot sounds." Unlike resilient noise, riot sounds upset the biopolitical management of life and death. These sounds are "riotous" because they upset the macro-level equilibrium that resilience discourse is designed to maintain. Like any good riot, riot sounds make "normal" life difficult to navigate.

This transformation of punk negation into riot sounds happens on "Delete Yourself," which reworks and recontextualizes the main guitar riff from The Sex Pistols' punk classic "God Save The Queen." ATR's musical recontextualization of the Pistols' riff mirrors MRWaSP's *political* recontextualization of queerness and queer death. If queer death traditionally manifests as negation—as, for example, the "No Future" Lee Edelman writes about—in neoliberal MRWaSP "queer" death takes the form of divestment. This type of divestment is "queer" because it targets insufficiently resilient sexualities and sexual practices. "Delete Yourself" reinterprets the Pistols' punk negation into a type of divestment or failed resilience. Pushing what Tavia Nyong'o calls "the fundamental and productive misprision between punk [music] and queer [theory]" (107), this chapter uses ATR's music to consider how biopolitically queer death might work as a *political* response to neoliberal demands to invest in "normal" life. In other words, I think ATR shows us one way to go into the death.

In what follows, I will first discuss the traditional concept of death-as-negation in both the Pistol's song, and the song's use in the work of queer theorists Lee Edelman and Jack Halberstam. I then argue that "Delete Yourself" describes a neoliberal, biopolitical concept of death, death as carefully-administered divestment. Finally, I use Deleuze & Guattari's discussion of drugs, and Ronald Bogue's Deleuzian reading of death metal to explain how "MIDIjunkies" and "Into the Death" frustrate and upset the biopolitical management of death. In these songs, ATR corrupt resilient investments in and intensifications of regular "normal" life by diverting these investments so they feed back into death. Rather than treating death as a nadir of intensity, these songs *intensify* it ...that is, they go *into the death*. I conclude the chapter by showing how going into the death turns resilient noise into riot sounds, sounds that bend the circuits of social normativity. But, to start off, let's talk about the Pistols, classic punk, and classical liberalism.

1. Death as Negation or An-Arche

Since it emerged in the Enlightenment, classically liberal humanism has been the West's dominant epistemic and evaluative paradigm. It organizes the world according to ideals of teleological (goal-oriented) development, authenticity, rationality, and autonomous agency or choice.[53] In such a context, "no future" is a radically queer, punk claim because it challenges the value of progress. Similarly, "anarchy" is a radical response to modernity's rigid insistence on *arche*.[54] The tension between the musical structure and the lyrical content in The Sex Pistols's "God Save the Queen" clarifies how "no future" functions as a negation of European Modernity's *arche* of progressive development.

So what goes on, musically, in this track? Though its lack of guitar solo and stripped-down aesthetic make it a conventionally punk reaction to glammy excess, "God Save the Queen"—especially its harmony, formal composition, and instrumentation—is a rather conventional tonal rock song in the key of A. (The A chord is easy to play on the guitar, hence its common use in punk songs.) The song begins with a riff that plays the leading tone, G#, against the tonic, A. A very powerful and common way of creating tension, the same strategy is used in the well-known *Jaws* theme. This riff also concludes the song. The journey from and back to this riff includes a foray into E in the two bridges with lyrics, and into B in the instrumental bridge near the end. E is the dominant (V) of A, and B is the dominant of E. So, the song uses a lot of very conventional harmonic gestures, like modulation to the dominant, to compose an even more conventional overall song structure. We begin in one key, progress through a few key changes, and then return back to the original key. This harmonic narrative is the song's musical *arche*: it teleologically progresses from home, through some obstacles, and back home again.[55] It doesn't negate or reject the laws of tonal harmony so much as distill them to their essence.[56] It begins in A major, modulates to E (i.e., to the dominant) in the choruses, and ends up back in A major, the outro elaborating the same D-C#-A riff that appears in the intro, except with a C# minor instead of a C# major. "God Save" isn't *musically* an-archic; it follows a conventionally teleological harmonic itinerary from tonic to dominant and back to tonic.[57] However, this shift from major to minor at the end suggests that this order may be a front for something more insidious. The song doesn't end *precisely* where it began, but in a slightly darker place. The song's *arche* leads it toward negation.

This negation is most evident in the song's lyrics, especially the refrain "no future," which is echoed in the title of Edelman's book, *No Future*. This Pistols song is a parody of the British national anthem, also titled "God Save the Queen." With lines such as "long live our noble Queen," and "long to reign over us," the national anthem uses the image of the monarch's future (her long life and reign) as a means to consolidate British national identity—the "we" or "us" in the song. "We" are the ones whose future is realized with the Queen's continued reign. In this context, "no future" is a powerfully resonant challenge not just to the Queen, but, more importantly, to the "we." The Pistols' "we" are those who lack the future promised by the Queen's reign, the people written out of post-industrial, neoliberalizing Britain—bare life, the precariat. But, as neoliberalization renders everyone increasingly precarious, what happens to the ongoing stability (the future) of the State and the national "we"? That's what the last part of the song discusses: it's not just "us" who have no future, but "you" and, indeed, the national imaginary itself. Whereas the national anthem creates solidarity through an imagined future, the Pistols' song creates solidarity through the negation of that imagined future. "No Future" negates he things that cohere through narrative of futurity, progress, and teleological development, like both songs' (the Pistols' and the national anthem) harmonic structure.

Though the lyrics of the Pistols' "God Save" show us how "no future" functions politically, the music doesn't help us figure out what "no future" would *sound* like. How does one negate the *arche* of traditional Western rock and pop musics? And what would be *queer* about that sound? Lee Edelman's book "No Future" suggests what queer negation might *sound* like, *musically*. Working from Hitchcock's *The Birds*, he argues that queer death *sounds* like meaningless repetition, "random signals," white noise, or "electronic buzzing"—more like The Normal or Cabaret Voltaire than The Sex Pistols, really.[58] For Edelman, queer death is the negation of teleological rationality, the *an* in *an-arche*. This sounds like noise—anarchic, disordered sound, sound that does not trace a coherent narrative from one moment to the next.

This noise is queer because it refuses to conform to the imperative to *reproduce*, that is, to populate the future with phenomena that continue and develop established legacies (like, obviously, children). Queer sounds do not reproduce themselves (e.g., by developing variations on a theme); they merely repeat. Repetition is key to Edelman's notion of queer anti-futurity and death. Following from what he identifies as the "repetitive insistence of the sinthome (*No Future* 56), Edelman argues that meaningless, un(re)productive repetition is what gives queerness (what he calls "sinthomosexuality") its negative force. Traditional Western sexual, epistemic, and aesthetic structures over-emphasize "reproduction" in order to conceal the presence and importance of repetition (sameness and lack of progress).[59]

This is more or less the exact claim that African-American Studies scholars Tricia Rose and James Snead make about the way Western music "secrets" repetition. According to Rose,

Snead claims that European culture 'secrets' repetition, categorizing it as progression or regression, assigning accumulation and growth or stagnation to motion, whereas black cultures highlight the observance of repetition, perceiving it as circulation, equilibrium...: 'In European culture, repetition must be seen to be not just circulation and flow, but accumulation and growth. In black culture, the thing is there for you to pick up when you come back to get it. If there is a goal...it is always deferred; it continually 'cuts' back to the start...'

As Rose and Snead indicate, Afro-diasporic musics tend to foreground repetition and, rather than trying to create a sense of evolutionary continuity—what Edelman calls "the genealogy that narrative syntax labors to affirm"—use "cuts" to create loops, which are then repeated over and over again. In the same way that a DJ cuts into the breakbeat and loops it back to the beginning, sinthomosexuality is, as Edelman describes, a "textual machine...like a guillotine," that uses the cut to "reduc[e] the assurance of meaning in fantasy's promise of continuity to the meaningless circulation and repetitions of the drive." The mutual privileging of repetition and "the cut" is one of the main ties between Edelman's theory of queerness and Afro-diasporic cultural and cosmological views. The queer-critical potential of looping, cutting, and the rejection of teleo-eveolutionary development is also central to J. Jack Halberstam's work in queer/trans cinema. For example, "queer time" involves the refusal of "growing up" (subjective evolutionary development to "normal" adulthood), and the "reveal" of a transgender character breaks linear narrative development by forcing viewers to re-visit prior scenes in light of new knowledge about a character's gender identity.[60]

The similarities among Edelman, Halberstam, and Snead and Rose should not be surprising. They are not just responding to the same interwoven networks of privilege and oppression, but to a specific way of understanding power: "reproductive futurity" and the European ideology of teleological "accumulation and growth" are both classically liberal frameworks whose centering of wholeness, resolution, development, and assimilation encourage the elision and misconstrual of "repetition."[61] Negation (like cutting) and repetition (like looping) are counter-hegemonic responses to a specific white supremacist, heteronormative *arche*, one premised on teleological development, accumulation, and growth.

Sounds are meaningless, random, and "noisy" only when evaluated against a specific standard of audiological significance, logic, and musicality.[62] Noisy an-arche sounds queer and illogical only to ears tempered by a *logos* that privileges development, teleology, euphony, virtuosity, and rationality. Neoliberalism, however, doesn't care about linear progress, teleology, or euphony; in fact, as I have argued earlier in the book, neoliberalism courts and incites damage, glitch, and imperfection. Neoliberalism co-opts classically queer negation and critical black aesthetics, redistributing their negative, critical force and putting it in service of privileged groups.

Atari Teenage Riot's citation and reworking of the guitar riff from the Pistols'"God Save" illustrates negation's waning critical power, and the implications of negation's co-optation for hardcore music aesthetics and the politics of both noise and of queerly racialized death. The riff's musical recontextualization from classic punk to digital hardcore parallels the neoliberal recontextualization of death, race, and sexuality. In the 20 years between "God Save" and ATR's "Delete Yourself," queerly racialized death was "upgraded" to be compatible with biopolitical MRWaSP. On ATR's album*1995*, death appears not as negation (the *an* in an-arche), but as disinvested, "bare" life.

2. Death as Divestment or Non-Resilience

Atari Teenage Riot is a German digital hardcore band active (with some interruptions and lineup changes) from 1992 to the present.[63] Their musical influences range from classic punk to hip hop to techno, and they are one of the most well known bands in the digital hardcore genre. Digital hardcore usually refers to a distinctly 1990s style of extreme techno, and is best described as post-cyberpunk techno or the electronica branch of post-punk hardcore.

In this section, I contrast ATR's use of the guitar riff from the Pistol's "God Save" with the Pistols' original as a way to open out a broader conversation about shifting politics and technologies of negation and "death." On ATR's first album, *1995*, the band's reworking of classically "negative," counter-hegemonic strategies like maximalized repetition, cutting, and noise/distortion parallels then-contemporary shifts to a more overtly biopolitical treatment of queer, black social death. If, in the classical conception, death takes the form of negation (the active subtraction of life, the cutting off of a promised future), in neoliberalism death is what happens when society refuses to make sufficient investments in your life. Resources are carefully diverted away from you because it's not in society's interest to make you live.[64] "Death" is the fate of people who are institutionally and structurally denied the benefits of their own resilience. Reworking the *musical* terms in which queerly racialized social death is expressed "Delete Yourself" is a microcosm of the broader ideological transformation of death from negation into biopolitical divestment. So, let's start by looking at the music.

(a) A Punk Riff, Upgraded to Digital Hardcore

Atari Teenage Riot's 1993 "Delete Yourself (You Have No Chance To Win)"[65] reproduces the main guitar riff from the Pistols' punk classic and uses it—both the riff itself, and the melody implied by the riff's chord progression—as the basis of a cyberpunk-y digital hardcore track. I will first discuss their *musical* reworking of the riff, and then consider the reworked riff together with the rest of the song.

ATR use the A-D-C#-D-A riff in two ways: they directly cite it, and they rework it into a mid-pitched, distorted synthesizer melodic motive. First, the instrumental melody in the chorus (the parts where the song's title is repeatedly sung) is a loop Alec Empire playing, on an electric guitar, an exact copy of the "God Save" riff. Second, the riff's chord progression is the basis of the verses, though this time it is programmed into a mid-pitched distorted synth. Each verse consists of 8 repetitions of this progression. In both the choruses and the verses, the original guitar riff is broken up and interrupted. In the choruses, the sample is overshadowed by percussion, most notably by a bass synth, which is just as much a part of the musical foreground as the guitar riff. The bass in "Delete Yourself" has more of a rhythmic than a harmonic function: the bass doesn't outline the chord progression (as in a traditional tonal song); rather, it punctuates and embellishes the riff's rhythms. Because both bass and riff are competing in/for the musical foreground, the bass track obscures and interrupts the cohesiveness of the riff. The smooth flow of the riff is broken up, interrupted, contorted. "Delete Yourself" uses rhythm to *interrupt the functionality of the riff's harmonic progression, to de-functionalize the harmony.*

The de-functionalized treatment of the riff is a microcosm of "Delete Yourself's" overarching compositional structure. In "God Save," the functionality or teleological *progression* of the chords is what organizes the song: we start out with consonance, this is challenged by various dissonances, but ultimately we return to consonance. "Delete Yourself" uses the same musical material (the riff) to a different effect. By de-functionalizing the riff's harmony, it takes the "progress" out of "chord progression." "Delete Yourself" doesn't really "progress." The modular alternation among verses, choruses, and the break is more determinative of the song's structure than any development or goal is.[66] The major source of tension and release in the track comes from the alternation between verses and choruses, not from some big hit or climax. Put simply, "Delete Yourself" takes the teleological harmonic element of "God Save" (i.e., the riff) and interrupts it, undoing its ability to structure the song as a progressive development through dissonance. "Delete Yourself" abandons classically liberal ideals of teleological development—there's no chance to win because there's nothing to win in the first place.

Importantly, the techniques ATR uses to de-functionalize the riff's harmony—cutting, looping, rhythmic repetition—are features of *both* black electronic music aesthetics, and queer anti-futurity/negativity/failure. The "digital hardcore" aesthetic is significantly indebted to Black Atlantic genres like techno, hip hop (the "into the red" or overdrive aesthetic Tricia Rose identifies in hip hop), and jungle (e.g., in the use of hyperfragmented and complexly reworked samples of the "Amen Break"). These strategies are also similar to the techniques and effects Edelman identifies as "sinthomosexual"; for example, "electronic buzzing" results from feedback, overdriven effects, and dead air. However, in appropriating these strategies, ATR has repurposed their negativity so it works like (dis)intensification.

(b) You Have No Chance To Win

These *musical* differences indicate "Delete Yourself's" deeper *ideological* and *philosophical* departures from "God Save." "God Save," both in itself as a year-zero punk song, and as it has been used in postmillennial queer theory, remains within the confines of a classically liberal humanism that posits death as the negation or interruption of teleological progress. For example, "futurity" (or the lack thereof) is relevant to Modern/ Enlightenment subjects who develop and, indeed, progress.

However, the classically liberal enlightenment subject is *not* the subject of biopolitical neoliberalism. For this subject, *life itself*, not progress or development, is the primary point of identification and organizing structure.[67] Or, as Jeffrey Nealon explains it, the classically liberal subject is concerned with *maintaining its integrity as it progresses through the future*, whereas the neoliberal subject is concerned with *optimizing its life*. The classically liberal subject is concerned with *authenticity of experience* (all leads back to me, to my true inner Self) whereas the neoliberal subject is concerned with *optimized intensity of experience*, wherever that may lead.

All this is to suggest that "No Future!" — in both the Pistols' and Edelman's declarations — is a critique of the *classically liberal subject*, and the *classically liberal state* (e.g., the constitutional monarchy). "God Save" argues that the promise of a future is bankrupt, i.e., that the liberal bourgeois British state, and all its trappings, have no future. "Delete Yourself," on the other hand, *critiques the neoliberal subject and the neoliberal state*: the "life" they invest in and administer is bankrupt. As they say in their 1995 track "Into the Death," "life is like a video game with no chance to win." "Delete Yourself" takes this idea one step further. The song's spoken exposition says that life isn't just *like* a video game, but that "cyberspace" and "reality" melded: "This is not just another video game...Cause reality is shit and cyberspace is gone." "Cyberspace" here is not the 90s virtual reality world of goggles and immersive images. "Cyberspace" can be read as a metaphor for the data-fication of "meatspace" (embodied, "real-life" existence). In order for life to be biopolitically adminis-tered — that is, managed like a market — it has to be quantified. Thus, in biopolitical neoliberalism, meatspace is increasingly expressed and understood in terms of *data* (birthrate, death rate, obesity rate, credit rate, unemployment rate, facebook profile, etc.).[68] Life is data, data is life. The lyrics meld meatspace and cyberspace because this is what biopolitical neoliberalism already does. This isn't just another video game, but life during biopolitical wartime.

If "cyberspace" is the biopolitical reduction of meatspace-life to data, then *we already exist in "cyberspace."* Moreover, biopolitical "cyberspace" isn't a state we can progress through and exit—there's no drive to "get out." [69] Instead of progressing forward toward some goal, we are caught in feedback loops...loops from which we can emerge resiliently, with profits, or precariously, just barely surviving. The command to "delete yourself" is a response not to the classically liberal demand to reproduce and progress toward the future, and but the ever-present neoliberal demand to live or let die. Similarly, "Delete Yourself's" losers aren't abject "flowers in the dustbin," but players who stuck in the game's grind with no possibility for success.

Following the guitar riff from "God Save" to "Delete Yourself," I've shown that the musical differences between the two songs track broader, deeper philosophical and political differences. Pistols-style negation is a historically and ideologically specific concept of death (the power to take life) and social non-belonging (abjection, constitutive exclusion). Just as ATR musically rework the Pistols's riff, neoliberalism *upgrades* negation so that death and social non-belonging are compatible with biopolitical logics of investment, intensification, and compounding interest. The next section considers biopolitical death in more depth: first ideologically, then musically.

(c) The Biopolitics of Death

i. Death as divestment

In MRWaSP, death is the effect of divestment, not exclusion. You're allowed to play the game, but you aren't given enough resources to finish it, because your flourishing is not sufficiently beneficial to society to justify further investment. In biopolitical neoliberalism, "life" is a competitive, deregulated marketplace of success and vibrancy; from this perspective, life *is* a game in which there are winners and losers. We are supposed to believe that anyone who plays can, with the proper skill and strategy (that is, with proper resilience), eventually win. But, this belief is incorrect: there are classes of people who don't even have a chance. For example, "Into the Death" claims that "our life is what they control," and it is controlled not so much by repression as by disinvestment. If, as Elias sings, "there's no good reason to keep you alive," you are left to "die, die, die." In other words, you aren't given the resources—or even the opportunity to procure the resources—you need to pull yourself up by the bootstraps.

For example, when the Berlin Wall fell, the new German state had to decide how to best allocate its resources. Without a clearly-drawn national border to separate "healthy" individuals and institutions from precarious, unsustainable ones, the distinction had to be made in other terms. [70] Whose lives were worth fostering, and whose weren't? Using reunification as an excuse to neoliberalize, Germany redistributed its resources to invest in both those groups/individuals who could be competitive and successful in globalized liberal democratic capitalism, and its own image as a progressive, multicultural liberal democratic state. If your individual resilience contributed to the nation's resilience, then you got a chance to win.

Resilience discourse produces a permanent underclass of precarious redshirts. These redshirts are fodder for other players' successes; their guaranteed death is what gives others a chance to win.[71] Some might call this group relegated to death "bare life." [72] Scraping by, barely surviving, unable to profit from the surplus value one's labor generates (e.g., by storing up the 'life' or 'credit' one needs to win a video game), "bare life" is the other side of resilience discourse. Biopolitical death isn't the negation of life, but insufficient resilience. Understood through the lens of resilience discourse, biopolitical death is not a subtraction, opposition to, or rejection of life, but an investment in "unviable" practices, practices that may help you survive, but won't help you win. Just as resilience intensifies "life," death intensifies "unviability."

Queerness and blackness are carriers of biopolitical death because this death is the fate of what or whomever was too racially and sexually "unruly" (to use philosopher Falguni Sheth's term) to reproduce and support post-racial, post-feminist, "homonational" society. Instead of constitutively excluding impurities, MRWaSP maintains the ideal balance of diverse elements by *divesting* itself of those who cannot success-fully keep up with the demands of modern life. Live in a way that doesn't upset this balance, or we'll leave you to die. In MRWaSP, death is biopolitical.

ii. Queer death, musically resignified

ATR's *1995* is, in many ways, an album about the biopolitics of death.[73]

Musically, *representations or expressions of death-as-negation are "remixed" to work biopolitically.* Conventionally black/queer-critical techniques like cutting, looping, and distortion don't interrupt but *overwhelm*—they work less like deconstruction (breaking down grand narratives) and more like a distributed denial-of-service (DDOS) attack (overloading servers with excessive demands).

Tom Briehan's *Pitchfork* review describes how their emphasis on repetition, noise, and rhythmic/timbral overdrive come to be interpreted as experiences of biopolitical death. "Their specific chaotic combination," he argues,

added up to German-accented ridiculousness ("Deutschland! Has gotta! *Diiieeee!*") screamed over hyperspeed 808 pounds and digitally treated guitar fuzz; it seemed scientifically engineered to annoy as many people as possible. It was impossible to dance or talk or read or drive or do *anything else* while they were playing.

In Briehan's experience, ATR's "hyperspeed 808 pounds," the "fuzz," and their "scientifically engineered" sonic nuisances are all *overwhelming*—they interrupt his ability to perform at all, let alone at his best. He's trying to resiliently push himself to his limits, but these sounds overclock him past the point of bouncing back. His attention is so overwhelmed by ATR's music that it is just on the verge of failing (at dancing, talking, reading, or driving). ATR's music is so intense (so fast, so densely noisy) that it jams both hegemony's and Briehan's ability to invest in and capitalize on himself. It makes him, in other words, precarious.[74] This feeling of precarity, then, is an affective expression of biopolitical death...the biopolitical death that multi-racial white supremacist patriarchy puts in assemblage with blackness/ queerness. This is one way the musical aesthetics and compositional choices on *1995* express or reflect the experience of queerly racialized biopolitical death.

To further explore both ATR's use of intensification to express the phenomenon of biopolitical death, its racial/sexual politics, and their role in the mainstream appropriation of queer/black critical responses to biopolitical death, I consider, in the next section, an interpretation of two more tracks on *1995*, "MIDIjunkies" and "Into the Death."

3. Taking MIDIjunkies Into the Death

"MIDIjunkies" and "Into the Death" form a triptych with "Delete Yourself." They share musical material and lyrical references; for example, the apparently non-metrical noodling at the end of "MIDIjunkies" fades into "Delete Yourself," and "Into the Death's" line "Like is life a video game with no chance to win" summarizes its "Delete Yourself"'s lyrical content, just as "Into the Death" directly references to "MIDIjunkies"'s title. These songs are essential components of "Delete Yourself"'s account of biopolitical death. In "Midijunkies," an allusion to Deleuze & Guattari's *A Thousand Plateaus*, illustrates exactly how neoliberal "control societies" control for biopolitical death.[75] "Into the Death" suggests one way to jam these mechanisms of control, illustrating how the queer necropolitics of "No Future" can be upgraded to contest the resilient production of life. Instead of recycling death into life, noise into signal, "Into the Death" intensifies sonic overdrive and breakdown. Making noise noisier, it queers resilience, bending its circuits to invest in death rather than (normal) life.[76] However, because this musical queering of resilience relies on the appropriation of black Atlantic underground musics, "Into the Death" also suggests that neoliberal race/gender/sexuality politics complicates already-fraught histories and politics of cultural appropriation among straight black, white queer, and queer of color musical subcultures.

(a) MIDIjunkies

In classically liberal, modernist regimes, repetition, looping, and electric buzzing were illegible to hegemony, and thus queerly racialized alternatives to it. However, by the 1990s, these queerly racialized sounds register as standardized deviances that technology already controls for. Specifically, they're preprogrammed right into MIDI interfaces, VSTs (Virtual Studio Technologies), sequencers, samplers, and all sorts of other electronic music media. MIDIs (and other electronic instruments) give easy access to traditionally counter-hegemonic black/queer critical strategies of repetition, looping, and electronic buzzing, strategies that were developed by repurposing music tech to work in non-standard ways.[77] Standard issue consumer audio tech gave users easy access to intensities that are excessively high or excessively low, and thus might *appear* to undermine hegemony's attempts to keep things within limits. However, as

"MIDIjunkies" warns, this apparent transgression is only a faux subversion: MIDI overdose fucks *you* up, not hegemony.

As Deleuze and Guattari argue in *A Thousand Plateaus*, drugs can induce a sort of faux-subversion of neoliberal logics of intensity (in Deleuze's terms, "control society"). According to them, getting fucked up on drugs mimics the experience of radical critique—what they call "deterritorialization." Drugs "change perception," alter its speed and intensity, and thus can reorganize epistemic and perceptual frameworks (TP 282), making perceptible what was, in hegemonic regimes, imperceptible. Psychedelics do this, amphetamines do this, even alcohol and caffeine do this. However, they argue that in drug use, "the deterritorializations remain relative" (TP 285) because highs are finite and everybody comes down at some point. Drug use happens in "the context of relative thresholds," like human physiology and drug chemistry, "that restrict" drug use to the "imitation" of deterritorialization (TP 284). Drug addiction even further restricts the possibilities opened up by drug use: addicts go "down, instead of high…the causal line, creative line, or line of flight" opened by drug use "turns into a line of death and abolition" (TP 285). In other words, drugs fuck up *junkies*, not hegemony…The trick is that hegemony convinces these "junkies" that their dejection is actually transgressive, even though their deviations are already standardized and accounted for. These losers fail in terms that hegemony is entirely comfortable with. For example, the American basic cable programs "Intervention" and "My Strange Addiction" transform individual losers into revenue streams; their addictions aren't disruptive, but normalized damage that fuels the contemporary culture industry.

ATR's song "MIDIjunkies" treats MIDIs as drugs in the DeleuzoGuattarian sense. MIDIs can be used in ways that make artists feel like they're fucking shit up, subverting hegemony's *arche*…but the do so in very carefully controlled and limited ways. One might think these electronic tools allow us to intensify repetition and noisiness beyond the limits of human perception or kinesthetic capacity. However, all hardware and software have limits: knobs only go up to 10, so to speak (and however you measure it, potentiometers do have mechanical and electrical limits). In DeleuzoGuattarian terms, MIDIs make planes of consistency *within* a plane of organization (i.e., the technological and mechanical limits of the MIDI program, the potentiometers on the control devices, etc.). The most prominent example of this "druggy" effect is the song's use of apparently unmetered sound. To the causal listener, the last part of the song—about 4 minutes in, after the bass drops out and all that's left are various treble synths—might appear to abandon the song's solid 4/4 and veer off into nonmetric noodling (the same noodling, notably, that begins "Delete Yourself"). There is no regular bass or percussion pattern to follow, so casual listeners could easily loose the downbeat. This section seems to exemplify what Deleuze and Guattari call, "a liberation of time, Aion, *a nonpulsed time for a floating music,* as Boulez says, an electronic music in which forms give way to pure modifications of speed" (TP 267; emphasis mine).

But these sections are not unmetered. The noodling still falls into four-bar phrases: every four bars, the musical motive changes slightly. The song itself is only *superficially* non-metric. More deeply attentive listeners, such as the fans dancing along at shows, kept meter with their bodies as they fervently pogoed up and down to the beat (in lieu of the bass and percussion tracks doing it for them).[78] "MIDIjunkies"'s apparently nonmetric breakdown rests on a very tight metric foundation. Similar approaches are found in African-American music. For example, in the *Moonwalker* version of Michael Jackson's "Smooth Criminal," there is a vocal breakdown that, to the casual listener, is composed of aleatory, non-metric groans and moans. As the video's staging shows, Jackson is in control throughout, carefully orchestrating what looks like unmanaged chaos (e.g., he keeps time by snapping his fingers or moving his body). As the *music* in MIDIjunkies shows, this apparent transgression of metric *arche* isn't, in fact, a transgression. "Drug"-induced excesses are, as Deleuze and Guattari put it, ultimately faux deterritorializations.

I think it's important to read "MIDIjunkies" through Deleuze and Guattari not only because ATR had explicit connections to Deleuzian thought (e.g., Empire's involvement with Mille Plateaux records), but also because its critique of druggy, free-floating, meterless time clarifies one of the main limitations of José Esteban Muñoz's concept of ecstatic queer utopianism. He theorizes ecstatic utopianism through both queer/punk performance and through comparisons to MDMA, once commonly referred to as ecstasy ("molly" is the preferred street name nowadays). For Muñoz, ecstasy—literally ek-stasis, excessive, ornamental, non-functional pleasure that transgresses the limitations of straight time and commodity capitalism—is both a critique of and alternative to Edelmanian negativity. Instead of the negation or rejection of the future, ecstasy is, as Muñoz explains via Marcuse, "the liberation from time" (133), specifically, the linear progressive rationality of "straight" capitalist time (as represented, for example, by Marcuse's concept of the performance principle).[79] Queer ecstasy is an excessiveness that works, like a drug, as "a surplus that pushes one off course, no longer able to contribute labor power at the proper tempo" (Munoz 154). However, what both Deleuze & Guattari and "MIDIjunkies" demonstrate is that this druggy, irregular temporality is, in neoliberalism, decidedly not queer—it's the very measure of healthy deregulated economy (of capital, of desire) in which rigidly controlled background conditions generate increasingly eccentric foreground events. This deterritorialization is only relative; not even time is liberated because in neoliberalism, labor power is *supposed* to be offbeat and irregular.[80]

The real junkies here are the ones addicted to classically

liberal concepts of death and resistance as negation—the ones who think "flowers in the dustbin" are actually oppositional, and not the compost fueling neoliberal biopower. Non-metrical music is an-archic, and like the Pistols, treats death or negation in a classically liberal framework. Because neoliberalism always-already co-opts death, randomness, and an-arche, these strategies do not challenge biopolitical hegemonies. Neoliberal regimes use biopolitical administration to regularize death; a normalized variable, death is not a form of distortion. The task, then, is to *distort death*. This is what happens on "Into the Death," which *hyper-intensifies* biopolitical or metric regulation.

(b) Into The Death

Drug users believed that drugs would grant them the plane, when in fact the plane must distill its own drugs (D&G TP 286).

"Into the Death" distills death, makes it *too intense*. Instead of negating, opposing, or anarchically deconstructing resilience discourse and MRWaSP biopolitics, the song approaches them in their own terms—intensification and divestment, making live and letting die. "Into the Death" plugs technologies of "life" (investment, amplification, resilience) into death. Bending hegemonic circuits, "Into the Death" distorts biopolitical death beyond the parameters set for it, parameters that optimize the viability and resilience of privileged populations and institutions. Sonically, these distortions manifest as what band leader Alec Empire calls "riot sounds." In this section, I'll first explain what ATR mean by "riot sounds," and then use "Into the Death" to illustrate how they work sonically. Finally, I will consider how "riot sounds" might work as a model for anti-racist queer political responses to neoliberalism. A "drug" distilled from biopolitics' own plane, investments in death bend MRWaSP's circuits, inciting a riot in the management of life.

If an-arche is the negation of order, "rioting" is the *intensification* of order. Empire describes "riot sounds" as "functional music," a sort of biohacking: "with the way we program the beats and use certain frequencies, it has this effect on your adrenaline." ATR use MIDIS and other biopolitical/algorithmic tools to produce abnormal, inappropriate effects and affects:

> It's the riot sounds, man...There's something about distortion when it's applied in a certain way... that creates these overtones, and it does something with the brain. It triggers certain senses that we can't explain with normal music science, the way we know it maybe from Western European music.

ATR aren't losing or forfeiting control, but taking a specific, albeit atypical, type of control—they're distorting sound waves in "certain way[s]," ways that must be precisely, expertly hacked. To make a "riot," soundwaves and brainwaves have to be carefully identified, targeted, and manipulated. Rioting isn't anarchy, it's biopolitical management for counter-hegemonic ends. ATR takes the tools biopolitical neoliberalism uses to invest in life, like algorithms (statistical data, synthesizer patches), and applies them instead to death—that is, to processes that reduce the viability of MRWaSP capitalism. It carefully, microscopically, and vigilantly *intensifies death*. So, for example, while neoliberal management strategies invest in promoting flexibility and adaptability, riotous, queer management strategies invest in the opposite—stringent, uncompromising order.[81]

It seems counterintuitive to say that stringent order is the way to contest social control. That's because classical liberalism treats anarchy and negation as remedies to the hegemonic insistence on order and discipline. However, *resilience discourse normalizes disorder*; anarchy and negation are the means of capitalist production and MRWaSP reproduction. As Steven Shaviro argues,

In the control society, or in the post-Fordist information economy…the only fixed requirement is precisely to maintain an underlying *flexibility*: an ability to take on any shape as needed, a capacity to adapt quickly and smoothly to the demands of any given form, or any procedure, whatsoever" (PCA 15).

Neoliberalism uses biopolitical management to optimize flexibility. Precise, exact quantization can undermine this "one requirement." The key is to craft a texture that's so rigid it won't shatter and produce damage that can be plugged back into resilience circuits. This rigidity will confuse ears tuned to expect flexibility, distortion, and aion-like deterritorialization. That's why it sounds riotous.

"Into the Death" illustrates this type of riotous inflexibility in two ways. First, the tempo seems to stretch and give, even though it remains rigidly steady, snapped perfectly to a 4/4 metric grid throughout. The sections without a bass synth on every beat might *seem* to have a more relaxed tempo than the sections with it, but the song's tempo is a consistent 188bpm. This rhythmic precision is also behind the song's second example of riot sounds: the "MIDIs," which are actually TR-909s, distill their own drugs/distortions. Machines can be more precise than human perception; they can, as Ronald Bogue puts it, "accelerate (or decelerate) metrical regularities until they" *appear to* "collapse or run out of control" (97). Blast drumming is a particularly clear example of such intensified metric regularity. As Bogue explains, blast drumming is one "tactic of accelerating meters to the point of collapse," produced through the "cut-time alteration of downbeat kick drum and offbeat snare, the accent being heard on the offbeat but felt on the downbeat" (99). According to Bogue, blast drumming uses ultra-precise rhythmic patterns to confound listeners' ability to perceive the established meter. The meter, in this way, distills its own "drug," its own distortions. But it's not the *music* that's distorted, it's our perception that's distorted. We hear exacting, precise musical technique as anarchic distortion. Blast drumming is one example of how rigid, strict adherence to *arche* produces "riot sounds." Riot sounds aren't anarchic, they're just the opposite. But, they *feel* like a riot in our ears because our senses aren't nimble and flexible enough to keep up.

Blast drumming is a common feature of death metal, and ATR use it in "Into the Death."[82] On this track, the already-overwhelming percussive "blasts" are intensified and exaggerated even further. ATR uses drum machines to accelerate blast beats beyond what a human drummer can perform.[83] In the version on *1995*, hyperaccelerated blast beats appear at: 0:14-0:15, 1:02-1:04, 2:12-2:13, 2:17-2:18, 2:20-1, and at the very close at 3:12-13. The cluster of blasts in the middle of the song coincide with lyrics that critique classically liberal models of resistance. Elias says, "maybe we'll sit down and talk about the revolution and stuff/But it doesn't work like that," the "but" emphasized with the 2:17-18 blast. Because ATR juxtapose these blasts with a critique of traditional leftist ideas, we can interpret the blasts as an alternative model of critical political practice. But what's critical and political about these blasts?

Bogue claims that blast-style metric destabilization produces Deleuzian bodies-without-organs—i.e., a complete scrambling or roll-back of organizational structures, an-*arche*.[84] It has a different effect in "Into the Death." This song does not produce a body without organs, but a precisely-engineered political tool.[85] In ATR's song, dissolution is not the point. The TR-909 never actually devolves the meter into actual or apparent chaos. The drum machine manages rhythm so precisely that it becomes, from the perspective of hegemony, unmanageable. Neoliberalism aims to optimize flexibility; in "Into the Death," these managerial techniques and instruments work *too perfectly*, producing *rigidity* rather than flexibility. This hyper-quantization and intensification of metric regularity articulates a counter-*arche*. It is a way of queering biopolitical management, managing for ends other than the "normal" ones.[86]

How exactly is this hyper-exact management an intensification of biopolitical death? This is where the second form of "riot sounds" factor in. ATR's work remixes or reroutes the networks that regulate the distribution of life-intensity (privilege or death), so that management produces "abnormal" results. They intensify precisely what shouldn't be intensified—bare life. Hegemony manages death to make sure it stays at a specific level of intensity (e.g., "equalized" in relation to other levels/channels). Instead of plugging death into the intensification of privileged lives, which is what neoliberalism does, "Into the Death" reroutes the engines of intensification and plugs them into death. In the same way that riot sounds are made by rerouting sound signals through MIDIs, samplers, and drum machines, riots are made by rerouting investment from life to death. Rioting is an intentional bending of the circuits of power.

In neoliberalism, the critical potential of queerly racialized death is not found in negation, but in intensification. If "life" is unviable, unwinnable, then the only place to go, the only thing to do, is go into the death. Instead of playing the game to win (or to lose), you play the game's algorithms themselves. This involves plugging the resources normally put to capitalization (i.e., winning) back into death, overdriving it so that it does something the original algorithms haven't accounted for. The product is not necessarily chaotic or unintelligible, as non-metric time/body-without-organs would be—it is just not the optimal outcome for maintaining and maximizing hegemonic relations of privilege and oppression. Thus, this intensification of death is what starts a riot. Overdriving death, turning death up, will affect and distort "life": keeping with the signal metaphor, alterations to the nadir of a curve or sine wave will also affect its apex. If death is something controlled in order to better manage life, then inhabiting death queerly will fuck neoliberal hegemony's algorithms, fuck up its management of life.[87]

Death is technically illegible to neoliberal "power over life," as biopolitics is primarily focused on administering and investing in *life*. [88] However, if death is beyond neoliberalism's grasp, it could be a site of counter-hegemonic insurgency. So, neoliberal hegemony has a vested interest in managing death, in co-opting and feeding death back into life.[89] "Into the Death," then, incites a riot by making death newly illegible, at least for a while. Death, in this song, is no longer an indirectly perceptible side-effect, but an excessive blast of perceptual data. Hegemonic institutions aren't equipped to handle that surge of input, so they can't stop it from blowing the monitors, so to speak. At the level of gender/race/sexual politics, intensified death blows up the processes that channel success to already-successful populations, and away from precarious ones.[90] It distorts the assemblages that balance and equalize flows of privilege, resources, life…and death. Death is no longer (at least momentarily) distributed in a way that allows for the successful reproduction of MRWaSP. The bent circuits don't manage life and death in ways that maintain an optimal balance of MRWaSP resilience.

4. Bending the Circuits of Biopolitical Life

ATR's *1995* shows us, in both its music and its lyrics, how the circuits of biopolitical intensification and divestment work, and how they can be bent. While I've spent most of this chapter discussing the first-order musical and political stakes of biopolitical death, there is also a metatheoretical dimension to my project. Queer, trans, feminist, and critical race theories are not just things to be applied to the study of popular music, noise, and sound. Popular music, noise, and sound studies are also methods of queer, trans, feminist, and critical race theorizing. As I have tried to show in this article, opening our analyses not just to music, but also to technical discussions of how songs work *as music* can really help our theorizing about other things, like death and politics.

ATR's 90s work articulates exactly how queer and Afro-diasporic aesthetics get associated with neoliberal, *biopolitical* death. This biopolitical death is a *different concept of death* than the one generally discussed in the academic debates about Edelman's "No Future" thesis. Thus, following the *musical* line of flight from classic 70s punk to 90s cyber(ish)punk does more than just expand our archive: recontextualizes the *political* conversation. In particular, it clarifies how queer death (a) is not limited to sexuality, to gays and lesbians, but is assembled with specific configurations of blackness, and (b) is not inherently, but only strategically, counter-hegemonic. Not only is "queer death" controlled for and managed as a condition for the "life" of homonationalist whites, but actual death as "queer" (in the sense of illegible) is also accounted for by the power over life. "Queer death" is an already-standardized deviation. Thus, it must be intensified beyond the point of standardization in order to be a resource for critical theoretical and political work. ATR's work responds to neoliberalism by *going into the death*. Interpreted in this way, their work on *1995* queers the biopolitical management of life (and death).[91]

To do this, ATR didn't have to invent new strategies out of thin air; they often drew on work by black punk and electronic musicians. Hanin Elias's vocals are influenced by X-Ray Spex's Poly Styrene, and Empire's composition is influenced by Underground Resistance.[92] If the punk/hip hop/disco explosion represented the mainstream co-optation or gentrification of black/queer negativity, then ATR's digital hardcore could be considered cyberpunk's co-optation of biopolitical death.[93] In a way, ATR are upgrading Pistols-style white hipsterism, identi-fying with and appropriating *marginality* or *precarity* rather than exclusion and abjection, upgrading "love and theft" for the digital age. Negation—regular, conventional cutting, looping, repetition—had already been so thoroughly co-opted into mainstream pop music that it no longer sounded or felt avant-garde. To make sonic death properly "hardcore," ATR had to *intensify* these negative strategies until they became something other or more than simple negation. Anyone could play at being an "outsider," but it was more radical and avant-garde to assert one's *precarity*. Just as mid-20th century blues-rock practices of white hipness fetishize some styles of gendered racial subalternity as means to white bodily pleasure and receptivity, millennial hardcore genres appropriated and homonationalized formerly "queer" death, using it as an index of radical, alternaboy cred.[94] (For example, the cover of Marilyn Manson's 1998 album *Mechanical Animals* condenses goth, death, and genderqueer embodiment into the primary symbol for white heteromasculine countercultural oppositionality.)

Appropriating black/queer aesthetics in a mutually-intensifying assemblage, ATR could stay ahead of mainstream cooptation, still sounding hardcore even as house, techno, and hip hop entered mainstream pop aesthetics. From this perspective, ATR are like the hipsters who move in to an economically disadvantaged neighborhood—the aesthetics of biopolitical death—and revamp it just enough to make it attractive for large-scale redevelopment and gentrification. This puts death back in the service of privileged lives, and the overall viability of MRWaSP capitalism. Queerly intensifying death or bending the circuits of biopolitical life-management *might* still viable responses to multiracial white supremacist heteropatriarchy. However, as I discuss in chapter four, this is going to *sound* differently in 2014 than it did in 1995.

ATR's musical appropriation of biopolitical death precipitated its wholescale cooptation by mainstream pop. Lady Gaga's work, which I discuss in chapter four, is a prime example of this cooptation; monstrosity and death function, in the Gagaverse, as the opening act in performances of resilience. But before I get to Gaga's work, I need to talk more fully about the politics and aesthetics of resilience. The next chapter focuses on the transformation of riot sounds—either in the form of distorted music, or wild and crazy "gaga feminism"—into resilient noise.

Resilience is a tool for MRWaSP normalization. In its role as a gender ideal that "feminine" subjects must embody, hegemonic femininity also cuts the MRWaSP color line, separating out viably "multi-racial" from the precariously black and queer. In aesthetics, this manifests as what I call, after both Steven Shaviro and Patricia Hill Collins a "post-cinematic" controlling image. Resilience discourse upgrades the male gaze—instead of objectifying women, it puts them to work, "controlling" them, in a typically neoliberal way, through deregulation. As Beyonce's "Video Phone," shows, women are "free" to overcome the male gaze because this free market in women's agency boosts the overall efficiency of multi-racial white supremacy.

3

Look, I Overcame!

In *Radical Philosophy*, Mark Neocleous argues that the ideal of "resilience" has replaced the ideal of "security," both as a structure of individual subjectivity and a principle of social/national policy. Briefly, he defines resilience as "the capacity of a system to return to a previous state, to recover from a shock, or to bounce back after a crisis or trauma." Resilience is an ethical and political ideal, a sort of transformation of Nietzsche's "what doesn't kill me makes me stronger" into a universalizable maxim (yep, a categorical imperative): "you *ought* to be stronger." Strength, here, is figured as *flexibility* rather than rigidity; instead of preventing bad things from happening, you are optimally prepared to meet any and all challenges. Resilience is the ability to recover from disaster, to turn, as Chicago mayor Rahm Emmanuel would say, a crisis into an "opportunity to do things you think you could not do before.[95] So, as an ethical imperative, resilience might look something like this: you are inevitably damaged, you will always be threatened with death, and you ought to overcome the threat in a way that does not deplete your resources, but in fact grows them—you ought to become stronger.

"Resilience," Neocleous argues, "connects the emotional management of personal problems with the wider security agenda and the logic of accumulation during a period of crisis." To illustrate this connection, Neocleous uses the example of a "young woman...dominated by an overpowering and angry bully of a man" thinks resilience is the "solution to her problem." Neocleous's choice of example tells us something about the gender politics of resilience. While anyone can be the victim of domestic abuse, patriarchy makes domestic abuse a problem that disproportionately affects women (indeed, gender norms contributed to economic situation of the woman in Neocleous's example—it is conventional that women follow their male partners' careers, and she "moved in with him to land a job in his town"). As feminists have long argued, these "private" struggles are thoroughly enmeshed with broader, "public" systems of privilege, like patriarchy. Neocleous assumes as much, and uses this one woman's experience as a microcosm of the macrocosmic phenomenon he analyzes in the essay: "the only thing a sad, lonely, and oppressed young woman thinks might help her turns out to be the very same thing being taught by the world's largest military power," and this commonality "takes us from mundane tips about how to live well to the world of national security, emergency planning and capital accumulation."

Why is it that the clearest hinge between subjectivity and the social manifests in a woman's gendered experience as a woman? Why is *women's* emotional management of their *feminized problems as women* the ideal example of the logic and practice of resilience?

Changes in properly feminine subjectivity (which means, privileged feminine ideals) reflect not only this shift from security-thinking to resilience-thinking, but also from classical white supremacist patriarchy to MRWaSP. This chapter tracks those changes. In the first section, I discuss shifts in ideal (white) femininity, from fragility to what I call the "Look, I Overcame!" (LIO). The LIO is a specific iteration of resilience discourse, one that involves both *overcoming* (resilience) and *looking*. The looking in LIO discourse is different than the looking involved in classic feminist concept of the male gaze. Instead of gazing, LIO resilience is a type of post-cinematic (to use Steven Shaviro's term) controlling image. I develop this concept of post-cinematic controlling image through a reading of Beyonce's "Video Phone." Then, in the second part of the chapter, I argue that Beyonce's song and video "Diva," in a quasi-accelerationist

Afrofuturist response to "Video Phone's" post-cinematic controlling images, blows up resilience discourse.

1. Good Girls Are Resilient

(a) Fragility

Traditionally, ideal (by which I mean: white, bourgeois, able-bodied, cisgendered) femininity required the performance of fragility. As Iris Marion Young explains, normative femininity trains women to:

> approach a physical engagement with things with timidity, uncertainty, and hesitancy. Typically, we lack an entire trust in our bodies to carry us to our aims....*We often experience our bodies as a fragile encumbrance, rather than the medium for the enactment of our aims.* We feel as though we must have our attention directed upon our bodies to make sure they are doing what we wish them to do, rather than paying attention to what we want to do through our bodies. (Young 34; emphasis mine).

As Young argues, traditionally feminine body comportment is tied to traditionally feminine structures of subjectivity. For a body to feel and be felt as feminine, it must be fragile. A fragile body is both unable to support one's intentions and desires and in need of support and therapeutic control/discipline. Fragile, feminine bodies can't do what you want them to, so they need constant attention to "make sure they"—both women and feminine bodies—"are doing what we wish them to do." Feminine bodies—and the people who have them—need thera-peutic monitoring and control to keep their fragility in check. Thus, for example, women are held to less punishing physical standards in athletics or military training; this 'protects' their supposedly weaker, more fragile bodies from overexertion.

Similarly, both advertisements and the medical community constantly exhort women to monitor all aspects of their bodies (breast self-exams, weighing oneself every day, food diaries, diets, etc.) to make sure their bodies don't get too out of control. By compelling women to embody fragile femininity, patriarchy both prevented them from taking full advantage of their bodies, and allowed itself to take more full advantage of them (e.g., through paternalism).

As an ideal and a disciplinary technique, fragility marks race and class-based distinctions among women, separating out the "good" women from the "bad." Traditionally, only white, bourgeois, cis/straight women are really fragile. Working-class women, non-white women, some trans- women, and butch/masculine-of-center women are stereotypically less fragile than the "ideally" feminine woman. Manual labor makes your body strong, not fragile; black women are often expected to be "bulletproof divas," as Lisa Jones puts it; transwomen's bodies are often called out for having features that are too "strong" (e.g., brow ridge); and some butch subjectivities center on the rejection of fragility and vulnerability.

Fragility traditionally separated privileged femininities from rougher, less dainty, less privileged ones. Now, however, fragility is increasingly attributed to minority women, especially third-world women of color, who are represented as precarious victims in need of rescue. This shift, which discuss in the next section, is the effect of neoliberalism's restructuring of ideal femininity. MRWaSP rewards privileged women for being resilient.

(b). Resilience and overcoming

Neoliberalism replaces fragility with a new feminine ideal. As Neocleous puts it, "rather than speak of fragility and its (negative) connotations, we should be speaking of resilience and its (positive) connotations." In post-feminist society, feminine identity and corporeality shouldn't be a drag, because we've solved patriarchy, right? Nowadays, ideally feminine subjects are expected to overcome the burdens traditionally associated with femininity: *they must overcome the fragility they've learned to embody as women.* Post-feminist society assumes that women are always-already damaged by patriarchy. All women are feminized, but "good" women visibly overcome the negative effects of feminization. In other words, women's gender performance is a two-step process: femininity is performed first as damage, second as resilience. This performance involves emotional and affective labor on oneself and one's corporeal schema—or, in the language of mainstream feminism, one's "body image."

This individualized emotional and affective labor is what Autumn Whitefield-Madrano calls the "therapeutic narrative" of feminine body image. In contemporary Anglo-American culture, good girls must "problematiz[e] something essentially human— cognizance of our own bodies—and fram[e] it as something that we must overcome... We've turned our relationship with our bodies into a therapeutic narrative" (Whitefield-Madrano). "Real" women—such as those portrayed in the Dove "Real Beauty" campaign—must recognize that traditional ideals of fragile, victimized femininity are damaging and pathological— which, you know, they are. Recognizing one's damage is, after all, the first step in many therapeutic practices, such as the 12-step model used in Alcoholics Anonymous. A good girl's consciousness is always-already raised, so to speak, and that's part of what makes her a "good" feminine subject: she, unlike regular women, is smart and strong enough to possess a critical self-awareness. This awareness is not necessarily an undesirable thing. The problem is that this is only half the picture; it naturalizes traditional forms of misogyny as *faits accomplis,* things you are powerless to change. Stopping short of a systematic critique of patriarchy as an institution, this type of consciousness-raising treats patriarchy as problem for women to solve individually. Instead of changing the world (because nobody can, there is no alternative, etc.), we must change ourselves.

To change ourselves, we must overcome our past damage. This overcoming is the step in performing resilience. Resilient overcoming isn't therapy, but as Whitefield-Madrano emphasizes, a therapeutic *narrative*—the aim isn't a cure, but the narrative process itself. This narrative, as Whitefield-Madrano analyzes it, includes all the elements of a traditional narrative: an exposition, a build to a crisis, a moment of crisis, and, if not a resolution, a sublimation:

> Key to the therapeutic narrative are four things: 1) a once-whole, once-healthy self that was damaged by 2) a negative incident or pattern that incites a protective formula, which 3) leads to suffering—but luckily we have 4) self-awareness, the key to returning to one's natural state of pure psychological health through a full understanding of one's "damage." Enter the inordinate focus on women's bodies and its adherence to the therapeutic narrative: the once-innocent girl, the incident of damage, the bodily self-loathing, and, by the time the tale is told, self-acceptance.

First, one has to constantly rehearse one's damage—you have to establish it (in the exposition, or item 1) and undergo it (development, item 2) until you reach a crisis point (item 3), which allows you to sublimate your damage into health. It is assumed that no woman is "naturally healthy" in her immediate, un-self-aware state; the "once-whole, once-healthy self" is a myth, much as the Garden of Eden is a myth. Damage is the "natural" or immediate state of the female body/psyche. That's what I mean by the claim that resilience discourse "naturalizes" damage. "Natural health," then, is something that has to be *accomplished* by therapeutic labor. (This is consistent with Foucault's claim in

Birth of Biopolitics that neoliberalism treats nature as an effect, not an immediate given.) Damage is *necessary* to health. So post-feminist neoliberal patriarchy doesn't resolve or fix traditional forms of misogyny—rather, it solicits them and incites them, but for different, non-traditional uses.

As Whitefield-Madrano indicates, women still ought to feel their bodies as encumbrances, as sites of damage and suffering. Unlike Young's account, in which this encumbrance is an impediment that arrests transcendence, Whitefield-Madrano's analysis shows that this encumbrance is now the very *medium for* transcendence—it does not prevent you from doing, but provides you the very materials with which you *can* do something. You have to be damaged and/or have damage in order to have something to overcome. So, while traditional feminine ideals equated goodness with virginity (fragile innocence and/or innocent fragility), nowadays lost innocence is, as Whitefield-Madrano suggests, a *prerequisite* for demonstrating one's goodness. As Neocleous argues,

> Good subjects will 'survive and thrive in any situation', they will 'achieve balance' across the several insecure and part-time jobs they have, 'overcome life's hurdles' such as facing retirement without a pension to speak of, and just 'bounce back' from whatever life throws, whether it be cuts to benefits, wage freezes or global economic meltdown...

In resilience discourse, moral or ethical goodness the profit one reaps from a specific type of therapeutic self-labor (I talk more about the political economy of resilience in the conclusion). "Good" girls are the ones who show a continual, active commitment to overcoming their damage, like the negative body image they've internalized from the media. So, women must do the work of overcoming damage inflicted by multi-racial white supremacist patriarchy, and in a twist of particularly cruel irony, this actually *reinforces* and *strengthens* patriarchy. With the narrative of therapeutic overcoming, patriarchy has figured out how to convert so-called "feminist" practices—like the Dove Real Beauty campaign, like French anti-veiling laws—into its own power supply.

Post-feminist therapeutic narratives don't just recognize that women are damaged by sexism, but *require* them to be damaged. Without misogynist feminine body ideals, what would women have to overcome? Sexism, then, is not a bug but a feature. Because it's not the sexism that needs collective overcoming, but individual women that need to be "resilient" in the face of unavoidable, persistent sexism. This is not about overcoming patriarchy, but about upgrading it.

(c) Resilience and MRWaSP

The classic virgin/whore dichotomy was often used to mark differences between white women, who were stereotypically good and virginal, and non-white women, who were stereotypically bad, unruly, and impure. The LIO narrative re-cuts the virgin/whore dichotomy to function in MRWaSP. "Good girls" are resilient, whereas "bad girls," insufficiently feminine subjects, continue to be fragile and in need of rescue and/or protection. If women of color are resilient enough, they are included within MRWaSP privilege; if they are insufficiently resilient, they are further marginialized as women of color. Think, for example, of the way formerly negative stereotypes about African American women are being revalued—their independence, toughness, fierceness, when combined with appropriate class/gender/sexual privilege, is not a negative, masculinizing thing, but a distinctive and valued feature of their black femininity. So, you have songs like Ne-Yo's "Miss Independent" and Webbie's "I-N-D-E-P-E-N-D-E-N-T" positively valuing black women's resilience in a very explicit way.

Resilience is, in effect, an index of one's inclusion within and normalization to MRWaSP. It takes resources to be resilient—you already need some capital (of both the human sort and the old-school money/resources sort) to be able to recover from a crisis rather than slide further into it. It takes money to make money, as the cliché goes. So, for example, Angelina Jolie can turn grief at her mother's death from breast cancer, and fear of her own susceptibility to the disease, into a double-mastectomy that becomes the basis for a sensational and widely-discussed op-ed in the nation's most prominent newspaper, the *New York Times*. Jolie, a wealthy celebrity, has the money and the time to invest in the very, very expensive testing and surgery—she doesn't have to negotiate with insurance companies, employers, or even childcare providers. *Resilience amplifies already-existing privilege.* Though it seems like a meritocratic practice—anyone can pull themselves together through hard work and commitment—it isn't. Practicing resilience is one way to further one's investments in MRWaSP, and to reap profit from it.

Resilience narratives allow individual women to capitalize in their damage in ways that generate surplus value for MRWaSP and neoliberal capitalism. For individual women, this thera-peutic self-work is an investment in their human capital. Therapeutic labor shapes them into properly "feminine" subjects, into "good" women. Having a normally gendered self, and all the so-called "benefits" that come with it, are the return or profit women get from this investment. This labor *makes them into women*, and thus allows them to be recognized and socially valued as such. The inverse is also true: those whose perfor-mances of this labor are insufficient and/or unsuccessful aren't "real" women—they may be bad women, non-white, non-bourgeois, trans*, queer, disabled women, etc.

Resilience makes women marketable sexually (as femme), ethically (as 'good'), and commercially (as productive laborers). It's not just MRWaSP that benefits from resilience: resilience is uniquely tailored to maximize women's productivity for neoliberal capitalism. In many ways, resilience is an updated version of traditional "women's work," the unwaged work required to reproduce the laborer (like laundry, cooking, and cleaning). Instead of reproducing the implicitly male wage laborer, resilience invests in the implicitly feminine affective or communicative laborer. In this way, resilience is profitable for neoliberal capitalism—it's the kind of labor the entrepreneurial subject does on herself. I'll discuss the role of resilience as labor more fully in the concluding chapter.

It's not just individual women (as entrepreneurs of themselves) and neoliberal capitalism that profit from resilience; the institution of MRWaSP also profits from women's resilient labor. Resilience discourse helps MRWaSP run more efficiently. The therapeutic narrative functions like a sort of cloaking device that allows patriarchy to go on the offense without having to spend resources defending itself from attack. MRWaSP *disavows* its own existence by loudly claiming that traditional patriarchy is something "we" have overcome. There are two versions of this claim, both of which are variations on the "it's not us it's *you*" line. First, this "you" can be an individual woman. Sexism and misogyny are, in this view, private psychological damage. Patriarchy thus seems like an individual pathology and not an institution facilitating all sorts of economic, epistemic, political, and sociocultural activity. Just as rape culture blames individual women for systematic, cultural problems, MRWaSP blames its victims and obscures its ongoing existence as a system of social organization. It's not just individual women who are scapegoated. In the second version of MRWaSP's "it's not us it's *you*," this "you" refers to supposedly "backwards" non-bourgeois subcultures—the unenlightened, unreconstructed "them" against which we define "us." MRWaSP scapegoats poor and working-class black men, "Muslim" men, rural/evangelical whites, and other supposedly traditional or primitive subcultures for any patriarchy and misogyny that it can't blame on women. This scapegoating is very evident in the music videos I discuss in this chapter and in chapter four. *I will show how pop music reveals, both in its politics and its aesthetics, the racialized and gendered political economy of neoliberal capitalism.* Pop music is a powerful instrument for analyzing resilience discourse because resilience must be performed as a spectacle for others. Women don't just need to overcome; their overcoming must be seen and heard.

(d) "Look, I Overcame!"

Resilience must be performed explicitly, legibly, and spectacularly. Overcoming is necessary, but insufficient; to count and function as resilience, this overcoming must be accomplished in a visible or otherwise legible and consumable manner. Overcoming is a type of "affective labor" which, as Steven Shaviro puts it, "is productive only to the extent that it is a public *performance*. It cannot unfold in the hidden depths; it must be visible and audible" (PCA 49n33). In order to tune into feminine resilience and feed it back into its power supply, MRWaSP has to perceive it as such.

"Look, I Overcame!" is the resilient subject's maxim or mantra. Gender and race have always been "visible identities," to use philosopher Linda Martin Alcoff's term, identities strongly tied to one's outward physical appearance. However, gendered/racialized resilience isn't visible in the same way that conventional gender and racial identities are visible. To clarify these differences, it's helpful to think of resilience in terms of a "Look, I Overcame!" imperative. "Look, I Overcame!" is easy to juxtapose to Frantz Fanon's "Look, a Negro!", which is the touchstone for his analysis of gendered racialization in "The Fact of Blackness." In both cases, looking is a means of crafting race/gender identities and distributing white patriarchal privilege. But, in the same way that resilience discourse "upgrades" traditional methods for crafting identities and distributing privilege, the "looking" in "Look, I Overcame!" is an upgrade on the "looking" in "Look, a Negro!"

According to Fanon, the exclamation "Look, a Negro!" racializes him *as* a black man. To be "a Negro" is to be objectified by the white supremacist gaze. This gaze fixes him as an object, rather than an ambiguous transcendence (which is a more nuanced way of describing the existentialist concept of subjectivity). "The black man," as Fanon argues, "has no ontological resistance for the white man" (BSWM 110) because, as an object and not a mutually-recognized subject, he cannot return the white man's gaze ("The Look" that is so important to Sartre's theory of subjectivity in *Being & Nothingness)*. The LIO narrative differs from Fanon's account in the same way it differs from Iris Young's account of feminine body comportment: in resilience discourse, objectification isn't an end but a means. Any impediment posed by the damage wrought by the white/male gaze is a necessary prerequisite for subjectivity, agency, and mutual recognition. In other words, being looked at isn't an impediment, but a resource.

Resilience discourse turns objectification (being looked at) into a means of subjectification (overcoming). It also makes *looking* even more efficient and profitable than simple objectification could ever be. Recognizing and affirming the affective labor of the resilient performer, the spectator feeds the performer's individual overcoming into a second-order therapeutic narrative: our approbation of her overcoming is evidence of our own overcoming of our past prejudices. This spectator wants to be seen by a wider audience as someone who answers the resilient feminine subject's hail, "Look, I Overcame!". Just as individual feminine subjects use their resilience as proof of their own goodness, MRWaSP uses the resilience of its "good girls" as proof that they're the "good guys" —that its social and ethical practices are truly just, and that we really mean it this time when we say everyone is equal. For example, the "resilience" of "our" women is often contrasted with the supposed "fragility" of Third-World women of color. Or, in domestic US race-gender politics, the resilience of some African-American women (their bootstraps-style class ascendance) is contrasted to the continued fragility of other African-American women, and thus used to reinforce class distinctions among blacks. There are a million different versions of this general story: "our" women are already liberated—they saved themselves—but, to riff on Gayatri Spivak, "brown women need saving from brown men." Most mainstream conversations about Third-World women are versions of this story: discussions of "Muslim" veiling, female circumcision, sweatshops, poverty, "development," they're all white-saviorist narratives meant to display MRWaSP's own resilience.

Look, I Overcame!" upgrades "Look, a Negro!" by (a) recycling objectification into overcoming and (b) compounding looking, so that one can profit from others' resilience, treating their overcoming as one's own overcoming. This upgrade in white supremacist patriarchy requires a concomitant upgrade in "looking." This shift in looking practices parallels developments in film and media aesthetics. As Steven Shaviro has argued, the values, techniques, and compositional strategies most common in contemporary mainstream Western cinema—like Michael Bay's *Transformers*—are significantly different than the ones used in modernist and post-modernist cinema, and that these differences in media production correlate to broader shifts in the means of capitalist and ideological production. Neoliberalism's aesthetic is, he argues, "post-cinematic." This post-cinematic aesthetic applies not just to film and media, but to resilience discourse. Its performance practices and looking relations configured by the "Look, I Overcame!" imperative, resilience is, in a way, another type of post-cinematic medium. In the next section I use Shaviro's theory of post-cinematic media to identify some specific ways in which traditional patriarchal tools are updated to work compatibly with

MRWaSP resilience discourse. The looking in the "Look, I Overcame!" narrative is not the same kind of looking described by concepts like "the male gaze" or "controlling images." This looking is a type of deregulated MRWaSP visualization.

2. MRWaSP Visualization

Resilience is necessarily performed for others: your overcoming has to be *seen* as such. The looking, as I argued, is just as important as the overcoming. But what sort of looking? What kinds of looking relations do resilient performances instantiate and/or presuppose? How does "looking" work? Whom does it position in relation to what common things or activities? What assumptions (about epistemology, about aesthetics) does resilience discourse embody? Especially because it begins with the incitement and admission of damage, how and why does resilience discourse make us feel good? Where is the aesthetic pleasure in resilient looking? Why do we like to perform resilience and see resilience performed? What's pleasurable about showing our overcoming, or viewing others' resilience?

Because film and media theory has a lot to say about the politics and aesthetics of looking, I will use it, specifically Steven Shaviro's work on "post-cinematic" or "post-continuity" media, to unpack the "looking" in the "Look, I Overcame!" narrative. Analyzing resilience discourse as a set of performance practices, visual methods, and looking relations, I treat it as a "post-cinematic" medium. The compositional techniques and aesthetic values that characterize post-cinematic media parallel the socio-political techniques and ethical values that characterize resilience discourse. Where classically cinematic aesthetics and liberal politics employ a series of binaries (subject/object, inside/outside, depth/surface, white/black, and male/female) to (re)produce white supremacist patriarchy, resilience discourse uses deregulated, "post-cinematic" processes to (re)produce MRWaSP.

The "looking" in resilient "Look, I Overcame!" narratives is fundamentally different than the kinds of looking assumed in traditional feminist accounts of women's objectification, such as Laura Mulvey's concept of "the male gaze" and Patricia Hill Collins's theory of "controlling images." The first part of this section explains what the male gaze and controlling images are, and how they are grounded in classical liberalism and (Hollywood) cinema aesthetics. The second part uses Shaviro's work on post-cinematic media to upgrade these two concepts so they are compatible with post-cinematic aesthetics and MRWaSP politics. The looking in the "Look, I Overcame!" narrative isn't a gaze or a controlling image, but a *deregulated visualization*. This concept of MRWaSP visualization will help me unpack the gender-race politics of Beyonce's "Video Phone," which I will discuss later in part three of this chapter.

(a) Old-School "Male Gazing" and "Controlling Images"

Laura Mulvey's concept of "the male gaze" and Patricia Hill-Collins's notion of "controlling images" are touchstones for feminist analyses of media. However, they were developed through analyses of historically-specific methods of racialized/gendered image making. Mulvey's "male gaze" is explicitly cinematic: it is, as the title of her famous article indicates, the structure of "visual pleasure" in classic Hollywood "*narrative* cinema." This sort of cinema privileges development, resolution, and wholeness—these are what cinematic discourses invest as sites of desire, pleasure, and meaning. Similarly, as I will argue later in this section, Hill Collins's concept of controlling images presumes a classically liberal subject/object binary, and thus the specific controlling images she identifies work like cinematic images, even when they appear in other media.

"The male gaze" is Mulvey's term for the structural, formal, and technical methods used in classic Hollywood cinema to naturalize patriarchal looking relations and masculine subject positions. That is, masculinity is the lens that brings otherwise incoherent, disparate elements into focus as a coherent whole. The camera, not the male/masculine protagonist, is the ultimate "bearer of the look," the male gazer behind the fourth wall's Oz-like curtain. Even though the male protagonist appears to be the one controlling the cinematic narrative, he isn't—the camera is.[96] Cinematographic, directorial, and editorial labor have made the story unfold with a sense of necessity and inevitability; everything works out in a way that makes the masculine protagonist appear to have more power or agency than he actually does. The hero, for example, always gets the girl and defeats the bad guy(s). (This hero can be female, but her relationship, as subject to feminized objects, makes her a masculine cinematic element. I'll talk more about feminized objects and masculine subjects in the next paragraph.)

This compositional labor obscures the fact that our self-image is always more ideal and perfect than our actual self; in real life, nobody always gets the girl and defeats the bad guys. By identifying with the camera, the audience adopts the perspective of an ideally effective agent, the entity who's *really* pulling the strings in this story. They misrecognize the "camera's" agency (which is really the work of cinematographers, directors, editors, and, well, the entire film crew) as their own. Thus, as Mulvey argues, "the camera's look is *disavowed* in order to create a convincing world in which the spectator's surrogate can perform with verisimilitude" (844). The spectators' belief in their own potency and agency requires the fantasy of the fourth wall. Similarly, men/masculine subjects can believe they are autonomous agents responsible for their own accomplishments only by obscuring and denying the privileges that patriarchy constantly provides them. Obscuring both the work of cinematographic art and of femininity/women, the male gaze makes both classic film form and conventional patriarchy seem more coherent and natural than they really are.

The male gaze performs obscures both of these facts at the same time, often by means of fragmenting and objectifiying whatever in the film is feminized (e.g., women characters). This prevents feminized cinematic elements from attaining the development, resolution, and wholeness expected of a film's primary narrative features (like the protagonist). For example, classic cinema often chops up women's bodies into their constituent parts through, for example, "conventional close-ups of legs (Dietrich, for instance) or a face (Garbo)." (Mulvey 838). Unlike fully human, fully-realized subjects, who exist, as Mulvey claims, as desiring subjects in three-dimensional space, female body parts are two-dimensional, "flat" (833) objects of desire. We see their fragmented body parts as merely images for our consumption, not as people we wish we could be (in Mulvely's psychoanalytic terms, as "ego ideals"). We enjoy having them, not being them. In this way, fragmentation is a means of objectification—it makes women available as objects for us by preventing them from being subjects themselves. Reducing women to body parts treats them as a collection of sub-human objects who are incapable of ever developing into a fully-realized subject. The male gaze doesn't just objectify "women"; it also subjectifies "men." Or, more accurately, narrative cinema subjectifies the gazer as male by objectifying the film's feminized elements. Its composition distributes objectification to women/femininzed elements of the film, and subjectivity to men/masculinized elements of the film. This is what Mulvey means by her famous phrase, "woman as image, man as bearer of the look" (Mulvey 343). In this way, the "male gaze" is a collection of distinctively cinematic techniques—fragmentation, objectification, subject/object binaries, and the disavowal of the camera—for reproducing patriarchal gender roles and relations.

Patricia Hill Collins's concept of "controlling images" is similarly cinematic in its assumptions and its logic. Unlike

Mulvey's concept of the male gaze, which applies primarily to representations of white women/femininities, Hill Collin's theory of controlling images analyzes the representation of black women/femininities in US pop culture. The "images" Collins discusses are concepts or stereotypes—though she does give many specific examples, the mammy, welfare queen, black lady, breeder, and hoochie are all archetypal abstractions. While these concepts are not themselves images, they *work* like cinematic images. You could think of them as specialized cameras that mediate the "gaze" directed at black women. The white patriarchal gaze sees black women *only* in these terms, and makes life even extra difficult for black women who do not conform to these stereotypes. Though they are quite different at the level of specific tactics, the "male gaze" and "controlling images" are both manifestations of the same "cinematic" strategies, including binarization, objectification, and disavowal.

Subject/object binaries are central to Hill-Collin's conception of controlling images.[97] As she argues in *Black Feminist Thought*, white supremacist patriarchy institutes a set of binaries— black/white, women/men (PHC 70)—and uses these binaries to both mark race/gender differences and to assign relative value to them. Race/gender binaries are inextricably tied to the subject/object binary. "Objectification," she argues, "is central to this process of oppositional difference. In binary thinking, one element is objectified as the Other, and is viewed as an object to be manipulated and controlled" (PHC 70). To call, categorize, or treat someone as a feminized or racialized "other" is to reduce them to a passive object, and also to assert one's authority, as a subject, over that (mere) object. Because, in Hill Collins's view, "domination always involves attempts to objectify the subordinate group" (PHC 71), then controlling images "control" via objectification.

Hill Collins uses "controlling images" and objectification to theorize political and economic exploitation (PHC 74)—it's black feminist theory, not, at least not primarily, film theory. However, the process of objectification she describes is analogous to the processes of objectification used in indexical cinema and the male gaze. For example, controlling images, like the male gaze, controlling assist in a disavowal. Just as the camera naturalizes the male gaze, controlling images naturalize exploitation, making it appear normal, right, and justified (PHC 78, 85). In Mulvey's account, the cinematic spectator's sense of mastery and agency requires the disavowal of the camera's mediation. Similarly, in Collins's account white supremacist patriarchy's self-presentation as neutral liberal meritocracy requires the disavowal of the ideological work (that is, the control) done by these images: "the mammy image was designed to mask this economic exploitation of social class" (PHC 74), she argues. If we disavow the construct-edness of the mammy images, and treat as unmediated fact rather than as a selectively-edited "image" or stereotype, this "shifts the angle of vision away from structural sources of poverty and blames the victims themselves" (PHC 80). Thus, just as the objectification of (white) women masks the role of the camera in structuring cinematographic relations among images, the objectification of black women masks the role of hegemony in structuring political, social, and economic relations. As Collins puts it, controlling images "diver[t] attention from political and economic inequalities that increasingly characterize global capitalism" (PHC 76).

The male gaze and controlling images are powerful tools for analyzing and critiquing traditional white supremacist patri-archy, their "cinematic" logic and assumptions, such as objectifi-cation and the coherent, self-present, self-determining subject. However, this means that they're ill-suited to address "post-cinematic" technologies like multi-racial white supremacist patri-archy and resilience narratives. MRWaSP is "post-cinematic" because it uses the methods and techniques of post-cinematic media to organize and operate race/gender/sexuality-based political and economic hegemonies. *It upgrades cinematic objectification and disavowal into "post-cinematic" resilience.*

(b) MRWaSP Resilience

Neoliberalism upgrades regulatory systems into deregulated ones. In economics, this means controlling the market's background conditions, rather than market activities themselves; market activities thus appear to operate "free" of direction.[98] For example, instead of instituting a single-payer health care system, one that ostensibly gives individuals no "choice," the Affordable Care Act (aka "Obamacare") allows people to "choose" among a highly circumscribed range of options (huge corporation A versus huge corporation B)—superficially this appears as 'free choice,' when in effect background constraints are basically a mode of soft coercion. In the same way that it restructures political economy, neoliberalism revamps the basic organizing principles of art.

Regulatory, cinematic practices of objectification, fragmentation, and disavowal have been upgraded into deregulatory, post-cinematic resilience. Section (a) addresses the difference between the male gaze/controlling images and deregulated MRWaSP visualization. Objectification and fragmentation are techniques with which the male gaze and controlling images regulate and exclude *femininity* in order to control the negative effects of damage. Compositional processes, on the other hand, are *de*regulatory techniques for producing feminized damage as a resource. Section (b) addresses the difference between the kinds of aesthetic pleasure produced by gazing/controlling, on the one hand, and visualization, on the other. Whereas the "visual pleasure" (a.k.a. "scopophilia") in the title of Mulvey's article on the male gaze comes from conquering feminized damage, the pleasure in post-cinematic media comes from resiliently overcoming damage—that is, from making oneself into something like Tiqqun's "Young Girl" (the ideal form of neoliberal human capital).

i. Compositional Processes: "Post-cinematic" media upgrades the logic and methods of classical narrative (tonality, the novel, Hollywood cinema) and modernist counter-narrative (like New Wave cinema or hip hop), reworking them into deregulatory practices like open works or generative processes. Regulatory techniques (like narrative, cinematic suturing, the male gaze, and controlling images) damage women for the purpose of excluding them from the undamaged work of art. Radical modernist and post-modernist works recuperate feminized damage as a means of *deconstructing regulations* (i.e., as a means of anti-art practice). In both modernist and post-modernist aesthetics, there is a preestablished formal logic, and femininity is instrumentalized in both constructing and deconstructing that logic.[99] Deregulatory techniques, on the other hand, liberate feminized damage so it can be directly put to work.

Deregulatory works are organized so they don't *seem* organized. Instead of following a pre-given formula, like narrative or tonality, visualization reveals the emergent order in an otherwise an-archic swarm. Structure "can only be apprehended bit by bit...and from moment to moment, through the constructive action of 'linking' one space to another" (Shaviro PCA 37). I call this technique "compositional process," because it shares aspects of Bruno Latour's concept of "compositionism" and composer Steve Reich's notion of "gradual process." [100] "Musical processes," Reich explains, "determine all the note-to-note (sound-to-sound) details and the overall form simultaneously. (Think of a round or infinite canon.)" (Reich, 34). Or, as Latour puts it the "micro- and macrocosm are now *literally* and not simply symbolically connected (BL 381). Unlike improvisation, which happens on top of a strictly regular formal architecture (e.g., a soloist improvising over fixed chord changes and phrase-lengths), this "'just-in-time' production" (Shaviro PCA 53) is a method of generating emergent order: the moment-to-moment details unfold simultaneously with and *as* the overarching structure. Compositional processes are flexible and irregular.

"Looseness or arbitrariness...is in fact the very *point*" (Shaviro PCA 74) of structures designed to generate *visual (or sonic) damage*. "Engineered so as to maximize shock" (Shaviro PCA 80), compositional processes are designed to cultivate aesthetic damage, which manifests, for example, as fragmentation, disjunction, lack of narrative/tonal center or goal, and lack of regular meter or temporality. As I discussed in chapter one, deregulated works can be "entirely incoherent, yet immediately legible to anyone" (Shaviro PC 80) because *the superficial chaos is intentionally produced and controlled for by the work's immanent structure.* If regulation limits and prohibits irrationality and incoherence, deregulated visualization leverages and exploits it. "Things don't need to harmonize, or fit together" (PCA 53) because deregulatory MRWaSP visualization explicitly *affirms* the damage that harmonization or integration is designed to obscure. In this way, MRWaSP visualization naturalizes feminized fragmentation, objectification, and incoherence.

MRWaSP visualization "controls" feminized damage by amplifying it and putting it to work generating resilient aesthetic/human capital. So, following Shaviro's analysis, if the cinematic gaze controls by organizing its visual field into active/passive, motion/stillness, subject/object hierarchies, MRWaSP visualization uses compositional processes, "modulation," and "feedback" to do its work (PCA 16). [101] Sonic and visual "events," like a sample or a post-production effect, "interpenetrate and feed back upon one another" (Shaviro PCA 52) so that a "film's sheer *density* of incidents and references baffles our efforts to 'translate' what we see and hear into something more abstract, more metaphorically palatable and easily manageable" (Shaviro 78; emphasis mine). It's like a DDOS for our eyes, ears, nerves, and brains. We're given more sensory data than we're capable of processing, so we have difficulty separating the signal from the noise. As Shaviro puts it, "the headlong rush...is all" (80). Dissonance, then, is the effect of overwhelming "noise" — either literal noise, or biopolitical/statistical "noise."

Being overwhelmed by something too big and/or strong to resist is a feature of conventional femininity and feminine sexuality (especially in rape culture); for example, there's the fantasy of being swept off one's feet. Traditional European aesthetics strive to contain and domesticate overwhelming affects and sensations. For example, Kant's feeling of sublimity is, as Christine Battersby and other feminist aestheticians have argued, a masculine conquest of potentially overwhelming, and thus feminizing, feelings.[102] MRWaSP visualization, on the other hand, treats the experience of overwhelming sensory-affective experience as a net gain, not as a loss of control (because, in a deregulatory scheme, there's no 'control' to lose). Feminized damage is now a resource, not a deficiency, a form of subjectivity and value-production, not a type of objectification and aesthetic/economic devaluation. Or rather, feminized damage is a resource and not a type of devaluation and desubjectification for otherwise privileged women, like professional white women who can "Lean In." Damage that isn't explicitly situated in a LIO narrative is treated as evidence of pathology. Persistent, unproblematized objectification are attributes of supposedly "voiceless" or "invisible" women who need to be saved and spoken for. MRWaSP visualization separates out resilient populations who can bounce back from sensory overload from precarious ones who can't.

MRWaSP visualization banks on sensory overload. This overload is the aesthetic equivalent of the "shock" in what Naomi Klein calls "shock capitalism".[103] "A variation on Machiavelli's advice that injuries should be *inflicted 'all at once'*" (7; emphasis mine), Klein explains, this idea of crisis or shock is the foundation for contemporary practices of (re)development, privatization, and investment. In post-cinematic media, shock-doctrine methods generate a surplus of pleasure. Post-cinematic media are designed to generate, amplify, and transmit damage so that we can *hear, see and feel* the damage we (or the characters we watch and identify with) ought to overcome. All that damage "makes sense" to audiences as fodder for a spectacular thera-peutic narrative: Look, it must be overcome! Whereas the male gaze and controlling images create the effect of coherence by blurring 'damaged' (feminized, blackened) elements out of focus, *deregulated MRWaSP visualization puts damage at the center of our attention.* The damage doesn't just make sense, it *feels good.*

ii. Pleasure: Without the security of universal structures, one must resiliently craft functional resources out of any and everything. Performing or viewing compositional processes, you never know what you're going to get, what material you'll have to work with, or what output performers will present you with. Thus, performers and audiences need to be flexible—they must turn damage (incoherence, accidents, chance occurrences) into a performative resource and/or listening pleasure.[104] Resilient subjects take pleasure in "feeling the burn," as the saying goes. For example, Taio Cruz's 2012 single "Hangover" treats a hangover as something to gleefuly celebrate, evidence of one's "work hard/play hard" cred. Don't get me wrong—hangovers *hurt.* But resilient subjects *savor* and crave that damage like vampires do human blood, because it's their fuel. It feels good to avow damage as what can be or has been overcome.

Resilience discourse habituates us to affirm and avow our damage. In the same way that Pavlov's dog is just following his programming when he or she drools upon hearing the sound of a bell (because he or she has been trained to associate that sound with the pleasure of eating), we're just following our programming when we find aesthetic pleasure in being overwhelmed by dissonance—we've learned to associate that feeling of overwhelming damage with the pleasure of, feeding our human capital, our "selves," if you will.

This is a very different model of pleasure than the pleasure in gazing or controlling, which comes from avoiding damage. "Visual pleasure" as Mulvey argues, is generated by the narrative devices that resolve or obscure challenges to the subject's autonomy. Failing to acknowledge the work done by the camera allows the protagonist/gazer to feel more powerful and autonomous than he is. Subject/object binaries have the same effect, allowing the gazing subject to feel like he isn't also the fragmented *object* of someone else's gaze.

The gaze is the means by which a classically liberal, modernist subject identifies and abjects objects from himself, as subject, and from society. Because the exclusion of the object is what constitutes the subject as such, this exclusion—in, for example, the form of resolution or closure—is invested as the site of traditional aesthetic pleasure. Modernist avant-gardes, on the other hand, produce "damaged goods," works or subjects whose imperfections critique and oppose dominant aesthetic and ethical norms. In post- or critical-modernity, transgression of exclusionary boundaries is the site of aesthetic pleasure. Examples of this include Dada artists' exquisite corpses, Afro-modernist antiphony, and feminist art's use of ugliness and disgust (e.g., in Orlan's work). Such practices transgress norms of coherence, homophony, and beauty as a means to critique them. This is why Mulvey argues that feminist film and film criticism ought to "make way for a total negation of the ease and plenitude of the narrative fiction film" (835).

MRWaSP visualization *avows* and normalizes visual, compositional, and affective damage, recycling modernist transgression into raw materials for the neoliberal culture industry. Damage isn't something subjects avoid, or which subjects do to objects—

damage is the means and medium of subjectification. Post-cinematic looking is a feedback loop in which we make visible, for others, our own self-objectification. To be recognized as a resilient subject, one must be seen by others as actively monitoring oneself (e.g., through quantified self practices like diet or exercise tracking). Because these practices collapse "image" and "bearer of the look" into the same role, conventional subject/object distinctions don't make much sense. So, instead of producing conventionally gendered male gazers and feminine objects, post-cinematic visualization produces both *resilient MRWaSP visualizers* and *pathological, toxic black holes* (i.e., vampiric drains of light, energy, momentum, and so on). The next section focuses on this toxicity and the role of non-resilient women of color in MRWaSP visualization.

(c) Toxicity: The Other Side of MRWaSP Visualization

MRWaSP visualization racializes "non-resilient" women as black. Whereas traditional virgin/whore dichotomies separate out "pure," virginal white women from everyone else, MRWaSP resilience separates out "toxic" black women from everyone else. As Jared Sexton explains, "the gaze of the new raciology... enabled by new visual technologies" such as "digital media" (238) coincides with and facilitates a "move beyond the black/white binary and toward a black-nonblack binary" (256). In MRWaSP, the overcoming of blackness and its supposed toxicity is what composes the multi-racial "we" as such. And that overcoming is, as this quote from Sexton suggests, facilitated by "new visual technologies" and "digital media." The concept "MRWaSP visualization" ties these two aspects of Sexton's argument together. In this section, I use it to describe and analyze how digital social media actively produce insufficiently resilient populations as both toxic and black.

Instead of objectifying and/or silencing women, MRWaSP visualization amplifies black women's (comparatively) unrestricted voices so they can provide non-black women with an opportunity to perform resilience for their social media networks and/or for big data (and, importantly, to accumulate the human capital that results from such performances). For example, just as mainstream non-black feminists have frequently and (in)famously decried black women's so-called aggressive bullying, trashing, and "emotional savage[ry]" as "toxic" (Goldberg 2014), Mark Fisher has argued that "intersectional" feminist activism on digital media vampirically drains the lifeblood of the progressive, radical left. Michelle Goldberg's essay "Feminism's Toxic Twitter Wars" describes the "dysfunctional, even unhealthy" culture of Twitter feminism as

> toxic. Indeed, there's a nascent genre of essays by people who feel emotionally savaged by their involvement in it—not because of sexist trolls, but because of the slashing righteousness of other feminists.

This toxicity drains what Goldberg identifies as the "revivifying" boost the internet gave to feminism. It does so by establishing a constant tenor of fear among digitally-engaged feminists. However, this constant state of anxiety and readiness is a feature not a bug. It is the normal and desired state of affairs in resilience discourse.

There must always be vampires for "us" to overcome. In both Goldberg's and Fisher's essays, feminists, especially feminists of color (often identified through the metonym "intersectionality"),[105] are tasked with manufacturing the raw materials— negative affects like guilt or anxiety—on which "good" subjects labor, and, through that labor, generate human capital (e.g., radical cred, moral/political goodness, proper femininity, and so on). White feminists subject WOC feminists to something like a controlling image of toxicity and disease so that they, the white feminists, can be seen as uplifting the online community into something respectable and safe.

Though Suey Park calls this "gentrification," resilience is actually quite distinct from gentrification. Gentrification implies eventual domestication and securitization: the point is to get rid of the toxic, decrepit, crumbling elements and make them 'nice' again. As Park puts it, the aim of gentrifiers is to "cleanse 'pollution' by erasing undesirable influence." Resilience discourse normalizes toxicity and decay—even though individuals learn how to deal with them, they never go away. The material constraints and affordances of Twitter—its "wildness" and disconnection from existing patterns of interpersonal communication—seem to be specially designed to incite and amplify never-ending cycles of toxicity, *and that's the point*.[106] From this perspective, Twitter is an engine for generating, channeling, and amplifying black femininity as the toxin for which "good" women—women that, as Goldberg describes, are "earnest and studiously politically correct"—are responsible for cleansing from society (cleaning up always is women's work, right?).

Analyzing Twitter toxicity as an instance of resilience discourse clarifies how "good" white femininity is designed to perform the work of anti-blackness. Instead of securing and protecting us vulnerable white women from the evil black threat, MRWaSP leaves us vulnerable to so-called "threats" so that we can demonstrate our agency, our independence, our post-feminist subjectivity in bouncing back from and eliminating that threat. Moreover, the toxicity narrative treats black women as themselves problems, not people with problems: they can cause toxicity, but they cannot experience it. Thus, "the invoking of 'toxic'" (Park) obscures and naturalizes the gendered and racialized precarity faced by black women. Similarly, when Fisher decries "the VC's [Vampire Castle's] work of constantly stoking up reactive outrage," he basically victim-blames "toxic" feminists for embodying cultural labor that's foisted on them—

sort of like how anti-black rape culture blames black women for embodying the controlling images the white male gaze foists on them. Notions of "toxicity" and "vampirism" rewrite the virgin/whore dichotomy for neoliberal feminism and capitalist cyberspace—a.k.a., MRWaSP visualization. *The supposed "toxicity" of Twitter feminism and feminists is one example of how MRWaSP visualization produces some women as toxic so that others can be resilient.*

(d) Summing Up MRWaSP Visualization

In media like Twitter or data visualizations, the LIO imperative does the work conventionally accomplished by controlling images and the male gaze—namely, it organizes media so they *amplify* white supremacist patriarchal institutions, values, and subjects. MRWaSP visualization is *a deregulatory process for generating damage and feeding it back into compositional/social processes so that it amplifies already-existent relations, structures, and institutions.*

Looking is a necessary element in resilience narratives: it's not just that you must overcome, but that your performance is seen, public, and available for consumption by others. Resilience is designed to generate human capital, and this capital *circulates*—in the market, as a means of social interaction—*as spectacle.* MRWaSP visualization, its aesthetics and its technical conventions, is an essential feature of the political economy of resilience. That's why the argument I made in the first half of this chapter is important, that is, the argument that the "Look, I Overcame!" narrative is a post-cinematic technology, that it organizes our relations to ourselves and to others with the same methods, concepts, and values that organize post-cinematic media and aesthetics.

So far this chapter has addressed the "visualization" part of MRWaSP visualization. In the next section, I use Beyoncé's "Video Phone" to flesh out the MRWaSP aspects of it. I'll address the relationship between "Look, I Overcame!" narratives,

MRWaSP, and post-cinematic methods and aesthetics. "Video Phone" uses the methods and aesthetics of post-cinematic media to adopt a gaze—or better, a style of visualization—that is distinctively post-feminist and post-racial.

3. Watch Beyonce Overcome: "Video Phone" & MRWaSP Visualization

The traditionally cinematic "male gaze" makes gendered subject/object divisions, and then naturalizes these categories by disavowing its own role, as "camera," in creating them. Beyoncé's "Video Phone," however, *explicitly foregrounds the camera*—it's the title of the song, after all. In so doing, the video also acknowledges and affirms the male gaze and the damage it has done to women. This is just one example of the various ways "Video Phone" uses MRWaSP visualization to organize its compositional form, its aesthetics, and its race-gender politics. In this section, I use "Video Phone" to illustrate the mutually-implicative relationships between the visualization techniques I discussed in Part Two of this chapter and the MRWaSP politics of resilience discourse. "Video Phone" clarifies how post-cinematic media like video phones and their attendant social media platforms are uniquely suited to help women broadcast their resilience and make their overcoming both visible (legible to others as spectacle) and visualizable (legible to big data). It also shows how these media work in conjunction with resilience discourse to produce a MRWaSP frame that visualizes non-elite black people (and aesthetics) as pathologically sexist and racist.

"Video Phone" has all the main elements or steps in a LIO narrative: it affirms the male gaze as damaging, recycles that damage into feminine subjectivity and human capital, and estab-lishes non-bourgeois black men and women as the source of any and all ongoing patriarchal damage. Though this section separates these stages out from one another and places them in a sequence for the sake of *analytical* clarity, in real life these elements often interact in ways that can't be neatly untangled into a linear protocol. Affirming damage, recycling it, and taking out the remaining trash—these are more like prisms I will use to separate out some colors or frequencies so we can pay more attention to the nuance of each hue or wavelength. That said, let's begin with the first step, affirming one's damage.

(a) Step One: Affirm your damage

In traditional cinema, the fourth wall (i.e., the disavowal of the camera as mediating the image) props up the male gaze—the "gaze" has to seem natural and normal, not the result of artifice.[107] Obscuring the gaze's infrastructure (i.e., the camera, patriarchy), the fourth wall lets the gazer feel and appear more autonomous than he actually is. (If the gaze depended on some one or some thing, it wouldn't be the free activity of an independent subject.) The fourth wall also obscures the infrastructure that objectifies women and femininity, and makes their situation seem natural, normal, and inevitable.

MRWaSP visualization knocks down the fourth wall. It demands that we recognize both the artifice of the camera and past racism and sexism. Video Phone" does this on a number of levels. First, the title and the lyrics explicitly name the camera and discuss the parameters of its use. It names the *device*, and not a media object, like a sext or a sex tape, because it's the means of production, not the product (which is what a sext is), that needs to be "outed." Second, "Video Phone" outs the camera's gaze *as male* by substituting cameras for the heads of the male characters and showing Beyoncé's character's reflection in the lens-eyes of a camera-dude. This doesn't just out the cameras as such, it outs cameras as male gazers. Post-cinematic media often out the camera. "Video Phone"'s outing of the camera is an instance of MRWaSP visualization because it outs *the male gaze*. In order for Beyonce's character to visualize her resilience, she has to first make visible the damage done to her as a woman.

"Video Phone" subjects Beyonce's character to two kinds of feminizing damage. First, her image is stuttered and fragmented throughout the video. Visually chopped and screwed, Beyonce's character exhibits symptoms of traditional cinematic feminization. Second, she is objectified as her character performs sexualized dance moves while wearing revealing costumes and poses for the camera-headed male characters in the video. In this way, she occupies the feminized position as object of the male gaze. But unlike the feminine objects of the male gaze, whose role is to unselfconsciously embody damage, Beyonce's character performs her explicit awareness and command of it. Lyrics frame objectification as something Beyoncé invites *and controls*: record me, she commands, because controlling the video phone is how I control and handle you. She can handle the male gaze because that's what resilience *does* — it is a method for processing the male gaze, as raw material, for use in LIO narratives. The male gaze may damage her, but it does not control her — she controls it. Mere awareness isn't enough; her character must *affirm* that damage as empowering for her as a (resilient) *feminine* subject.

Beyonce's character invites the male gaze because she needs to be seen overcoming *this look*. Affirming the damaging gaze as male is what makes her, as victim of that damage, legible or visible *as a woman*. Her character positions herself in front of the camera, as the object of both its' and men's gazes, to produce that image, the evidence of damage for her to overcome. She performs this overcoming in two ways. First, the lyrics begin with a catcall, and Beyonce's character responds to it by undermining it: you can't look at me, but you can put me on your video phone. This demand to move from traditional gazing, with its clear subject/object dichotomy, to video-phone style prosumer consumption/production, is how Beyonce both overcomes "the male gaze" and asserts her resilience — she's no mere object, but a prosuming entrepreneur. Second, throughout the video she captures, tortures, and eventually executes the camera-headed male dancers. So, even though she may objectify herself in front of a camera, she has transformed this performance from a damaging to an empowering experience.[108] Beyonce's character overcomes not just the feminized damage wrought by the male gaze, but also the anti-black feminized damage of controlling images. Her character may perform traditional "hoochie" and "jezebel" (and even "black lady") stereotypes, but only to demonstrate both her and "our" (middle-class American audiences') overcoming of them.

Instead of inhibiting Beyoncé's character, the male gaze and controlling images provides her with the opportunity to demonstrate her resilient subjectivity. She uses her video phone and its attendant social media platforms to recycle past damage and re-invest it in what Rob Horning calls a "data self."

(b) Step Two: Recycle That Damage, Girl!

In the video for "Video Phone," Beyonce's character performs for her (potential) paramour's video phone and for our computers, smartphones, and tablets. This performance is the process through which she *composes* a resilient feminine self. Overcoming the male gaze, Beyonce's character emerges as a distinctly *feminine* "data self."

Originally Rob Horning's term, the "data self" is one way that human capital is personified, one way we subjects of neoliberalism understand ourselves as "people." Unlike the traditional Modern subject, who is a pre-existing, authentic, autonomous being that is either accurately or inaccurately represented by media, the data self is the product of algorithmic mediation. As Horning explains, the data self:

> emerges through information processing (sharing, being shared, being on a social graph, having recommendations automated, being processed by algorithms, and so on). As information is processed and assimilated to the archive of self,

it begins feeding into the algorithmic systems that report back to us the true nature of what we really are (Horning GAFS).

In other words, I am my Facebook timeline, my Instagram/Vine accounts, my Amazon purchase history/wishlist, my search history on Google or my listening history on Spotify or YouTube, etc. For example, there are applications that will analyze your social media accounts to tell you who your closest friends are, who influences you and whom you influence most, what words you use most often in your statuses, what your most common moods are, and so on. Or, you can take an online quiz that will tell you which character you are in a popular TV series, which philosopher you are, or which city you most belong in. Instead of confessing who we are to our therapist or priest, data reveals it to us. Thus, in order to exist at all, I have to make myself into the media objects that then get shared, tracked, and fed into algorithms. "We are *only* what we express and share" (Horning, GAFS).

The data self, like post-cinematic media in general, *dynamically composes itself*. The overall 'self' emerges as a macro-scale effect of moment-to-moment, micro-level interactions among various bits of data. As Horning argues, "real selves (real in the sense of being influential in networks) emerge through the process of information processing." (Horning, "dumb bullshit").[109] Objectification or better "capture" is *necessary* for becoming a data self: to be crunched, you have to first be a number.

To be a data self, to be a recognized member of neoliberal society, Beyonce *has* to put herself in front of the camera as an ongoing media performance that can circulate, both itself and in commentary, on YouTube, twitter, tumblr, be made into parodies and spliced into gifs, etc.[110] Her circulated images are "necessary collateral, mandatory passports to participate in a consumer society gone 'social' (Horning GAFS). So, the camera's gaze isn't an impediment, but a *precondition* to her recognition as a 'real' person, someone who belongs and contributes to society. Means for producing, consuming, sharing, and editorializing, video phones are *gateways* to economies that confer personhood and measure value in terms of views, shares, likes, reblogs, and other metrics of social/human capital. Beyonce's sexy, femme data self is not an objectified image but a performative process. She's a *visualization* of data, not an object of a gaze.

MRWaSP works as and through the algorithms that crunch all the data generated by devices like video phones, not directly as and through the devices themselves. Similarly, the recipient of a sext isn't really the individual to whom you send it (a male gazer), but "the cloud." (In "Video Phone," both individual men and individual cameras are so superfluous Beyonce can destroy them.) When you send a digital image from your video phone, that image is stored on the cloud somewhere, most likely by both your carrier/ISP and by whatever app you're using. The cloud doesn't *see* you—it processes, stores, and redistributes abstractions (i.e., the code for your video message). MRWaSP algorithmically *visualizes* you, makes you legible to yourself and others as a self, as human capital. Turning traditional patriarchal damage into "content" to upload and share, Beyonce's character recycles that damage...not in a way that liberates her from patriarchy, but in a way that incorporates her more fully into MRWaSP.

Performing for video phones, Beyonce's character composes a data self...and not just any data self, but a specifically gendered one. Because she overcomes the *male* gaze, her character performs *feminine* resilience. Broadcasting that overcoming everyone to see, comment on, and share, her feminine resilience is legible, visualizable, profitable. But her character's resilience isn't just gendered—it's also raced and racializing. In "Video Phone," all the representatives of the male gaze are non-white men. Why does "Video Phone" present *feminine* resilience as the overcoming and, indeed, execution, of apparently misogynist non-white men?

(c) Step Three: Take out the remaining trash

In the final stage of MRWaSP visualization, post-feminist patriarchy most obviously manifests as a form of *multi-racial* white
supremacy. Here, the visualization process gets rid of all
noticeable vestiges of sexism and racism by scapegoating non-
elite people of color (generally "third world" or urban poor) and,
less frequently, insufficiently neoliberal whites (rural poor/
working class, radical conservatives, religious fundamentalists,
etc.). As I argued in the introduction, visible sexism and racism
is inconsistent with the neoliberal myth of postracialism and
postfeminism. So, MRWaSP visualization resolves that paradox
by making visible sexism and racism *look black*. Remember, white
supremacy becomes "multi-racial" by including everyone *but*
blacks, and just as white supremacy can be embodied by
someone who is phenotypically not white, blackness can be
embodied by people who are phenotypically not black. MRWaSP
visualization renders specific people and populations black. It
does this by assigning a person (or group, or institution) responsibility for sexism, racism, and other "backwards" and inefficient
or unhealthy phenomena. Tying Beyonce's character's resilience
to her overcoming of black male gazers, "Video Phone" is a clear
example of this this aspect of MRWaSP visualization.

Especially because Beyonce is phenotypically black, her
character's performance of resilience hangs on the character's
disidentification from what MRWaSP considers "black." And
that's what "Video Phone" visualizes. Here, Beyonce, in various
states of swimwear-undress, demonstrates her overcoming of
traditional male-gaze style objectification by executing a stereotypically misogynist black man. I've already discussed how the
video visually presents the male gazer as a man of color. The
lyrics reaffirm this, and, with references both to his verbal dialect
and his sartorial style (white tshirt and droopy pants), specify
him as a member of working-class, urban black culture.[111] These
vocal and fashion cues establish the racial, class, and cultural

identity of the man fixing—or attempting to fix—Beyonce's character as the object of his gaze. Following Regina Bradley's analysis of Beyonce's use of Houston dialects, we can infer that this man is a southern, working-class, non-bourgeois black man.[112] This kind of "working class, southern, cassette tapes" type of "masculin[ity]" is, as Zandria Robinson argues, a source of "discomfort" for "a black middle class that views itself as fundamentally distinct from poorer blacks." So, "Video Phone" associates the male gaze with the very black men that don't get folded into middle-class MRWaSP respectability. And these are the men Beyonce's character controls, captures, and executes; they are what she overcomes.

Black rappers have long been white supremacist patriarchy's scapegoats. As bell hooks and plenty of others have argued, concerns about the excessive misogyny in rap are often racist ploys to scapegoat black men, making them seem responsible for the misogyny that is actually a central feature of white supremacy, too.[113] These videos update this trope to function in a MRWaSP context. Non-bourgeois black men must be eliminated by female characters so that dominant society can prove it is *both* post-racial (they're bad because they're misogynist, not because they're black) and post-feminist (misogyny is limited only to this "primitive," backwards subgroup from which women can defend themselves).

By executing *this* particular representative of "the male gaze," Beyonce's character affirms her inclusion within multi-racial white supremacist patriarchy. She separates herself from supposedly unhealthy, non-resilient blackness and, in so doing, shows that unlike victimized women of color, Beyonce is resilient, capable of overcoming objectification and exploitation *and*, importantly, capable of disidentifying with the men who are supposedly responsible for that objectification and exploitation. Gaga's "Telephone" performs more or less the same thing. The collective overcoming of stereotypically misogynist black men is what cements the cross-racial bond between Gaga and Bey's characters, and thus affirms the "multi-raciality" of multi-racial white supremacist patriarchy.

On the one hand, "Video Phone" presents Beyonce as a resiliently respectable woman, one who uses the human capital she garners from her conquest of non-bourgeois black men and the misogyny they represent to mainstream audiences as her buy-in to multi-racial white supremacist patriarchal privilege. On the other hand, the *music* in the song's introduction does somewhat complicate this performance of respectability. This is just one of many instances where, to use Regina Bradley's terms, Beyonce plays "what we *see* of and about Beyonce" against "what we *hear*" from and about her. Though "Video Phone"'s video tells us the story of feminine resilience & MRWaSP visualization, the song's introduction refers us to an entirely different narrative of neoliberal black femininity. The introduction's music references the end of "Diva," which is two tracks before "Video Phone" on *I Am...Sasha Fierce*. "Diva's" video coda features the music from the beginning of "Video Phone"—the same syncopated, high-pitched, chime-like synth loop over trappy drum machines crescendos into a line of lyrics from "Video Phone." The reference establishes a clear, unmistakable connection between "Diva" and "Video Phone." But what does this connection *do*?

"Diva" complicates the resilient-good-girl/precarious-bad-girl dichotomy (which, as I argued earlier, is an upgrade on traditional virgin/whore dichotomies). The "diva" is entrepreneurial but not properly resilient, and bad but not precarious or victimized. The Diva figure takes resilience discourse, feeds it back into itself, intensifying it to diva-like excess. These excesses warp the feedback process so that the strategies and techniques that ought, under normal conditions, amplify MRWaSP resilience discourse, actually corrode it. In a way, she embezzles the profits of resilience discourse (human capital, for example), using them for her own ends. She out-hustles the "hustle," which, as Lester Spence argues, is "not so much an alternative as a hip-hop inflected spin on the concept of human capital" (Staring 17).

4. Q: Are We Not Human Capital? A: We Are Diva.

As Lester Spence has argued, in the first decades of the 21st century, mainstream hip hop culture embraced entrepreneurship as both a practice and a masculine ideal. Hip hop artists not only brag about their entrepreneurial skills in their songs, they *are* CEOs of multiplatform brand enterprises. Hip hop upgraded itself, moving "from the street corner to the corner office." Beyonce's husband, Jay-Z, often raps about his translation of street-honed skills to boardroom strategy; Sean Combs (Diddy), Dana Owens (Queen Latifah), 50 Cent, and even Beyonce herself (e.g., with her House of Dereon fashion line) are other examples. In hip hop culture, entrepreneurship is often framed as a gendered LIO narrative: war-on-drugs racialized, gendered, and class-inflected damage is the very basis of entrepreneurial rap-game success. For example, Mark Ecko, speaking in *Entrepreneur* magazine, says that "the nature of hip-hop and the dynamic that spawned hip-hop is innately entrepreneurial...It's something made from nothing." In hip hop culture, entrepreneurship is often a performance of resilient black *masculinity*—it's one way for black men to work their way into respectable MRWaSP society. Instead of overcoming the male gaze, these entrepreneurs overcome a stereotypically black masculine pathology—the street "hustler." The differences and similarities between entrepreneurs and hustlers are widely debated, but in general the hustler has the same "game" as the entrepreneur, minus the latter's performance of bourgeois respectability.[114]

"The Diva," as Beyonce's song claims, is the feminine incarnation of the hustler figure. Manifesting in her swagger, tough-talking, embrace of violence, even her cigar smoking, hustler masculinity saturates Beyonce's performance of the Diva role. As I will argue in this section, Beyonce's Diva kings on—that is, the Diva *queers*—the hustler as "hip-hop inflected spin on...human capital" (Spence 17). "Kinging," as Jack Halberstam explains, "reads dominant male masculinity and explodes its effects" (IAQTAP 127). Beyonce's Diva explodes *both* hustler masculinity and resilient, "Look, I Overcame!" femininity by feeding them back through one another on a circuit bent and distorted by Afrofuturist posthumanism. As I will explain below, Diva's drag isn't limited to gender; the *posthuman* aspects of Lil Wayne's and Klaus Nomi's masculinities are central to Beyonce's performance of her Robo-Diva persona.[115] Beyonce's Robo-Diva kings on or bends the circuits of *both* hustla entrepreneurialism and resilience discourse, transforming these modes of MRWaSP human capital production into a "bankrupt form" (Halberstam IAQTAP 130). That's the Diva's hustle—queering the circuits of MRWaSP production, she redirects their outputs back to her pockets. Her apparent compliance is really just a front for her own long con.

For example, "Diva"'s video bends the circuits of conventional LIO resilience. The video displays all the trappings of a "Look, I Overcame!" narrative, but the Diva's performance acts as an accelerant that burns up damage rather than overcomes it. The first scene in the video is a shot of a car trunk overflowing with disassembled white female mannequins—the fragmented, damaged objects of the traditional male gaze. At the end of the video, after "Diva" has finished and the soundtrack shifts to the syncopated, chiming hook from "Video Phone," Beyonce's character sets the car alight. (As she strikes the match and walks away, Beyonce's character wears, on her left hand, the robot glove she dons in "Single Ladies," and which is central to her Robo-Diva persona, which I will discuss at more length in a moment.) The visual spectacle, here, isn't her objectified body, nor is it her overcoming. In fact, even though her body is sexualized, Beyonce's character's body is never presented as *damaged* by that sexualization. Beyonce's character doesn't positively affirm her damage as a character-building exercise— she never "reclaims" or "owns" it (e.g., by tearing up magazine images or by executing some representative of the male gaze, as in "Video Phone"). She doesn't *embody* damage; rather, she *wreaks* it. The most visually spectacular moment in "Diva" is the huge explosion, that is, Robo-Diva's *sabotage* of resilience discourse. She gives us something to look at, just not what the "Look, I Overcame!" narrative wants us to see. This diversion redirects the outputs of resilience discourse.

Beyonce's "Diva" doesn't rob us of pleasure—we'd probably be really upset if she did. Rather, she redirects our pleasure away from its normal object (we're expecting to look at her overcoming), and toward an abnormal one—here, the explosion. Queering audience pleasure in this way, Beyonce's Diva diverts investments in resilience—both her performative work and the audience's "really subsumed" labor—so that their dividends line *her* pockets, not MRWaSP's. We watch her annihilate the damage that she's supposed to own and transform into resilient human capital. Success and opportunity purposely wasted, gone up in smoke, "Diva'''s pile burning mannequins echoes the pile of burning cash in "The K Foundation Burn A Million Quid."[116] Just as kinging "explodes" normative masculinity, "Diva's" hustle "explodes" the gendered, racialized, and aesthetic norms of resilience discourse. Sending its power supply up in smoke, Beyonce's Robo-Diva's *bankrupts* MRWaSP resilience.

This visual trick isn't Robo-Diva's endgame; it's merely a means to an end. Her explosive, visually spectacular sabotage of distracts our attention from her *sonic* hustle. While we're looking, waiting for her to overcome, she's using sound and music to divert the flow of human capital to her own, alien coffers. The first image we have of Beyoncé is her fabulously shod feet as they count out the rhythm for the song (this echoes the introductory shot of "Video Phone," where she walks down an alley with a posse of men in dark suits). In fact, in the video we *hear* two of her steps/beats before we even see her feet. This opening clip establishes that the visual is merely a means to "Diva"'s sonic work. Similarly, in the song at least, the *music* defines "Diva" before the lyrics do. Musically, the song is built on a looped and chipmunked vocal sample: "Imma-a-Diva/Imma-Imma-a-Diva." This loop is the first bit of music we hear in the video (the footsteps lead directly into it), and is played for four measures before the vocals come in with the verbal definition: a diva is "the hustler"'s feminine counterpart. The song uses music to indicate what Beyonce means by "Diva"; the lyrics just elaborate this primary definition.

What does the music tell us a Diva is? Musically, "Diva" echoes Lil Wayne's 2008 single "A Milli," which was also produced by Bangladesh (Shondrae Crawford) and built on a looped vocal stating the song's title ("a-milli-a-milli-a-milli-a-milli-a-milli"). Musically, then, "Diva" is the female version of "A Milli." Beyonce's Diva is a female version of Weezy's specific style of hustling...which isn't limited to (Young) money, but also includes Afrofuturist posthumanism. For example, on *Tha Carter III*, the album on which "A Milli" appears, Weezy repeatedly emphasizes that he is a Martian.[117] If he's investing in himself, he's not producing *human* capital, but *alien capital*. So, if the Diva is the female version of Weezy's specific style of hustler, then the Diva is also a shareholder of extra-human capital.

Beyonce's visual performance of Afrofuturist Robo-Diva characters reinforces this sonic affiliation with Weezy's alien hustle/hustler. There are a number of components to this perfor-mance; some are more cyborg-like, such as the robot glove from "Single Ladies," and some are more explicitly alien. For example, in the same way that "Diva"'s *music* kings on Weezy's "A Milli," Beyonce's Robo-Diva character visually kings on another famous male "alien," Klaus Nomi, a queer German-American New Wave musician who performed as the extraterrestrial character "Nomi." Intermittently throughout the video, Beyonce wears an outfit that strongly recalls his iconic inverted-triangle tuxedo. Or rather, her outfit is Nomi's inverted-triangle tuxedo re-imagined as futuristic space suit or droid armor. As with her sonic Weezy drag, Robo-Diva's visual Nomi drag "kings" on both gender *through posthumanity*. That is, she uses posthuman performance to amplify the instability her race/gender drag generates.

Her posthumanity *is* her hustle—Robo-Diva embezzles human capital by laundering it as *post*-human capital (alien or robot identity). This is evident in the video's presentation of the Diva's work, her performative labor, as something that invests in and amplifies *posthumanity*. For example, in the middle of the video Beyoncé puts a horizontal fluorescent light at eye-level; this effect makes her character look like a Cylon (a robot/cyborg in the *Battlestar Gallactica* universe, which was, at the time the video was shot, the subject of a critically-acclaimed and popular television series). Shortly thereafter, the juxtaposition of lyical and visual content connects this cyborg identity to her status as a pop diva. The lyrics discuss the labor of the pop (rather than rap) game, the work of feminine gender performance that Beyonce Knowles (the person) has been doing since she was a young teen. While performing these lines, Beyoncé appears with a group of ambiguously-sexed golden androids (which are also references to the clearly female white mannequins from the introduction). Hunched over and arms akimbo, she is posed like a powered-down droid, just as the gloss on her skin gives her a plastic "glow". The juxtaposition of these images with those lyrics implies that black pop divas *are* droids, programmed from adolescence to perform as hyperfeminine cyborgs (e.g., with stiletto shoes as feminizing prosthetics).

Beyonce positively affirms this cyborg identity, but *not as something that damaged her*. The lyrics treat her work and experience as a source of her authority, her status as Diva.

Though the Robo-Diva's posthumanity *could* be seen as damaged humanity ripe for refinement into resilient human capital, Beyonce's *sonic* performance undermines any attempt to frame this as a LIO narrative. *We don't see her overcome, but hear her talk back.*

Just as Robo-Diva's *sonic* presence precedes and often supersedes her visual one, her noisy machinic excess drowns out her human damage (as the stereotypically silent subaltern or angry, loud black lady). Talking back, Bey's Robo-Diva makes sonic feedback loops that blow up "our" attempts to hear her confess her damage, just as she blows up the mannequins in the car. This happens about two minutes into the video, at which point Beyoncé emphasizes the line "ladies talk back" by making "talking" gestures with her hand. On the hand that makes this gesture, she's wearing the same robot glove she wears while igniting the trunk full of mannequins; this visual resonance implies that "talking back" is a similarly "explosive" response to patriarchal damage, and to resilience discourse. The video confirms that implication. Because there is no acknowledgement of silencing or hysteric shrieking, "talking back" doesn't appear as a reclamation of lost voice. It is instead a method of correcting people who underestimate one's authority.[118] The problem here isn't the Diva's—the person she's talking back to is the one who is dysfunctional and damaged. Talking back is, basically, saying "It's not me, it's *you*." It *reflects or refracts the damage back on MRWaSP.*

In this way, talking back resembles other "hollaback" tactics. "Hollaback" is a feminist response to street harassment that deflects the male gaze. Instead of focusing visibility on victims and their damage, Hollaback uses smartphone tech and social media to post images of the *perpetrators* of street harassment on a website, ihollaback.org. It feeds the male gaze back on itself, amplifying it so that it destabilizes the authority of the male gazers and the mechanisms of the male gaze (cameras, objectification, etc.). *Talking back feeds patriarchal damage back on itself, identifying patriarchy itself, not women, as the damaged thing that needs to be fixed.* Too much feedback—that is, too much noise—will blow a circuit or a speaker. Damage, here, isn't the fuel for a resilient overcoming, but an accelerant Robo-Diva uses to blow it up, much as she did with mannequins in the trunk.

Talking back, Robo-Diva uses sound to *amplify* Beyonce's human capital beyond the limits of the (merely) human. Just as the Robo-Diva persona is a form of posthuman drag that "kings" on Weezy's alien hustler, Beyonce's performance of that persona distorts or "kings" on resilient human capital—destabilizing it, making it too queer to be bankable as "human" capital (though it may be bankable as a different form of value). Robo-Diva's presence as a visibly post-human body is her ultimate drag performance. Her actual material form is, as the song's lyrics suggest, radio waves or streaming data. She's a Diva because she rules radios.[119] And, insofar as we're talking about "Beyonce" the pop superstar (not Beyonce Knowles the person), that's more or less correct. The character "Beyonce" *is* a collection of media objects—sounds, data streams, videos, and so on. To become "queen Bey," arguably the most globally successful female pop star of the contemporary era, Beyonce Knowles had to transform herself into sound waves, data streams, digital images, and electrical singers. So, to become an excessively successful, bankable star, Beyonce had to become "Beyonce". This "Beyonce," the one embodied by the Robo Diva, is not a singer on the radio, she is, as a singer, *the radio waves and streaming data itself.* Robo-Diva is, in other words, algorithmic. Instead of building human capital through resilience, she kings on human capital by becoming the logic of capital itself. She bankrupts the institution of human capital by robbing it of any "human" on which to capitalize.

Just as drag king performances trouble the naturalness and normalcy of supposedly "normal" masculinities, Beyonce's Robo

Diva blows up the practice of human capitalization, here in the form of resilience discourse. She uses various layers of drag (of Weezy, of Nomi, of capital itself) to find the "kingy effect within [the] otherwise mainstream" (Halberstam IAQTAP 129) discourses of resilient human capital. This "kingy effect" is the sonic shock wave that reverberates across "Diva" and "Video Phone," destabilizing "otherwise mainstream" interpretations of both works. In "Diva"'s video coda, *the shock wave from the exploding car changes the sonic texture*: the introductory hook to "Video Phone" plays as Beyoncé walks away from the car. *Sound* –here, the sounds linking "Diva" and "Video Phone" – provides the "kingy effect" in Beyonce's "Look, I Overcame!" narratives. Instead of resiliently executing the male gaze, as Beyonce's character does in "Video Phone," Robo-Diva blows up resilience discourse. She *feeds resilience discourse back into itself*, amplifying it so intensely that it melts the systems fuses and sets it alight. This sort of amplification produces noise/waste that can't be recycled, or can't be recycled fast enough, so it just accumulates like lint in a clothesdryer, courting combustion. In this way, "Diva" is a sort of accelerationist response to resilience discourse: she out hustles the hustle. In fact, her "kingy effects" strongly parallel the "navigational," "experimental...mode of acceleration" advocated by Alex Williams & Nick Srnicek in *#ACCELERATE Manifesto for an Accelerationist Politics*.

But accelerationism intensifies biopolitical imperatives—it's like cancerous growth.[120] Accelerationism is more or less the opposite of what I mean by going into the death. Whereas accelerationism intensifies and invests in life, the strategies I discuss in the next chapter—going into the death, melancholy—intensify and invest in, you guessed it, death. Moreover, accelerationism is often considered something that amplifies mastery;[121] I'm interested in practices that can't be captured by active/passive or virtuosity/failure oppositions because they call ideals of mastery, virtuosity, and, indeed, *resilience* into question. Melancholy—that is, misfired resilience, insufficiently profitable overcoming—is an alternative to biopolitical discourses of resilience and acceleration. Instead of resiliently recycling damage into human capital, melancholy goes into the death, investing in damage without properly overcoming it.

The next chapter contrasts Rihanna's and Lady Gaga's responses to resilience discourse. Gaga, like the Beyonce of "Video Phone," fully buys into the LIO narrative of feminine resilience and anti-blackness. Rihanna, on the other hand, is like neither the resilient Beyonce of "Video Phone," nor the accelerationist Beyonce of "Diva." Instead, she's a melancholic bad girl, an insufficiently resilient woman who does not overcome but invests in supposedly damaged blackness.

4

(Little) Monsters & Melancholics

Feminized, queered, disabled, racially blackened damage are the building blocks of resilience discourse. By recycling this damage, resilience upgrades liberal identity politics into neoliberal post-identity ones: I am [an abused woman/queer/disabled/anorexic/obese/etc.] and because I have worked to overcome the difficulties that come with that identity or situation, I am special and deserving of inclusion in some echelon of privilege. Resilience doesn't just produce a new, post-identity society; it also extracts surplus value from the individuals doing the work of self-overcoming...who are, by and large, women. As I argued earlier, the work of becoming a woman (the performance of MRWaSP femininity, the practices and behaviors that gender someone "feminine") is a means of producing both human capital for the resilient woman, and further profits for MRWaSP institutions. Lady Gaga's "Little Monsters" are a prime example of this overcoming and profiting from damage.

But some damage is more profitable *as damage*; hegemonic institutions benefit most when they prevent it from being recycled, composted, or appropriated. This is what Lester Spence calls the "exception" to neoliberalism's voracious subsumption of everything into capitalist production, on the one hand, and post-identity inclusion, on the other. This exception is embodied, Spence argues, in the racialized, gendered, socioeconomically-inflected "damage" represented by urban black masculinity. This damage is a constitutive outside of both neoliberal capitalism and MRWaSP. It can't be recycled because it is toxic to the system. Hegemonic institutions function most efficiently when this damage is fed back into the system *as excluded* — as *death.* The death of poor and working-class black men — the grist for the school-to-prison pipeline and stand-your-ground-style execution, for example—is what makes post-capitalist MRWaSP society possible. Their death is also central to many "feminist" pop music narratives, including Beyonce's "Video Phone," which I discussed in the previous chapter, and Gaga's "Telephone," which I will talk about in this one.

In this chapter, I use goth, both the music genre and the concept of "goth damage," to contrast Gaga's explicitly anti-black resilience with Rihanna's black feminist melancholy. If damage is a key feature of resilience discourse, goth, with its emphasis on damage, is almost a natural complement to resilience. Goth aesthetics—in music, in fashion, in visual imagery—are one way for artists to perform the "damage" they must later overcome...or, in Rihanna's case, not overcome. In Gaga's work, goth damage symbolizes the damage done to MRWaSP femininities by patriarchy, which is represented by stereotypically urban black men. In this way, her work clearly illustrates the role of anti-blackness in resilience discourse. Rihanna's *Unapologetic*, on the other hand, rejects both resilience discourse and anti-blackness. Her work doesn't overcome, but *invests in* gothy damage and stereotypically urban black men (namely, Chris Brown). Rihanna's work is not resilient, but *melancholic*. This melancholy isn't the failure to get over a loss (as Freud understands it); rather, Rihanna's melancholy is a way of actively investing in the biopolitical, MRWaSP death that blackness represents. Melancholy is a feminist method of going *into the death*. Rather than investing in damage, melancholy invests in MRWaSP's *exceptions*. Bending resilience discourse and MRWaSP aesthetics in this way, melancholy generates the wrong kind of noise: not the damaged, fragmented aesthetics of MRWaSP visualization, but the sounds that start a riot in MRWaSP aesthetics and the politics of resilience.

To fully appreciate what's so riotous about Rihanna's melancholic investments in death, you need to know how and why the loud, obnoxious production of noisy, gothy damage actually maintains order. So, though this chapter is ultimately about Rihanna and melancholy, I'll begin by looking at Gaga's post-goth resilience.

1. Gaga's Post-Goth Resilience

From pastel goth (a teen fashion subculture that updates classic goth style) to witch house to a New York Times article on hipster covens in Brooklyn, goth seems to be rising from the grave of passé 90s subcultures and into hipster and mainstream currency. The sounds conventionally associated with goth rock, industrial, and EBM (electronic body music) are now commonly used in both rock- and EDM-pop, mainstream hip hop, dubstep, and trap. For example, the winner of the 2013 Pazz & Jop poll, Kanye West's *Yeezus*, has more sonically in common with My Life With The Thrill Kill Kult and Nitzer Ebb than it does with mainstream rap (or rather, it represents the ever-narrowing convergence of the two).

The musical, sartorial, and visual appropriation of goth is a central feature of Lady Gaga's work on *The Fame Monster*, *Born This Way*, and *ARTPOP*. There, she uses goth damage as a symbol of and substitute for the gendered, sexualized damage women and queers suffer at the hands of heteropatriarchy. Goth signifiers are the medium in which she demonstrates her overcoming of her own damage—her femininity, her struggles with body image, her appropriation of homo- and trans-phobic damage, etc. As I will show in what follows, her proud performances of goth damage are analogs for the resilient performances of femininity and LGBTQ identity that her fans should ideally embody.

(a) Gaga's Use of Goth

Goth is a subculture, but it is also a genre of pop music.[122] So, because Gaga is also primarily a musician (she releases albums, singles, and music videos, and her career is organized around these works) it's important to ground Gaga's use of goth in her musical practices. There are many, many subgenres of goth music, with influences from traditional Celtic music to noise rock to acid house, and Gaga draws on this wide spectrum of goth musics. Gaga's goth influences range from industrial and EBM (e.g., on "Judas") to the more straightforwardly melody-focused goth-pop of bands like Siouxie and the Banshees, Depeche Mode, and Bauhaus. These influences manifest in specific musical choices and in overall aesthetics, in compositional structures, instrumental and vocal performance styles, and in lyrical content. Gaga acknowledges this influence in a press release for *The Fame Monster*, which states: "this album is a pop experimentation with industrial/Goth beats, 90's dance melodies, an obsession with the lyrical genius of 80's melancholic pop."[123]

With this explicit reference to goth/industrial, it shouldn't be a surprise that this album contains the most obvious similarity between any one Gaga track and any one goth-y track is between "Dance in the Dark" and Depeche Mode's "Strangelove." Early Depeche Mode was very synthy and proto-industrial, particularly their 1983-1984 releases *Construction Time Again*, and *Some Great Reward*. "Strangelove" appears on the 1987 album *Music for the Masses*, which takes the earlier albums' industrial and synthpop sounds in a more mainstream, poppy direction. (In fact, Depeche Mode's combination of industrial and mainstream synthpop is actually quite similar to Gaga's own aesthetic.) Both "Dance In the Dark" and "Strangelove" are composed around essentially the same treble synth hook, which appears as the introductory melodic hook in each song. "Dance In the Dark" pulls somewhat of an "Ice Ice Baby" on Depeche Mode's original, altering the hook's melody very slightly by adding a note or two; in "Dance In the Dark," a sequencer effect chops the hook's longer notes into a series of repeated eight-notes.[124]

Though many of her songs often make musical references to

goth and industrial musical conventions, "Judas" is perhaps the most obviously "industrial" in its overall musical aesthetic. With its 4-on-the-floor percussion and cyberpunky timbre of its melodic synth, the break has a very psy-trance/EBM feel. It would fit in quite well with something, say, from the KMFDM/My Life with the Thrill Kill Kult side project Excessive Force. "Judas," like many KMDFM songs, combines heavy instrumentals with quite poppy female vocals (think, for example, of "Juke Joint Jezebel," or Excessive Force's "Violent Peace"). Moreover, the song's tongue-in-cheek blasphemy—for example, Gaga's declaration of romantic love for Judas—is reminiscent of My Life with the Thrill Kill Kult's Christian-trolling. "Judas" cobbles together a number of goth/industrial musical conventions.

Gaga's musical debts to goth/industrial are also evident in ARTPOP, her most recent release as of this writing. According to music theorist and historian of industrial music S. Alexander Reed, the vocal delivery on "Applause" draws on Bauhaus frontman Peter Murphy's style.[125] For example, the low-range, relatively monotone way in which Gaga sings the chorus and the husky chesty-ness of her timber, as well as the way she slides into pitches (e.g., on the "I"s) and her use of vibrato at the ends of phrases resembles Murphy's ways of doing each of these vocal techniques, on everything from "Bela Lugosi" to his solo work.

Gaga's *music* owes a lot to the spectra of goth/industrial styles, conventions, and sounds. Though pop fans might not be familiar enough with goth/industrial/EBM to readily recognize the musical influences and references, her visual presentation is just as explicit in its appropriations of goth style. From meat dresses to lacy black Victorian veils to latex nun regalia, to the art direction of videos from "Alejandro" to "Judas" to "Bad Romance," Gaga's visual style is heavily indebted to goth fashion and aesthetics. "Bad Romance" is one of her most popular and highly-regarded pieces and was, at one time, the most viewed item on YouTube, ever. More importantly, because its cinematic narrative is a clear example of resilience discourse, "Bad Romance" ties Gaga's goth aesthetics to her use of "Look, I Overcame!" narratives.

The video uses the visual signifiers of goth monstrosity to demonstrate the grotesqueness of traditional gender and sexual norms/identities, to make visible the damage that Gaga's character overcomes. The video's costumes and props are heavily influenced by goth fashion; the first few scenes provide more than enough examples: In the introductory sequence, we see cast members with bondage wear, high-heeled platform combat boots, and Victorian-style furniture. Gaga is wearing eyeglasses made out of razor blades and a manicure evocative of barbed wire. The next scene shows seven white caskets with the word "monster" and a red Christian cross on the lid. Words on the screen tell us that this is the "Bath Haus of Gaga"—this phrase plays on the name of Gaga's creative team, Haus of Gaga, in a way that evokes not only gay bathouses, but also, and more importantly, the seminal goth band *Bauhaus* (whose track "Bela Lugosi is Dead" is the quintessential classic goth track). From the coffins emerge Gaga and six dancers, each dressed like an eyeless tree-monster. Even though everyone is wearing skin-tight latex bodysuits, the dancing in this scene is not at all sexual. Rather, it is clumsy, jittery, and awkward—more Frankenstein than freaking. Around the 2:15 mark, we see a nude Gaga whose lack of clothing emphasizes her body's grotesqueness rather than its sexual desirability. Her body is extremely emaciated; her vertebrae are exaggerated to the point that they resemble the ridges on the back of a reptile. On her head Gaga is wearing the mummified body of a long-fanged bat. There are plenty more examples of the video's use of goth aesthetics, but by now you get the idea.

The video's *aesthetic* damage—the disgusting, distorted, monstrous bodies and movements—evokes and amplifies the *sexist* damage Gaga's character suffers and, eventually, overcomes. Gaga's body performs the visual rhetoric of goth in order to demonstrate the damage patriarchy has wrought upon it. "Bad Romance" is about Gaga's conquest of the male gaze, the traffic in women, and rape culture. It shows her being commanded to dance for an audience of men, who then bid on her; one takes her home and, the video implies, tries to force her to have sex. Around this point in the video (about 3:30) Gaga's character appears in an Alexander McQueen "insect" suit with lobster-claw heels. Both the chartreuse hue of the outfit and the shape of Gaga's hairstyle suggest that she's not just any insect, but a praying mantis. Female praying mantises eat their mates after copulation; this fact foreshadows the video's concluding scene, in which Gaga uses a flame-throwing bra to immolate both the man who has purchased her, and the bed upon which she was presumably to be raped. Narratively, the video is a pretty typical LIO story: executing her pimp and lying next to his burnt corpse, Gaga's character spectacularly overcomes her patriarchal damage. But as we know, that overcoming must be preceded by the visible display of damage. Sexist damage manifests *aesthetically* in the video as goth style.

However, whereas goth aesthetics find the grotesque pleasurable and desirable, "Bad Romance" points out the grotesqueness of what heteropatriarchy tells us we ought to desire. As the song's title and chorus indicate, it's not about romanticizing "bad" things; rather, it's about pointing out the badness of conventionally-scripted pop song "romance" itself. The song presents "normal" heterosexuality (the male gaze, the traffic in women, rape culture) and as monstrous and horrific— patriarchy has us all "caught in a bad romance," so to speak.If traditional goth treats monstrosity and damage as aesthetic ends (they are pleasurable "in themselves," to use some terms from Kantian aesthetics), Gaga treats them as mere means. Goth damage is the medium for Gaga's resilience. Any pleasure we

---

take in the disgusting, gothy elements of her performance is merely instrumental; the real source of pleasure here is her overcoming. In this way, "Bad Romance" flips traditional goth scripts into post-goth resilience.

(b) Post-Goth Monstrosity for Post-Identity Politics

Traditionally, goth is an oppositional subculture. Goth's highly stylized aesthetics are the means by which goths subvert and resist mainstream norms. For example, as Michael Du Pleiss explains, "goth subculture articulates modes of empowering monstrosity" (166). Claiming a monstrous identity was a way to critique and refuse the normalization required to be recognizably "human." That is, affirming one's and/or others' monstrosity was both a way to positively value what the mainstream rejected, and a way to reject what the mainstream valued. With respect to gender and sexuality, goth monstrosity could, at its most progressive, challenge (or at least loosen up) hegemonic constructions of gender and sexuality, and affirm non-cis-normative and queer people, desires, and pleasures: "goths see no need to mourn the passing of the categories of gender and sexuality as they crumble into decay" (Du Plessis, 166; emphasis mine). Though goth often reaffirms and retrenches hegemonic gender, race, and sexual norms, it has and can, as Du Pleiss argues, be a queer and/or trans practice.

Though goth damage was conventionally a badge of one's opposition to the norm, and/or a way to impede mainstream appropriation, in Gaga's work, goth aesthetics, especially the trope of monstrosity, is a vehicle for MRWaSP inclusion. Because goth damage is a tool of the mainstream rather than a weapon against it, Gaga's approach to damage is *post-goth*, much in the same way that MRWaSP is *post-race*, *post-feminist*, and *post-identity*. From "Bad Romance" to "Monster" to the "Paparazzi"/"Telephone" dyptich, Gaga's post-goth approach to monstrosity is central to her performance of MRWaSP resilience.

Monstrosity folds women and queers into the mainstream while at the same time excepting non-bourgeois black men from it.

Gaga often uses monstrosity as a metaphor for the gendered damage done to women by patriarchy. For example, her song about rape culture and its normalization of sexually predatory hetero-masculine sexuality is titled "Monster." As the verses narrate a date rape, they identify the male perpetrator with a werewolf, a vampire, and a zombie. The more rapey he gets, the more monstrous he becomes. But as monstrous as he may be, he's not the most horrific thing in the song. Gaga's narrator repeatedly states that she may still, possibly, be open to loving the man who attacked her. In this way, the song evokes the idea of rape culture, the culture that socializes women to accept and tolerate sexual assault. Individual men may be monsters, but, as the song implies, patriarchal heterosexuality is the big bad in the castle from which post-feminist princesses rescue themselves.

Just as Beyonce's "Video Phone" frames black men for the damage done by the male gaze, "Telephone" (which features Beyonce, just as "Video Phone" features Gaga) represents this "big bad" as a black man, as though black men were singularly responsible for patriarchy's monstrous excesses, and overcoming patriarchy was simply a matter of punishing or eliminating black men. "Telephone" is the conclusion to the story begun in "Paparazzi." Like "Monster," these videos present heteromasculine sexuality as predatory. In "Paparazzi," Gaga's white male lover tries to kill her by throwing her over a balcony. Gaga does not die, and though *apparently* disabled by her injuries, she ultimately overcomes both her physical and her political damage. She kills her abusive boyfriend, and, by the end of the video, is sent to jail.

"Telephone" begins as Gaga is taken to her cell. Midway through the video, Beyoncé bails Gaga out of jail and they team up to poison Beyoncé's ex and a diner full of patrons—a sort of large-scale version of Gaga's tactics in "Paparazzi" (remember, this is the big bad in the castle, not just your regular villain). The video repeatedly characterizes Beyonce's ex as a stereotypically misogynist and brutish black man. We are introduced to him when he greets Beyonce's character with a "Where have you been ****?," which implies he calls her a "bitch." Immediately after this, the camera pans directly to Beyonce's cleavage, showing us that he looks at her breasts before acknowledging her face, and thus that considers her primarily a sexual object. He then gets up to go to the counter, where he has a confrontation with one customer and gropes another woman. He wreaks patriarchal damage everywhere he goes; pretty much everything he does is offensive in some way, evidence of his supposedly primitive thuggishness. He embodies the misogynist monstrosity that Beyonce and Gaga must spectacularly overcome. So, they kill him...along with the restaurant's other non-bourgeois patrons (Gaga's creative class dance crew/kitchen staff survives). In this way, "Telephone" sings more or less the same tune that "Video Phone" does: women overcome patriarchal damage by executing non-bourgeois black men.

"Telephone" takes "Video Phone"'s LIO narrative one step further. Beyonce and Gaga aren't just overcoming their own personal damage, but the American nation's damage, its history of misogyny and racism. In "telephone," Beyonce's ex embodies the race-consciousness and sexism that the MRWaSP nation must overcome to demonstrate its own multicultural, diverse resilience. Executing her ex and overcoming the damage he does to her, Beyonce's character also overcomes the damage he does to the nation. That's why Bey and Gaga's post-execution dance party looks like a veritable Fourth-of-July victory celebration. Both women dressed in American flag costumes (down to the nail art!). Their independent-woman resilience resonates with the Fourth's overtones of "independence." Resilient women are key features of the neoliberal, MRWaSP American nation—the resilience of "our" women is what distinguishes us from backwards nations in need of white savorism, drone strikes, and worse. That's why "Telephone"'s cross-racial feminist alliance succeeds completely where Gaga, working alone in "Paparazzi," succeeded only partially (she went to jail for killing her white boyfriend, but triumphantly escapes prosecution for mass murder). *Women "Lean In" to MRWaSP by rendering non-bourgeois black men as its "exception."*

"Bad Romance," "Monster," "Telephone": these pieces incite patriarchal damage—human trafficking, sexual assault, domestic abuse—so that Gaga can overcome it. So, whereas traditional goth practices use an identification with monstrosity as a way to achieve a critical distance from mainstream culture, Gaga superficially identifies with monstrosity in order to achieve a more fundamental dis-identification with the "real" monster: sexism, racism, and other identity-based -isms. These identity-based –isms make good MRWaSP post-identity subjects feel like monsters, which is why *identity-based –isms* are the real monster, the big bad. Gaga's performances of monstrosity are not identifi-cations with, but incitements of the damage that she ultimately overcomes. Thus, Gaga's use of goth is actually post-goth, in much the same way that neoliberalism considers itself to be post-feminist and post-racial: goth damage, like patriarchial and white supremacist damage, is something the good neoliberal subject overcomes incites for the express purpose of overcoming it. Identifying her fans as "little monsters," Gaga gives her audience the raw materials they need to demonstrate their own resilience and craft a LIO narrative after Gaga's own example. "Little monsters" grow up into resilient citizens.

(c) Gaga's Resilient Little Monsters

Gaga, like resilience discourse generally, uses damage as the means to achieve success in mainstream terms. Her spectacularly monstrous, disgusting, macabre performances are the first step in her own personally branded "Look, I Overcame!" narrative.

"Gaga feminism" — Jack Halberstam's term for the style of feminism Lady Gaga practices — is a highly aestheticized, gothy variation on resilience discourse. (For Halberstam, and for my purposes here, gaga feminism is a broader social phenomenon exemplified by but not limited to Lady Gaga's own feminist views and/or commitments.) Though Halberstam is at best ambivalent about the progressive potential of gaga feminism, it is pretty clear to me that gaga feminism is the neoliberal co-optation of queer riot sound and queer monstrosity.

"Gaga feminism," Halberstam explains, is "monstrous" (GF xii) because it is "unreadable" (GF xiii) in modernist, classically liberal terms. For example, "gaga feminists will see multiple genders, finding male/female dichotomies to be outdated and illogical" (26). If you think gender is an identity, a property the body and/or the self, treating gender as a playfully-composed assemblage makes the individual performing this assemblage appear like Frankenstein's monster — an unnatural mishmash of components. Gaga feminism treats this monstrosity as a feature rather than a bug, evidence of one's evolution past obsolete and reactionary values. As Halberstam argues, gaga feminists

> celebrate variation, mutation, cooperation, transformation, deviance, perversion, and diversion. These modes of change, many of which carry negative connotations, actually name the way that people take the risks that are necessary to shove our inert social structures rudely into the path of the oncoming gagapocalypse. Making change means stepping off the beaten path, making detours around the usual, and distorting the everyday ideologies that go by the name of 'truth' or 'common sense' (GF 143).

Gaga feminism takes apparently monstrous transgressions and re-frames them as a pleasurable, normal experiences. It re-brands the "negative connotations" of gender non-conformity, "celebrat[ing] it as a "necessary" feature of ethical subjectivity. *"Gender trouble" is the new normal.*

Gaga gender performance does not trouble MRWaSP, but fuels it. Gendered monstrosity isn't troublesome illegibility, but what makes one intelligible as a resilient person. This is evident in Lady Gaga's performances of a monstrously feminine body — a body that is gendered feminine, but that is not conventionally attractive. Traditionally, white cis-femininity involves *internalizing* the male gaze and its damage. Gaga, however *externalizes* it, making this damage legible on her body. For example, when Gaga performs a traditionally sexualized female body, she does so in a way that emphasizes it as an object of disgust, not desire. She explains:

> Well, yeah, I take my pants off, but does it matter if your pants are off if you've got eight-inch shoulder pads on, and a hood, and black lipstick and glasses with rocks on them? I don't know. That's sexy to me. But I don't really think anybody's dick is hard, looking at that. I think they're just confused, and maybe a little scared. It's more [Marilyn] Manson to me than it is sexy.[126]

Goth damage is sexy to Gaga, even (and perhaps especially) if it's going to scare and confuse people still too wedded to outmoded notions of gender and aesthetics. It is significant that she references 90s goth rock star Marilyn Manson on this point. As his stage name "Marilyn" (traditionally feminine) indicates, Manson often plays with gender cross- and dis-identifications. Unlike traditional glam (or even hair metal), Manson does not appropriate femininity to increase his sexual desirability; rather, he claims to "tr[y] my hardest to be as unappealing, as unattractive as I could be" (Manson; 1:32).[127] Manson uses his monstrously gendered body to dis-identify with mainstream bourgeois values. Gaga, on the other hand, emphasizes the desirability of the monstrous: it might not be sexy to everyone, but it's sexy to her. The pleasure she finds in her damaged feminine body, in affirming or 'owning' her unconventional desire isn't the scopophilic pleasure in being the object of the male gaze, but the pleasure of "winning" conveyed in/by LIO narratives. She's using her monstrosity to insert herself into resilience discourse; this both distances her from the "old" mainstream and identifies her with the new bourgeois norm. Gaga flips Manson's traditional goth script. In traditional goth, aesthetic damage is pleasurable because it's a medium through which goths collectively dis-identify with the mainstream. In resilience discourse, damage *interpellates us to the mainstream.*

"A feminism built around...embracing your darkness" (Halberstam 62), gaga feminism is a type of resilience discourse. Gaga feminism teaches us to affirm our damage, to positively regard the little monstrosities that were traditionally viewed only negatively. This "edgy" affirmation of damage encourages the perception, among its practitioners and observers, that it's innovative and avant-garde. Gaga feminism is a post-feminist, MRWaSP strategy neoliberalism uses to convince privileged women (and men) that they are sufficiently "progressive" and "enlightened," the "good guys" vis-à-vis "bad guys" like Christian and Muslim fundamentalists, whose pre-modern family-centrism doesn't mesh with neoliberal imperatives to development, capitalization, flexibility, globalization, and so on. *Neoliberalism needs privileged folk to individually "go gaga" so that society (relations of privilege and oppression) can stay the same.* So, when Halberstam says things like "Gaga feminism names...a politics of gender for the postcapitalist world we currently inhabit...Gaga feminism will not save us from ourselves or from Wall Street" (xv), we should take him seriously![128] Gaga is not anarchic; it is the very arche of multi-racial white supremacist patriarchy.

Just as gaga feminism normalizes gender trouble, gaga

aesthetics render riot sounds resilient. Lady Gaga's music takes the monstrous, riotous sounds of queer death (which I discussed in chapter 2) and upgrades them into MRWaSP visualization (which I discussed in chapter 3).

(d) "Gaga" = Riot Sounds Rendered Resilient

While it is true that "gaga feminism is...off-beat" and "best represented as a sonic form of *hesitation*" (Halberstam GF 5), this "stutter step" isn't a riot sound, but a sonic manifestation of resilient femininity. Sonic damage doesn't start a queer riot in biopolitical MRWaSP, but revives and energizes it. This is evident even and especially in Gaga's musical performance. Contrary to what Halberstam thinks, these "soundscapes full of stutters and clicks" are anything but "innovative" or "*misleadingly* pop in tone" (GF 62-3). Rather, it is *forthrightly* pop in tone. For example, as I argued in chapter one, vocal stuttering—or the post-production chopping of a vowel sound—has largely replaced melisma in contemporary US/UK radio pop. In Gaga's work, this stuttering happens most prominently on *Telephone* (the "eh-eh-eh"s). (Telephone is, perhaps not coincidentally, the work that most explicitly connects feminine overcoming to the execution of black men.) This type of vocal stuttering is just one way neoliberal pop normalizes sonic damage. Damage makes songs legible and coherent to mainstream audiences, for whom the appreciation of aesthetic damage is a way of i*dentifying with dominant narratives* of pleasure, subjectivity, and community (such as the LIO narrative and resilience discourse more broadly).

What Halberstam calls "the noisy riot of going gaga" (138) is the co-optation and normalization of Atari Teenage Riot's "riot sounds." The riot's noisy, damaged darkness isn't oppositional to MRWaSP aesthetics or politics. Like goth monstrosity, feminized damage, or even queer death, riot sounds are, in Gaga's work and gaga feminism more generally, the damage necessary to catalyze a spectacular performance of resilience.

(e) From Gaga to Melancholia

Mining the silver in the lining of every shadow-producing cloud, gaga feminism's post-goth style celebrates monstrosity; it is a particularly fabulous type of damage that can be extra-spectacular in its overcoming. Gaga-style monstrosity is a ticket to the upper echelons of mainstream culture. Interpreted in the most charitable way possible, Jack Halberstam's theory of gaga feminism is a good *descriptive* account of such domestications of noisy monstrosities and queer femme transgressions. However, it should not be taken as what philosophers call a *normative* account, that is, as an ideal toward which we should strive.

"Shadow feminism" is a concept Halberstam often uses inter-changeably with "gaga feminism." This conflation is, I think, mistaken. Following Halberstam's own understanding of these concepts, shadow feminism is the *corruption,* or, to use another of Halberstam's concepts, the *failure* of gaga feminism.[129] Gaga feminism is socially profitable: it extracts surplus value from gothy shadow practices, and pays that forward to neoliberal hegemony. Shadow feminism, on the other hand, is anti-social. It fails to capitalize on personal damage in ways that produce surplus value for MRWaSP and neoliberal capitalism. Shadow feminism is not *opposed* to the mainstream, but *entropic* to it. It bends gaga-style positive feedback loops into negative loops of melancholic decay. Thus, as I will argue below, in MRWaSP resilience discourse the route "into the death" is not via a gaga riot, but melancholic shadowplay.

Melancholic feminism ventures queerly into the death. Biopolitical death is, as Foucault describes it, "something that slips into life, perpetually gnaws at it, diminishes it and weakens it" (SMBD 244). Melancholia drains MRWaSP from within by inefficiently executing MRWaSP techniques. For example, melancholic feminism bends the circuits of MRWaSP resilience so they invest in blackness rather than produce it as exception. This prevents resilient circuits from functioning at the levels required to reproduce and maintain MRWaSP's optimal functionality. Melancholic circuits are poor conductors of MRWaSP power, and thus feel like investments in death.

The concept of melancholy I use in this book is different from traditional understandings of melancholia. Classical melancholia's pathology is based on classically liberal models of subjectivity, models built on ideals of wholeness, authenticity, and integrity. From this perspective, the melancholic is one who can't resolve or get over a loss (as Freud describes in his essay "Mourning and Melancholia), and melancholia is a failure to progress toward and attain a goal (wholeness, completeness, self-sufficiency). However, neoliberalism normalizes ateleological open-endedness; flexibility and adaptability are valued skills, just as compositing and dynamic emergence (as I discussed in chapter one) are common aesthetic strategies. From the perspective of neoliberalism, healthy, successful subjects are expected to exhibit features of classical melancholia's pathology; yet again, what was traditionally a bug is now a feature.

At the same time, melancholia is still a bug; it just names something different. Or, what's pathological about neoliberal melancholy is different than what's pathological about classical melancholy. In neoliberalism, melancholy is a pathology specific to resilience discourse. Melancholy is failed or inefficient self-capitalization, an insufficiently profitable venture. Melancholy feels like *an investment in death*. Melancholy is the *refusal to do the affective cultural labor MRWaSP capitalism requires of* potentially resilient people. When resilient positive feedback loops are bent into negative ones, melancholia is the result. In this way, melancholy is the contemporary analog to ATR's "riot sounds." Because the actual sounds ATR used to induce riots have been co-opted and normalized in contemporary pop, melancholic music *sounds* significantly different than ATR's accelerationist digital hardcore. It sounds, for example, like Rihanna's *Unapologetic*.

As I will argue in the next section, Rihanna's performance on *Unapologetic* bends resilience discourse into melancholic death-spirals. Like resilience discourse, Rihanna's character/persona incites damage. Her performance *intensifies* this damage instead of overcoming it. Amplifying individual damage into anti-social noise, her performance hijacks biopolitical strategies and tactics so they *invest in death*. Unlike "Video Phone" and "Telephone," in which resilient women spectacularly execute supposedly misogynist black men, Rihanna's *Unapologetic* repeatedly invokes her *ongoing attachment* to stereotypically misogynist black masculinity (e.g., in the figure of Chris Brown, her abusive ex-boyfriend). She rejects resilience discourse and its demand to overcome the damage MRWaSP attributes to black men. That is, she refuses to produce blackness, especially as embodied by a particular style of black masculinity, as what Lester Spence calls "the exception" to MRWaSP society. In this way, Rihanna performs a *melancholic* attachment to non-bourgeois black masculinity and to biopolitical death.

2. Rihanna's Melancholic Damage[130]

When Rihanna's *Unapologetic* came out in November 2012, critics and fans filtered their response to it through her continued professional (and perhaps personal) relationship with her abusive boyfriend Chris Brown. (He assaulted her outside the 2009 Grammy Awards ceremony, and this resulted in a huge and ongoing media spectacle.) The *Los Angeles Times*'s Randall Roberts opens his review with a discussion of the track that features Brown ("Nobody's Business") instead of the album's lead single, which was already on radio and had a video on YouTube. *Spin*'s Caryn Ganz treats Rihanna's "unapologetic love of Chris Brown" as central to the album's interpretation and cultural significance. Positioning himself as the white guy mansplaining to a black woman what's best for her, *The New York Times's* John Caramanica argues that Rihanna's attempt, on the album, "to make public art with the person who physically abused you is immature, pre-feminist, post-ethics." MusicOMH's Philip Matusavage takes the saving-brown-women-from-brown-men paternalism the farthest:

> to argue that the unpleasantness at the album's core doesn't matter ... is to enable the misogyny which fuels this record, where an overwhelmingly male group of songwriters play up Rihanna as an alluring cipher, flirting with danger while staring into the void. Whatever Rihanna's role in this album, it's to be hoped that she doesn't believe most of what she's singing here. As a record it is not only misguided, it's dangerous. We should not shy away from that.

Why is Brown the only lens through which so many people want to interpret the album? And, more importantly, why do so many critics (and fans) think *Unapologetic* is so "dangerous" and "post-ethics"?

The answer is: resilience discourse. We expect women, *especially* the women of color who are folded into MRWaSP normativity, perform racist-misogynist damage that either they resiliently overcome, or that we white saviors overcome for them. It's not the performance of damage that's got everyone so upset. Rather, they're upset at Rihanna's apparent failure to overcome that damage and capitalize on it. They feel cheated out of the cultural work (that is, a surplus value of human capital) that MRWaSP obliges her, as a black woman with global media visibility, to furnish for it and for its members. On this point, Roberts's review is especially revelatory. The album is, he argues, "a little *sickening*, because for the first time since the incident, her addressing the complicated issue feels not like a defense of love but a marketing maneuver, a way of *turning a negative into a positive"* [all emphasis mine]. Roberts hears the album as sickening because it exhibits an unhealthy approach to damage. Resilience is the healthy approach to: "good" women turn negatives like domestic abuse into positives (such as feminist cred, 'moral' bonus points, or even something like a blog or a self-help book deal). And this is what Roberts can't hear in the album—there's no proper resilience. The album is "sickening" because listeners cannot efficiently turn damage — domestic abuse, poverty, racism, etc. — into their own human capital. Listeners can't use their appreciation of the album as a way to demonstrate their status as "good" subjects (that is, their own successful buy-in to resilience narratives)...Except, perhaps, by concern-trolling and treating their attempts to save this brown woman from her brown man as a badge of our own cred in a multiracial white-supremacist patriarchy, as the reviewers have done.

If, as Roberts argues, *Unapologetic* turns a negative into a positive, it turns the *wrong* negative into the *wrong* positive, and amplifies the "wrong" affects. As I will show below, *Unapologetic*'s "positive" *embraces rather than overcomes* the "negative" (her relationship with Brown). Rihanna capitalizes on damage, just not in the "right" way, i.e., in a way that amplifies rather than obscures MRWaSP's own damage and pathologies. *Unapologetic*'s music, lyrics, and videos use melancholic strategies to spoil resilience discourse. Rihanna's melancholia is good-girl resilience gone bad.

The reception of Rihanna's album is intimately tied to contemporary gender/race/sexual (bio)politics, which are themselves constituted in and through neoliberal political economy. So, while this chapter is, at one level, an analysis of Rihanna's album and critical responses to it, this analysis is the basis of another, more meta-level theorization of how MRWaSP works and how one might formulate a queer, anti-racist, feminist responses to it. Rihanna's performance on *Unapologetic* suggests as feminist alternatives to resilience discourse and "Look, I Overcame!" post-feminism. Melancholy, as I read it, is how one might go "into the death."

I should also clarify that I take "Rihanna" to be a pop star who is the effect or product of the various culture industries; she is different than both Robyn Fenty, private citizen, and Rihanna the artist. "Rihanna" is the persona, not the person. This latter Rihanna, the persona performed by Fenty, is only *part* of this corporate person I'm calling Rihanna. Rihanna is the "corporate person" embodied and performed by Robyn Fenty, but which represents a collective, corporate process of production (artistic craft on Fenty's part, her artistic collaborators, management, etc.). As Shaviro suggests in *Post Cinematic Affect,* the pop star is the ideal neoliberal subject—the corporate person, entrepreneur of herself, pure spectacle constituted by media feedback. When I make claims about "Rihanna," I'm talking about this *corporate person* who is the assemblage of many things, and not reducible to any one person's intentions or agency.

So, on to melancholia: first, I discuss Rihanna's reworking of resilience. To do this, I'll look at the music on *Unapologetic,* particularly the song "Diamonds.". Then, I turn to the lyrics and the video for that song. After showing how her performance bends the circuits of resilience, I use "Pour It Up" to show how Rihanna bends resilient circuits so they invest in blackness as exception or blackness as biopolitical death. Finally, I will argue that Rihanna's investments in black masculinity—that is, her melancholic hang-ups—position her as a melancholic bad girl. This melancholic bad girl is different from both the resilient Telephoner or Video-Phoner, and from the accelerationist Diva, and that difference is crucial for understanding the political and aesthetic significance of melancholy.

(a) Musical Melancholia

Unapologetic sounds melancholic. For example, Caramancia

describes the album as "bored," "dull," and "bland." The song "Lost in Paradise," he writes, "buzzes and hums but does not take flight" as though it does not generate enough lift to rise above the album's affective doldrums, "sinking" instead, as Alex Macpherson writes in *Fact*, "into directionless drift." In a musical economy that values the "work hard/play hard" ethos (both David Guetta and Wiz Kalifah have songs based on this premise), *Unapologetic* does neither. Its music is just "meh."

The album's lead single, "Diamonds," in both its music and its video, evokes directionless drift and melancholic "meh." In a way, the song is structured like Ravel's *Bolero*: it's one long crescendo over a rhythmic ostinato. *Bolero*, however, goes somewhere—it has a goal, a direction (namely, the climax). "Diamonds," however, doesn't go anywhere; it's more an unending loop of soft peaks and valleys. The song rises and falls like a wave on the open sea, a wave that never gets to build and crest. This failure to crest is evident in the song's musical structure, which takes two different compositional techniques for building musical climaxes and under-realizes both of them.

First, even though it's not a properly tonal piece— there are no cadences, no resolution, no key changes, etc.—"Diamonds" has a harmonic structure that is rooted in the semiotics of functional tonality. The song is basically a loop of G Bb A (Bb) chords. It plays around with the minor-third relationship between G and Bb, and evokes D as an absent, spectral dominant/major fifth (A is the dominant of D, which is the dominant of G). The song continually circles around the minor third and the absent major fifth—the two main functional relationships in tonal chord structure. This looping can be heard as melancholic in two ways. First, its failure to get over the lost or lacking fifth (the "dominant" in music-theory jargon) is melancholic both in its evoking a palpable absence, and in its failure to utilize the dominant/tonic relationship to build and release tension. Second, the circling around the minor third creates the effect of a harmonic Bermuda triangle. The minor third is strongly associated with sad, depressed, melancholic affect—it's sad, whereas the leading-tone interval (i.e., the theme from *Jaws*) is more scary. Constantly circulating around and returning to this minor third, the song generates melancholic affects. "Diamonds" uses the language and semiotics of tonality to produce harmonic *melancholy*.

But the song's the chord changes are more middle-ground effects than fundamental structures; its underlying foundation has more in common with extra-tonal EDM-pop than with tonal pop. Many EDM-pop songs use a combination of a soar and a pause-drop to create a musical climax. Psy's infamous "Gangnam Style" and Baauer's even more infamous "Harlem Shake" both do this: they "soar" up to a peak of rhythmic intensity by increasing the rate at which a percussion and/or vocal pattern is repeated, then "pause" by dropping out (most of) the instruments for a bar before landing hard on the downbeat of the following measure. The pause delays "resolution," thus exacerbating tension and augmenting the intensity of the "hit" by creating a "harder they come, the harder they fall" effect. "Diamonds" also has a pause and a drop. The extra four-bar phrase between the last two choruses ("B" in the diagram below) functions like a pause.

Intro (4 bars)
A (4x4, or 16-bar verse)
B (4x4 or 16-bar chorus)
A1 (4x3, or 12-bar verse)
B – regular chorus
1 4-bar phrase (that leftover phrase from A1)
B

All but the barest accompaniment drops out during these four bars, after which it "drops" on the downbeat of the final chorus.

However, there's no soar up to this pause-drop. In the same way that the tonal dominant/fifth is invoked as an absence, the song is haunted by an absent soar. It never intensifies as we are led to expect it will. In fact, "Diamonds" doesn't just omit a soar, it *undercuts* it. As you can see in the formal diagram above, because the final verse (A1) is missing a four-bar phrase, the four bars that function as the pause are not an extra or surplus material—they're effectively borrowed from the shortened verse. "Diamonds" can intensify the final iteration of the chorus (the last "B" section) only by putting one of the verses in debt. The song doesn't resiliently bounce back from musical damage (the pause-drop) so much as merely break even; the surplus value the pause-drop produces isn't profit, but debt owed the last verse. . "Diamonds" short-circuits the pause-drop method; here, it cannot amplify and intensify, as it is expected to, only maintain it. This short circuit is the second way the song's compositional structure is melancholic: its music neither overcomes nor bounces back (that is, it's not resilient).

"Diamonds" feels aimless and dull because it lacks the spectacular crises and overcomings we have come to expect from contemporary pop songs. It feels, in other words, like a failed *musical* investment. "Diamonds" drains its musical resources, so it sounds and feels *musically* melancholic. Its vocals and video similarly short-circuit resilience discourse and produce a distinctly gendered, racialized melancholia.

(b) Siren Songs

Rihanna's vocal and video performance amplifies the melancholic feel of "Diamonds"'s musical form. She plays the role of Siren, but instead of seducing audiences with excess or transgression, she kills joy with melancholy. She's not going to cause your ship to crash into the rocks, but cut the engines and set you loose.

The video for "Diamonds" ends with Rihanna's character

floating—not even swimming or treading water, just floating face-up—in the water. Drifting directionlessly atop tiny ripples of water, there are no crises for her to overcome—no storm, no tsunami. The waves are gentile, soft, and regular. These watery ripples don't threaten Rihanna's character; in fact, they *support* her body as it floats. Unlike Ulysses, Rihanna's character neither meets any challengers, nor goes anywhere. She never makes it out of the song's Bermuda triangle of melancholy, never returns to solid Caribbean and/or North American ground.

This scene is even more clearly melancholic when contrasted to the video for Ludacris's 2012 single "Rest of My Life." Images of cresting waves feature prominently throughout the video; they are often located at moments of musical climax—that is, in the song's soars. The video uses these images as both a visualization of the soar (which, as I argued in chapter one, is a musical manifestation of resilience discourse), and resilience discourse itself. The lyrics describe various features of a macho-inflected resilience. They praise a life dedicated to living life on the edge and gambling with transgression, like drug use and partying too hard. For example, the very first lines riff on Nietzsche's infamous line "what does not kill me makes me stronger." So, even when we overstep our limits, we still win in the end—we get stronger. The image of the cresting wave is a metaphor for the lyrics' lesson: the only way to really live is at, and sometimes even beyond, full tilt. If these huge, potentially threatening waves symbolize resilience, then the tiny, gentle, supportive ripples in "Diamonds" illustrate the lack of resilience, i.e., melancholy. Unlike "Rest of My Life," "Diamonds" does not build up to a crest (i.e., a musical soar), so Rihanna just floats along with the undulating waves. She's not living life on the edge; she's just going with the flow.

"Diamonds"'s video ends by panning out on this shot of Rihanna floating in the water. We could interpret this as her being lost at sea—that is, as a crisis for her to overcome. But she doesn't. She doesn't struggle or fight back. This could be an opportunity for her to scream out in fear or yell for help, to really show off her vocal chops—she is a singer, and this is a music video, after all. But instead she silently drifts. (She's not drifting because she's dead or unconscious: the pan-out is preceded by a close-up of Rihanna opening her eyes, which implies that she's both conscious and alive, gazing at the camera.) Just as the song's musical form lacks a climax, a sonic crisis, "Diamonds" video lacks narrative climax or crisis—there are no peaks and valleys, just gentle ripples. There's nothing here for us to see or hear her overcome.

Rihanna's vocal performance is similarly un-spectacular throughout the album. Many critics fault her delivery for its lack of any emotional investment whatsoever, positive or negative. For example, Macpherson accuses Rihanna of failing to suffi-ciently make use of her emotional pain and trauma:

> Frequently, Rihanna seems as if she can barely be arsed to connect to the songs emotionally, opting instead to blare out ragged, aimless vocal performances. ("Just going through the motions / I can't even get the emotions to come out," she intones on "What Now": too bloody right).

Macpherson faults Rihanna's vocal performance not because it's bad, but because it's apathetic and "disconnected"—that is, it's a poor conductor or intensifier of affect. This performance is a problem because the one thing resilience discourse can't assim-ilate is apathy.[131] Rihanna's vocal delivery neither incites damage, by expressing suffering and pain, nor does it express struggle and/or triumphant overcoming.

"Diamonds" is musically melancholic because it short circuits the aesthetics of resilience, like the pause-drop and LIO narra-tives. Rihanna's performance on *Unapologetic* also short circuits the MRWaSP *politics* of resilience. That is, Rihanna fails to accomplish the *cultural* work MRWaSP demands of good, resilient women.

(c) Melancholia and the cultural labor of resilience

Jessica Hopper's *Pitchfork* review illustrates the connection listeners and critics made between *Unapologetic*'s musical melancholy and Rihanna's perceived lack of personal resilience:

> On one hand, it's tempting to give Rihanna props for broadcasting her all-too-real shortcomings. She's quite a distance from the tidy narrative we'd like, the one where she's learned from her pain and is back to doing diva triumph club stomp in the shadow of Beyoncé…But the measurable failure is the album's music. On a track-by-track basis, the songs make for dull labor, not worth our time and not befitting Rihanna's talent.

Hopper argues that Rihanna does not turn her damage into the best of all possible success stories. The "tidy narrative we'd like" is the LIO narrative in which pain is recycled into learning and adversity into triumph. Rihanna doesn't do the work of overcoming, so *Unapologetic* feels like it's left this "dull labor" for her listeners.

Hopper's review suggests that we could forget Rihanna's politics (her "inconvenient, messy truth") if only she made a banger—that we could overlook her failed personal resilience if her musical performance felt resilient. She could evoke all sorts of awful damage as long as she capitalizes on it in the right way, that is, in a way that saves listeners the "dull labor" of working through damage for themselves. This is what Rihanna's "We Found Love" does. Built around two utterly massive soars and with lyrics and a video about how a "hopeless place"—e.g., abject and disgusting council flats, an abusive relationship— becomes a place where "we found love," this song is overloaded with all sorts of resilience. "We Found" performs the *musical* and *affective* overcoming that is absent in "Diamonds." It turns damage into surplus value, rather than leaving that damage for us to process and recycle into something pleasurable. Unlike her work on "We Found," Rihanna's performance on *Unapologetic* fails to extract the aesthetic surplus value (the banger anthem) latent in the album's and the performer's damage. And *that's* why it feels melancholy, like a waste of resources like time and talent.

Why is Rihanna's failure to turn her personal damage into aesthetic surplus value seen as a waste of our time and hers? Why is its melancholic aesthetic viewed so negatively by many well-respected music critics?

As I've been arguing throughout this book, women's performances of resilient femininity do the gender and racializing work of MRWaSP: these performances both fold these women into MRWaSP privilege *as* properly gendered/racialized subjects, and render non-bourgeois black masculinity as the "exception" to MRWaSP pluralism and inclusion. This folding in and rendering out is the cultural labor of resilience, and it is all over contemporary US/UK pop radio. For example, white pop divas Kelly Clarkson and Taylor Swift have their own brands of good-girl resilience: Clarkson comes off as a bit more bruised and experienced, probably because she is older and more seasoned (and, notably, reads somewhat less bourgeois than Swift). Her catalog is filled with resilience narratives: "Stronger" quotes that infamous Nietzsche line "what doesn't kill you makes you stronger," and her biggest recent hit, "Since U Been Gone," is all about her post-breakup resilience. Swift also trades in post-breakup resilience. Her 2012 hit "We Are Never Ever Getting Back Together" is a sarcastic middle-finger to an ex-lover. "I Knew You Were Trouble" details the narrator's process of rationalizing and working through her breakup pain. Both Clarkson's and Swift's brands of femininity center on the triumphant overcoming of pain caused by failed romantic relationships and ex-lovers. The problem with *Unapolgetic's* Rihanna is that she doesn't reject Brown as "trouble"—she bounces back from the 2009 incident, but in a skewed, misdirected, *melancholic* way.

The problem with *Unapologetic*, as Hopper's review indicates, is that it isn't the resilience narrative we expect from female pop stars: neither Rihanna nor the music recognizably bounce back:

> The album is unapologetic but it's also airless, nearly hookless, and exudes a deep melancholy. Given these qualities, it's hard not to wonder where else the album might have gone. Would it fare better if the topics were the same but set to songs as combustible as "Don't Stop the Music"?

Even if Rihanna's isn't resilient, Hopper suggests that we still expect *Unapologetic's* music to be so. The album would be a success if its music overcame the damage Rihanna expressed in the lyrics. But, because the music fails to be resilient, the album "exudes a deep melancholy."

Melancholy is the practice, and melancholia the effect, of failing to successfully accomplish the resilient labor MRWaSP expects of you. *Unapologetic* is melancholic because it doesn't render Brown as exception—instead, it forces us to "hang in this dark space" with him—and thus fails to properly, profitably fold Rihanna into MRWaSP.

Unapologetic feels melancholic because it doesn't perform the cultural labor MRWaSP assigns to resilient femininity— rendering "violent" black masculinity as exception. *Unapologetic* also fails to perform the cultural labor MRWaSP assigns to the black entertainers it folds into its ranks, those it does not render as exception. Just it recruits women into patriarchy by putting resilient femininity to work, MRWaSP includes some styles of blackness into multi-racial white supremacy by putting *them* to work. (In fact, you could argue that the styles of blackness disqualified as "exception" are precisely those that can't be profitably "put to work.") Whereas Modernist and Postmodern white supremacist aesthetics treat blackness, as Kwame Anthony Appiah has put it, an "otherness machine," in MRWaSP, non-exceptional blackness works instead as an *affective amplifier*. Because some styles of blackness are conditionally incorporated within MRWaSP's privileged mainstream, they don't generate "otherness" as efficiently as do newer, more exotic and unruly racial identities do. For example, in the aftermath of Osama bin Laden's execution, images of a black US president were juxta-posed with those of the "Muslim" terrorist, creating an us-versus-them dichotomy in which the nationalist American "us" is represented by a Harvard-educated black man, and the "them" by a vaguely "brown" religious fundamentalist. So blackness — middle class, cis-gendered, normatively hetero- or homo-sexual — is still instrumental, but it's a different type of instrument. It "works hard/plays hard", amplifying the intensity of whites' affective comportments; black culture workers are like sous chefs, making white affective economies (e.g., nationalist fervor) work more efficiently for whites/white supremacy. With their "work hard/play hard" and "living life on the edge" tropes, black artists like Ludacris on "Rest of My Life" amplify white listeners' affective experience of "winning"—i.e., of privilege. On *Unapologetic*, Rihanna doesn't broadcast the suffering, the overcoming, or the "winning" that MRWaSP audiences can then receive and rehearse as their own.

Unapologetic is not the resilience machine fans and critics expect from neoliberal pop. It does not evoke damage, and when people try to locate damage in it, e.g., by interpreting it through Rihanna's relationship with Brown, that damage isn't spectacu-larly overcome. Instead, the album is read as an investment in Chris Brown, that is, in the in stereotypical thug-like black masculinities MRWaSP must render as exception. As I argued in the introduction, non-bourgeois black masculinity, often embodied in thug stereotypes, is one ginormous "tell" in

MRWaSP's post-racial poker face. The continued oppression of non-bourgeois black men (e.g., in the prison industrial complex, in stop-and-frisk, in unemployment figures, etc.) is evidence that multi-racial white supremacy isn't really 'multi-racial" after all. MRWaSP relies on women—both white women and women of color—to sweep this inconvenient evidence under the rug (sweeping up is, of course, stereotypically women's work). This is why, in "Telephone" and "Video Phone," the female protagonists demonstrate their resilience by overcoming the misogynist patriarchal damage embodied by non-bourgeois black male characters. *Unapologetic*, however, continues to be hung up on precisely the ties MRWaSP hegemony demands "good girls" sever. Rihanna, as we know from an earlier album title, is a "good girl gone bad." And she demonstrates this badness on *Unapologetic* by performing a melancholic (rather than Diva's quasi-accelerationist) identification with precisely the black masculinity MRWaSP resilience wants her to reject.

(d) No Phones, Just Melancholic Hang-Ups

Reviewers criticize Rihanna's continued attachments to what she ought to overcome—non-bourgeois black masculinities. Critics locate this attachment not only in *Unapologetic*'s implicit and explicit evocations of Chris Brown but also in Rihanna's own performance of black masculinity. They attribute Breezy-style, unprofitable black masculine unruliness to Rihanna herself. For example, Caramancia opens his review with the observation that:

> The 13th word of the first verse of the first song on "Unapologetic," the seventh album by Rihanna, is a curse, and she relishes it, *hitting the syllables hard, spitting them out sharply as if she hoped they might wound someone*. The song, "Phresh Out the Runway," is a chaotically dense spray of boasts over a *muscular*, scraping beat. Rihanna sounds

indignant and impressed with herself, proclaiming, *"Walk up in this bitch like I own the ho"* (emphasis mine).

With her violent, hard-hitting, misogynist delivery, Rihanna performs the stereotypical black masculinities that Gaga and Beyonce eliminate and overcome. Whereas Caramancia interprets her vocal delivery as hypermacho, Rihanna's visual performance in the video is, as Susan Elizabeth Shephard, Ayesha A. Siddiqi, and Sarah Nicole Prickett note in their *hairpin* roundtable, very femme and girls'-girly. Moreover, there are, as they note *no men* in the video, not even on the prop money Rihanna's character throws around (it has *her* image, not that of a dead president). There seems to be some tension, then, between the vocal/lyrical and the visual dimensions of Rihanna's performance on *Unapologetic*, a tension that is crystallized in "Pour It Up": Rihanna's vocal performance reads masculine and the lyrics reference men (for example, Rihanna's narrator talks about brokering a deal with Jay Z, the boss of her label at the time), but her visual performance reads femme and the video lacks references to men. Rihanna's toughness and aggressevity read, to Caramanica, as masculinity because they aren't framed as responses to specifically feminized damage, like domestic violence. Without that reference back to feminized damage, Rihanna's assertiveness looks and sounds like pathological masculinity, not resilient femininity.

"Pour It Up" ignores men because it is completely unconcerned with resilience discourse and LIO narratives. The lack of men in the video means that there are no monsters for her to kill, nobody for her and her gal-pals to render exceptional. As Siddiqi suggests, Rihanna's brand assertiveness is "a way to buck the victim narrative she found herself in after Chris Brown." This is a femininity that refuses to perform and capitalize on damage. Instead of shooting patriarchy's scapegoat, "Pour It Up" targets MRWaSP itself. By ignoring the imperative to spectacularly kill *a* man, "Pour It Up" eviscerates the very logic of, as Prikett put it, "all the men."

The femininity Rihanna performs in this video is thus not the resilient MRWaSP good girl, but a melancholic bad girl who makes bad investments and is a poor conductor of MRWaSP power. For example, Rihanna invests in herself in a way that changes the currency: is it *her* (not some dead white guy's) image on the money in the video, suggesting that she's transformed the very logic of neoliberal capitalism from M-M1 to M-R ("R" for "Rihanna"). In "Pour It Up," money is everywhere: as the refrain emphasizes, Rihanna's character, like every good neoliberal, sees everything in terms of an economic rationality—the fungiblity of "dolla" signs. Unlike any good neoliberal, everything Rihanna does, even throwing money away, always intensifies *her* money (rather than abstract, infinitely fungible money). Though every verse couplet begins with an activity that's expensive or wasteful, it concludes with Rihanna's statement that it hasn't cost her any of *her* money. Rihanna uses mere money to intensify and augment *her* money: this is the M-R hustle. She uses M to invest in R, and not to make more M (i.e., "M1") for MRWaSP capitalism. From this latter perspective, Rihanna appears to waste money on bad investments.

Investing in exceptional black masculinity would be one such "bad" investment. When Rihanna makes it rain by throwing a wad of cash into the air so it flutters down to the floor (which she does both in the lyrics, and in the video), she uses money in a way that *identifies* her with precisely the kind of black masculinity that she's supposed to overcome. This gesture doesn't increase her MRWaSP capital, but diminishes it. The waste of cash could be forgiven if we thought it was a good investment (like Luda's women, weed, and alcohol). But, from the perspective of MRWaSP, it doesn't come off that way. As Roberts's *Los Angeles Times* review puts it: "The opening line — 'Throw it up, watch it all fall out' — seems like an ode to getting sick, in fact, until it becomes clear that Rihanna is singing about money, strip clubs, doing shots of tequila and 'making it rain' with bills." Whereas "Rest of My Life" treats Luda's investments in "women, weed, and alcohol" as an ideal to celebrate, Roberts perceives a very similar gesture, Rihanna's investments in women and alcohol, as a waste. Given the similarity between the narrators' behavior in "Pour It Up" and "Rest of My Life", why is Rihanna's performance received so differently than Luda's?

As was the case with "Diamonds," the difference between Rihanna and Luda can be read in the water. As I argued earlier, "Rest of My Life" uses water to represent resilience. In *Unapologetic's* videos, water is a common element: it's in "Diamonds," in "Stay" (which features Rihanna crying in the bathtub), and in "Pour It Up." Here, the floor is a shallow layer of water, which occasionally ripples, and thus echoes the rippling waves in "Diamonds," where water symbolizes melancholy. Water serves the same metaphoric purpose on "Pour It Up." Here, the lyrics allude to the trope of "making it rain," and Rihanna's character performs this gesture several times in the video. In contemporary hip hop, "make it rain" is a metaphor that uses water to represent money. If, in Rihanna's *Unapologetic* universe, water represents melancholy, "making it rain" indicates melancholic use of money, bad investment practices, investing in the wrong things. Making it rain doesn't intensify the flow of MRWaSP capitalism to its peak; rather, rain diverts the current entirely, embezzling M into R. This investment strategy is melancholic because it invests in and amplifies the exception to MRWaSP resilience: unviable, unprofitable blackness.

Melancholy is the active investment in and intensification of what does not support the viability and vitality of MRWaSP biopolitics. Amplifying one's attachments to the very things resilience discourse demands one overcome, melancholy isn't the failure to get over a loss (as melancholia is classically conceived), but the failure *to get rid of something very specific*. In "Telephone" and "Video Phone," Gaga and Beyonce wash supposedly pathological black men out of their hair, thus also supposedly cleansing MRWaSP society of its last vestiges of sexism and racism. Their personal overcoming is a microcosm of post-racial, post-feminist society's own resilience, the positive feedback loop that supposedly recycles the damages of the past (racism, sexism) into a promising present and future. Rihanna's overcoming of the "angry" and "unruly" Chris Brown would amplify mainstream society's sense that it has "overcome" racism. However, by attempting to capitalize on her continued attachment to what we otherwise demand she overcome, Rihanna bends that positive feedback loop into a vicious, melancholic circuit. This generates *a whole hell of a lot of noise* — it impedes efficient extraction of the "signal," the messages, vicarious experiences and affective orientations that mainstream audiences to which mainstream audiences are tuned in and expect to hear. Some of this noise can and will be recouped— think of all the back-and-forth on social media the album generated: *somebody* profits from that. But this is a really inefficient production process—*Unapologetic's* melancholy has to be processed through another set of filters and resistors (e.g., social media) to produce the monetary value (for, say, Facebook), the human capital (self-congratulatory displays of what a great feminist one is), and the post-racist/feminist ideology that society demands of it. In addition to bending the circuits of resilience, melancholy often decelerates the processes of co-optation and recuperation by making it quite costly to recycle its noise back into proper signal. For MRWaSP to re-render melancholic performances into resilient ones, it has to add an extra step or two in the production process. But it must also continually police and control for melancholic performances. This policing diverts resources from other more profitable projects.

Melancholy isn't just failed or misfired resilience; it is the continual, compounded draining of neoliberalism's batteries. If resilience is a positive feedback loop, melancholia is a vicious cycle. Melancholic hang-ups bend resilient circuits into entropic ones; instead of amplifying life, they go into the death.

(e) Spiraling Downward Into The Death

Neoliberal melancholy often looks, on the surface, just like resilience. It takes the procedures and practices of resilience and uses them to invest in what MRWaSP otherwise renders as exception, what, as Lester Spence puts it, "cannot be remade for the purposes of capital" because it "does not operate according to market dictates" (38-9). Applying resilience to phenomena that, when remade as a market, do not generate sufficient surplus value for MRWaSP produces *melancholy*. Markets that don't operate according to MRWaSP's dictates are melancholic because they detract from MRWaSP's vitality.

For example, there is a whole subgenre of right-wing outrage journalism focused on people on public assistance who "waste" their money on supposedly frivolous purchases like manicures or name-brand apparel and electronics. In March 2014, the Tea Party News Network posted an online survey that asked "Do you agree with welfare recipients being forbidden to spend their taxpayer provided welfare money at lingerie shops, tattoo parlors, nail salons, jewelry stores, and anything other than food?" Similarly, the website somecards.com has a relatively large number of user-created ecards that reflect similar attitudes about the behavior of "welfare recipients." Many mockingly depict women living indulgent lives full of manicures and designer clothes, while simultaneously reinforcing the stereotype that uses "welfare recipients" as a code word for urban, working-class black women.[132] As Hill-Collins notes, "portrayed as being content to sit around and collect welfare, shunning work and passing bad values on to her offspring," the point of racializing this "welfare queen" stereotype is to "labe[l] as unnecessary and even dangerous to the values of the country the fertility of women who are not White and middle class," values such as (Black Feminist Thought, 87). The poll and the ecards give voice to a widespread worry that "welfare recipients"—that is, black women—are unable to properly execute the economic rationality we expect of good neoliberal subjects: they invest in the "wrong" things, in things that don't maximize the vitality and profitability of MRWaSP. Nails, hair, and clothes are investments in black aesthetics, in a black woman's own enjoyment of and satisfaction with her body. These small pleasures might be a way to "bounce back" from the daily grind of dealing with the increasingly baroque and repressive welfare state bureaucracy, and from, you know, constant, pervasive anti-black misogyny.

These melancholic behaviors might also be very canny investments in one's own human capital. As Tressie McMillan Cottom argues, poor African-Americans sometimes cultivate the appearance of upper-middle class respectability in order to accumulate the human capital necessary to successfully navigate MRWaSP institutions. She explains:

It took half a day but something about my mother's performance of respectable black person — her Queen's English, her Mahogany outfit, her straight bob and pearl earrings — got done what the elderly lady next door had not been able to get done in over a year. I learned, watching my mother, that there was a price we had to pay to signal to gatekeepers that we were worthy of engaging. It meant dressing well and speaking well.

So, designer clothes, nice jewelry, these things may seem like exorbitant purchases for someone on a very limited budget. However, if these investments actually help you navigate the institutions that determine your access to and the success of your interaction with the welfare system or the justice system, then these investments are actually quite savvy: the returns far outweigh the costs.

The return is access to more and better human capital than is usually granted black femininity; for example, as Cottom argues, her investments in a Jones New York suite "signaled that I was not a typical black or a typical woman, two identities that in combination are almost always conflated with being poor." Such signaling provides access to things otherwise denied to poor black women, to people with their type and amount of human capital: the benefit of the doubt, middle-class jobs, a mortgage, etc.

Without an account of the sexist racism that black women experience, this overinvestment in designer brands seems like a bad economic decision, a waste of resources. This is why mainstream society views such calculations as what Cottom calls the "logic of stupid poor people." But this "stupid logic" is actually a prime example of neoliberal economic rationality: it's a very thoroughly researched (often backed by generations of trial-and-error testing, as Cottom's many anecdotes suggest) and well-hedged bet. This rationality is thought to be "stupid" because it amplifies black women's human capital in ways that do not necessarily or optimally revitalize MRWaSP. Because MRWaSP must at least pay lip service to neoliberalism's idealization of individual free choice, it has to delegitimize the rationality of choices that aren't in *its* interest. That's why this logic is "stupid": this rhetorical move frames what would otherwise be seen as one free choice among others and as ignorance, pathology, or as a symptom of one's inability to make free choices for oneself. When white women and people of color practice resilience in ways that don't adequately support MRWaSP, they do not appear to be exercising free choice, to be choosing an alternative way of life. Rather, they appear to lack the capacity to choose—they're supposedly victims of poverty, ignorance, misogynist ethnic cultural traditions, and so on, capable only of "stupid people logic."

Melancholia is resilience that isn't socially legible as such. It's the application of resilient techniques—market-based calculation, balancing cost and benefit, investing in oneself—to material that MRWaSP cannot or does not want to capitalize on, to damage it does not want to recycle but render exceptional. Melancholia is the inability to recover from damage, to invest in oneself, *in a way that MRWaSP recognizes as "healthy."* "Healthy" subjectivity is supposed to work as a positive feedback loop on both the subjective and the social levels: gains in the microcosm are compounded and amplified at the macrocosmic level. Melancholy, on the other hand can become a pathological vicious cycle wherein gains at microcosm are *drains* to the macrocosm. At the individual level, melancholia is double-edged: because what is good for you isn't what's healthiest for MRWaSP, your good decisions will be punished and pathologized, not rewarded. Smart self-capitalization is derided as "stupid," for example. This sort of concern-trolling can be a way for MRWaSP to turn melancholic damage back into profit; it's an opportunity for healthy subjects to demonstrate their, well, health—that they know better, that they're not stupid, etc. This is why we should avoid getting troll-baited into fighting accusations of stupidity, toxicity, and so on: it's just co-opting our noise and turning it back into signal. Instead, we should focus our energies on changing the circumstances and institutions that make our survival appear toxic, that make investments in ourselves seem pathological and irrational.

Melancholia can, I think, be a way to do just this. Though MRWaSP will always try to recoup melancholic noise as resilient signal, there can be instances in which melancholia stacks the deck against MRWaSP so that any attempts to profit from melancholy, to overcome or co-opt its damage for monetary, aesthetic, and political gain are losing bets *for MRWaSP.* In such instances, melancholy diminishes the capacity at which neoliberal institutions can function. Instead of recycling this damage into more life (by overcoming it and/or rendering it exceptional), melancholy intensifies it, pushing it into the death.

Rihanna's *Unapologetic* is, as I've been arguing throughout this chapter, an example of this latter type of melancholy. *Unapologetic* may indeed be Rihanna's attempt to work through her relationship with Brown, through this attack on her, and the subsequent media scandal. It may be what Robyn Fenty needed to do for her own personal and creative health. But it doesn't do the work MRWaSP expects Rihanna to perform to maintain *its* health.

MRWaSP uses resilience discourse to fold "model" minorities into multi-racial white privilege. We can celebrate our supposed overcoming of racism if and only if we ignore the fact that resilience discourse allows women to "Lean In" to MRWaSP privilege because their overcoming and leaning-in actively produce blackness as exception, as pathology, as death. If our personal resilience is ultimately about white supremacist patriarchy's resilience, then perhaps it's in our own best interests to kill some of that joy, as Sara Ahmed would say? When resilience means performing the work of anti-blackness, we should reject its imperative to overcome. In contexts where "feminism" is evidence of one's resilience, critical feminist practice must be melancholic. We should actually amplify our noisy complicities with white supremacist patriarchy and not pretend that we've overcome racism and sexism. Rather than contributing to the ongoing viability of MRWaSP, it must push MRWaSP into the death.

Conclusion

Alternatives & Adaptations

Resilience is a technique that organizes both social relations and musical practices for the benefit of MRWaSP, its priorities and its values. It shouldn't be surprising, then, that the musical practices most closely tied to resilience discourse—the soar, the pause-drop—are featured in genres targeted, demographically, to the populations expected to be most resilient: pop audiences, multicultural millennials, teen and college-aged girls ("Young Girls," as Tiqqun might put it). Just as MRWaSP co-opted and domesticated resistance strategies and turned them into resilience discourse, it co-opted and domesticated the musics of oppressed groups and turned these noisy monstrosities into gaga-style pop aesthetics.

Resilience is a method for recycling noise into signal. It's also a form of labor—labor that, in the age of real subsumption and affective labor, is economic *because* it is cultural, affective, and psychological. Performed primarily by traditionally oppressed groups—above all, by the "multicultural" women MRWaSP encourages to work their way up its ranks—resilience both naturalizes traditional forms of oppression and produces new ones. These new oppressions are what I call MRWaSP: multiracial white supremacist patriarchy. Because music aesthetics are deeply political, neoliberal upgrades to traditional white supremacist, patriarchal politics also impact aesthetics—"the male gaze" becomes MRWaSP visualization, for example. This intertwining of politics and aesthetics makes it possible to hear already-existing alternatives to resilience discourse in the structure of songs like Rihanna's "Diamonds," or in her performance in "Pour It Up." We don't have to imagine an alternative to MRWaSP and to neoliberal capitalism—Rihanna's already developed one for us. Her alternative is specifically targeted at the techniques that subsume privileged women into its political, economic, and aesthetic means of production—namely, resilience discourse. Instead of recycling noise into signal, Rihanna's performance on *Unapologetic* bends this resilient circuit so that it invests in noise, that is, in currents and currency that diminishes the viability of MRWaSP. This practice of bending resilience so that it invests in "death" rather than "life" is what I call melancholy. Melancholic subjects are poor conductors of MRWaSP power.

In this conclusion, I consider some further elaborations of and alternatives to resilience, both as a (bio)political and a musical phenomenon. Given what we know about gender, race, and pop music from chapters three and four, I want to return to the discussion of biopolitics I began in chapter two and think about resilience biopolitically. This biopolitical lens clarifies the distinction between resilience discourse, which is a specific ideology and technique, and the alternative ways of coping and recovery that oppressed groups have always used to survive amid the damage of racism, sexism, and so on. A better understanding of this distinction makes it easier to develop critical and counter-hegemonic *alternatives* to and *maladaptations* of resilience. If resilience is a technique for investing in the *life* of MRWaSP, then perhaps making *bad investments*—that is, investing in *exceptions*—would suck the life out of, rather than support, MRWaSP.

Thinking biopolitically also clarifies recent adaptations in the soar and in pop music aesthetics. In the final section, I use Miley Cyrus's 2013 single "We Can't Stop" to argue that this post-maximalism coincides with, and is caused by, a shift in perspective from the entrepreneurial individual to the biopolitical population, from "I" or "me" to "we." Soar-style intensification has been maxed out, so the only way to further intensify a song is to push past maximalism into what sounds like minimalism. Though this superficially sounds like sonic de-intensification, it is actually the intensification of auditory and narrative *perspective*—not more sounds, but more ears. So, this move to more chill, more collectively-minded pop may is not an alternative to resilience discourse, but an adaptation and intensification of it.

1. Bad Investments

In chapter 2, I argued that the shift from traditional white supremacist heteropatriarchy to MRWaSP is intertwined with the rise of biopolitics, the power of and over "life." Resilience is one technique for producing the "life" or the "bio" in biopolitics. It takes potentially deadly or debilitating damage and recycles it into new, stronger, better life, both for the resilient individual, and, more importantly, for the groups and societies to which that individual belongs. Resilience is a positive feedback loop in which individual health augments and intensifies the "health" and "life" of the overall population. From this perspective, non-resilient practices seem, well, deadly. Because they're not sufficiently "lively," counter- or non-resilient practices can appear and feel melancholy. But melancholy isn't the only way to respond critically to resilience discourse.

Here I want to *zoom out* from the last chapter's narrow focus on melancholy and think more broadly about critical alternatives to resilience. If resilience is and has long been a way that marginalized and oppressed people respond to, survive, and thrive in the midst of oppression, now that resilience has been co-opted so that it's a normalizing rather than a critical, counter-hegemonic practice, how does one respond to the historical and ongoing damage of oppression in a way that doesn't feed MRWaSP? How do you survive and thrive in ways that don't produce "resilient" surplus value?

To answer these questions, it helps to *zoom in* on a more careful and nuanced definition of resilience. Resilience isn't just "recovery" or "bouncing back" in general, but a socio-historically specific technique and ideology: resilience is recovery that is profitable for neoliberal capitalism and MRWaSP. It is for their sake and well-being that resilience therapeutically re-makes individuals—not for the sake of these individuals themselves. Resilience, then, is a form of subjectification: it makes individuals legible as legitimate members of society who are entitled to the benefits of living in that society. In order to become legible as a real, full person, you have to perform specific behaviors, behaviors that efficiently accomplish the cultural, affective, and social labor required to maintain and reproduce MRWAsP. Groups who have been traditionally excluded from full personhood demonstrate their inclusion in the new, supposedly more diverse, tolerant, and progressive post-racial, post-feminist mainstream by practicing resilience.

Not all behaviors that could be described as "resilient" in the general, non-technical, dictionary-definition sense conform to the logic of resilience discourse. There are many, many ways to deal with damage and trauma, and people frequently recover, survive, cope, and flourish in ways that don't (adequately) support hegemony. These alternative methods of "dealing" don't perform the cultural, ideological, and material/economic labor that produces the surplus value hegemony needs for its continued growth and health. There are myriad ways to respond to the male gaze (and, frankly, myriad variations on the male gaze itself). Resilience discourse demands that women do this in a way that demonstrates a particular type of agency, strength, and overcoming of traditional patriarchy. Women must, for example, display their bodies as objects of *self*-love and admiration: flawed bodies and damaged psyches must be explicitly transformed into normal bodies and healthy psyches. In the spring of 2014, NBC's "Today" show featured a segment called "Love Your Selfie." This regularly-running segment is basically a course in resilience: it follows the damage-therapeutic work-spectacle logic I outlined in the introduction. As the

"Today" show website advertises, "will peel back the layers of their own insecurities, and will share the stories of people who are transforming the traditional definitions of beauty." Damage is revealed, transformed, and rendered as media spectacle. Body image narratives that don't conform to this damage-transformation-spectacle logic, such as veiling/modesty or fat positivity, are seen as pathological, and their practitioners are unintelligible as (real) women. These alternative body image narratives are responses to the male gaze that, for some women, work just fine. But they aren't intelligible as "resilience" because they don't feel like they're healthy for society, for MRWaSP—they don't generate the spectacular evidence of society's own overcoming of patriarchy, here in the form of the male gaze.

There are some ways of surviving and processing damage that aren't resilient in their form or logic. But it is also the case that some people, no matter how perfectly they execute this logic of resilience, will never be legible as properly "resilient". MRWaSP works only if certain groups are rendered exceptional. As I've shown in the last half of the book, the techniques by which some of Modernity's "others" fold (or lean) themselves in to mainstream society also fold specific groups *out*. *Resilience and exception are products of the same process.* Even when people from exceptional groups perform the very same kinds of "resilient" behavior for which MRWaSP rewards members privileged groups, this behavior reads as pathological rather than healthy. That behavior may be absolutely healthy for whomever performs it, but it is not, in the end, the most efficiently or optimally healthy behavior for MRWaSP.

Resilience manages individual-level noise so that it contributes to the overall health of MRWaSP as a system. Resilience discourse is a way of making *individuals* do the work of managing the overall distribution of life and death, health and vulnerability, so that the odds always lean ever more firmly in MRWaSP's favor. To counteract MRWaSP, then, we have to shift the overall distribution of life and death, tip the odds of surviving and thriving back in *our* favor. Feminism will be most effective when it targets MRWaSP at the macro- level, the level of the population, as I put it in chapter two.

But how can individuals effect macro-level change, especially change in a dynamic system that's able to respond and adapt to variability at the individual level? Working in concert, individuals may be able to turn that dynamism back on itself so that adaptations weaken rather than strengthen MRWaSP. In other words, we might be able to turn a positive feedback loop into a vicious cycle. Because neoliberal systems are designed to tolerate a few random outliers or deviants, such a project *must* be collective—it must involve a "statistically significant" sample. But how could we get *enough* people to make to make the kinds of decisions MRWaSP disincentivizes?

Perhaps we could encourage large numbers of people to make 'bad' (for MRWaSP) investments by changing the dis/incentives that motivate individual choices and behaviors. Neoliberalism needs the state to manage background conditions so that they support the market—in this case, the market in race/gender supremacy. Perhaps we can, collectively mis-manage these same background conditions so that the market—here, the market in racial/gender supremacy—collapses in on itself. This mis-management might begin by recognizing and accounting for the way that historical and ongoing white supremacy, patriarchy, and other forms of oppression differentially structure the background conditions in which we each, individually, make decisions. MRWaSP's post-racial, post-feminist perspective cannot account for the effects of past and white supremacy, patriarchy, ableism, heteronormitivity. (This inability means MRWaSP doesn't have a complete picture of the incentives and disincentives motivating decisions made by people in "exceptional" situations—that's why they appear "stupid" or unhealthy.) All of these oppressions deeply, deeply structure the material, economic, and social conditions in which we all make decisions. These conditions offer different incentives to different groups.

For example, YOLO risk taking is an ideal for neoliberal subjects—the greater the risk, the greater the reward. However, risk is not evenly rewarded and punished. As Anna North argues,

> It turns out there's good evidence that being the kind of person who...breaks the rules — can lead to success. But breaking rules doesn't usually go as well for women or people of color as it does for white boys, and changing that might be a necessary step toward equal opportunity.

In our post-Ke$ha world, there may be more cultural and social space for wild girls who like to party so hard they like to brush their teeth in the morning with bourbon (as the lyrics of "Tik Tok" suggest). But if that wild night out ends in sexual assault, because of rape culture—a background social condition—*women* will be blamed for mismanaging risk, for partying too hard, getting too drunk, dressing too provocatively, hanging out with the wrong people, and so on. Patriarchy means that women face a different set of incentives and disincentives than men; that different things are at stake in their choices.

I'm *not* arguing that we should make the risk/reward field more *level* for women, about giving them more equal opportunity to participate in dominant cultural narratives (in this case, the one that incentivizes partying past the point of hangover or diminishing returns). Rather, I'm arguing that we should change the background conditions so that both rape culture behaviors and YOLO entrepreneurialism just don't seem like such attractive investments anymore. Even changing our *understanding* of the background conditions to account rape culture could change the underlying narrative...maybe not right away, but after enough negative feedback gets in the system the background conditions will offer different sets of incentives and disincentives to perpetrators and victims of rape culture.

Changing our understanding of the background conditions is a start, and it may even be necessary, but it's not enough. This sort of consciousness-raising supports the supposedly "stupid" logic of poor and oppressed people. Validating these choices and the people who make them is a far cry from giving us less crappy options, options that are better suited to our needs, our survival, and our well-being. This "bad investment" strategy is a way to actually change these background conditions themselves. Once we recognize that white supremacy, patriarchy, and so on all organize background conditions so that they support the viability of only certain kinds of life, re-organizing and redeveloping these background conditions might be a way to both kill off MRWaSP and make everyone's lives (including the planet's) more livable. We can redevelop background conditions by re-investing resources in the background conditions themselves rather than paying them forward to MRWaSP. Instead of building human or social capital, these "bad" investments build the infrastructure to support the viability of the people and communities MRWaSP kills off as exception. They *redevelop background conditions so they are responsive to the needs of exceptional communities and individuals.* They provide options that aren't catch-22s, that support and encourage the alternative modes and narratives of well-being. For example, radical mental health collectives like The Icarus Project build both alternative narratives of mental health and alternative support networks outside the mainstream medical establishment. [133]

In some senses, I'm arguing that people should do what they've always done, which is build subcultural institutions that support your community in your terms. But this is supposed to be a social justice strategy, so this work can't be limited to the members of the communities or subcultures themselves. Those of us who have enough capital, enough privilege, to spare, we're the ones who need to bear the weight of these 'bad' investments. White feminists like me need to be the ones actively "wasting" our human and social (and capital) capital investing in enterprises that, from the perspective of MRWaSP, offer only bad returns. Resilient people (like Gaga or Beyonce) invest in themselves by producing exceptions as such. Because bad investments don't make exceptions, they don't make resilience, either.[134]

This "bad investment" strategy is different than white saviorism because white saviorism instrumentalizes 'exceptions' in service of building one's own human and social capital. Bad investments are *bad* because they deplete one's human and social capital. Though this example is more about hard capital than "soft" human capital, clearly illustrates how "bad" investments can be a strategy for social change. The Occupy-related project "Rolling Jubilee" buys debt (medical debt, credit card debt) not to collect it at a profit, as is customary, but to forgive it. According to one article in *The Guardian*, by November 2013 the group had forgiven nearly $15 million in personal debt. The members of this group are quite literally making bad financial investments (they're investing in debt on which they'll never see a return) as a method of making good social investments— investments that redistribute opportunities and resources away from the 1% (to use some Occupy jargon) and toward those with less capital. When people are less shackled to their debt, they have more opportunity to pursue whatever is healthy for them and their communities, even and especially if this is not the thing MRWaSP capitalism most benefits from, and most strongly encourages them to do. Attorneys with massive law school debt could, if that debt was forgiven, devote themselves to lower-paying public service work. This is not about helping people bounce back or be resilient (which just assimilates them to MRWaSP); rather, it's about giving people the resources and opportunities to be something other than either "resilient" or "exception." When you invest in the "wrong" things, you redistribute resources, resources that MRWaSP was otherwise counting on.

At bottom, this strategy of making "bad investments" really an argument for a more even distribution of care work. By "care work" I mean the labor required to support life and other types of labor—more or less the classically Marxist feminist understanding of "women's work" as the work required to reproduce the ongoing life of the laborer and the labor force. Caring, I understand it, is investing in others without expecting or receiving a return, in the form of human capital, to the people making the investments. Caring is a necessary job—humans are interdependent and vulnerable, so we can't always care for ourselves. And caring itself—giving without expectation or realization of return—is not inherently unethical, immoral, or violent. As feminists have been arguing for decades, it's the *uneven distribution* of care that's unethical, immoral, and violent. In late capitalist MRWaSP, caring is a bad investment because it doesn't build your human capital.[135] Because care work is such a bad individual investment, it is forced on exceptional populations, often as a way of reinforcing their status as exceptional (i.e., as unable to be re-made into a profitable market). In this light, saying that white and otherwise privileged feminists need to make bad investments means that we need to take responsibility for our fair share of the care work, the work that doesn't build our human capital, and which, in turn, doesn't maximize MRWaSP's own viability.

You might object that this language of "bad investment" stays within the overall neoliberal conceptual universe—that it relies on the same concepts and values as neoliberalism, but just deploys them to different ends. While I am staying within neoliberalism's conceptual universe, I'm doing so because I think it's the only way to have any meaningful impact on it. This is an ideology that cannot even imagine an outside, an alternative, an un-co-optable noise. Because such positions are unintelligible to neoliberalism, they won't gain traction. The counter-hegemonic strategies I've proposed in this book are, as Rita Raley puts it, "reiterative"—they are "radically transformational precisely because [they] exis[t] in dynamic interplay with [their] object" (135). [136] If macro-level systems are designed to dynamically respond to micro-level variability, then micro-level changes in the background conditions would eventually affect the macro-level balance of, say, health and wealth. Negative feedback loops compound micro-level actions into macro-level effects. This is a counter- or critically *biopolitical* strategy because it aims, ultimately, at population-level change. Melancholy, bad investments—these both turn resilient dynamism against itself, bending positive feedback loops into vicious cycles. They're ways of sending MRWaSP into the death and making a better life for everyone.

Now that I've articulated some political alternatives to resilience, I want to shift the focus back to adapting and evolving pop music aesthetics. The soar and the drop are, as I've been arguing, musical manifestations of resilience discourse: they turn musical damage into surplus pleasure. I've also treated the soar and the drop as analogues for *individual* resilience...mainly because that's how pop songs have used them. But, the crass maximalism of 2011-12ish is falling out of fashion; tastes and compositional techniques are adapting. In the next section, I trace these adaptations and argue that they coincide with a shift in perspective: these new tastes and techniques aren't modeled on individual resilience, but group- or population-level resilience.

2. Post-Soar Biopolitics: We Can't Stop

The soar is the musical analogue of the individually resilient person who understands themself as human capital. Just as this entrepreneurial subject understands themself in terms of investment and return on investment, the soar is also a practice of investment, a musical manifestation of neoliberal logics of intensification. In other words, the soar echoes the role of the *individual* person in biopolitical society.

The crassly maximalist soar I discussed in chapter one is well on the road to maxing itself out, both technically and aesthetically. For example, as I argued in the introduction, Harris's "Sweet Nothing," Harris had already *technically* maxed out soarstyle intensification, so the only way to make "Sweet Nothing"s soar *more* intense was to push it beyond maximalism into something more minimal sounding. Similarly, though the maximalist soar still has a strong foothold in EDM, pop seems to have maxed out its tolerance for soar-style intensification. Pushing the limits of our audition just doesn't bring the same bang for the buck as it once did. So, pop songs use new and different musical methods of intensification, methods that can, as in the Diplo and Grandtheft "Sweet Nothing" remix, sound like de-intensification. Just think of how chill Lorde's songs sound compared to your average Skrillex single. Or, think of Katy Perry's "Roar": it has a soar, but a very, very tame one; it intensifies, but it stays far from pushing anybody's limits.

There are still plenty of songs with soars, but, as Alex Niven has noted, "we are seeing…something like the sublimation of the Soar…now The Soar also seems to be giving expression to more genuinely populist sentiments." Niven is right that the soar is being "sublimated" or reworked into something bigger. Interestingly, he implies that this sublimation isn't so much in how the soar *sounds*, but in the "instinct" or "sentiment" behind it, what it *"expresses."* On this point, Niven is, I think, absolutely correct: as a musical technique, the sublimated soar retains everything but the original soar's maximalism, and the de-intensification of the soar effects a shift in perspective from individual to collective. "Everywhere you look in the chart music of the moment," Niven argues, "themes of collectivism and contemporaneity are being pushed front and centre...'We' is fast replacing 'me' as the pronoun of choice for producers seeking to latch onto the pop zeitgeist of the 2010s." Niven misidentifies the "we" who is the subject and addressee of these songs. He thinks the "we" is modernity's revolutionary collectivities (e.g., the proletariat coming to class consciousness). But that's not who this "we" is. These songs give voice to the biopolitical population as a "we" and an "us." If the soar echoes the structure of the individual, entrepreneurial subject, these post-soar developments echo the structure of the *biopolitical population as corporate subject.* Instead of the competitive individual who "soar[s] above its airwave rivals," this new breed of pop song *gives voice to the overall biopolitical average,* the statistical distribution of more and less resilient entrepreneurs and exceptions. At this macro scale, every individual soar feels pretty average compared to all the others. No matter how gaga anybody goes, from this vantage it all seems tempered and moderate. *That's* the sublimation: sound becomes perspective.

A really chill song about partying gone out of control, Miley Cyrus's 2013 single "We Can't Stop" is a perfect illustration of this sublimation. The lyrics are a hymn to deregulated excess, partying hard and doing whatever one wants (indeed, Miley has somewhat replaced Gaga and Ke$ha as the most outrageously gaga of female pop stars), but, as the title suggests, the subject of the song isn't "me" but "we." If everybody's going full throttle, even the most excessive diva behavior won't disrupt the overall vibe. That's why, as the opening line says, there's "no drama" when "we" party without limits or rules. There aren't individuals with competing interests at this party, just the collective "we" and what it wants.

With a "laidback...vibe," as Bianca Gracie puts it, the song's music also follows this "no drama" rule. First, there's no dramatic energy propelling the song forward: just as the lyrics suggest that the "we" is caught in a feedback loop it can't stop, the music keeps spuriously cycling through verses and choruses without moving forward or backward.[137] Second, there's no dramatic climax. In most EDM-pop of this era, the bridge climaxes in a soar and/or a drop, which then leads back to the final repetition of the chorus. "We Can't Stop" puts a *vacuum* at the end of the bridge: the percussion drops out entirely, leaving only some synths and Miley noodling around on some "yea-eh-ah-ayh"s. Miley's vocals don't build, but *decay* over time. The rhythmic intensity of her syllabifications actually *decreases* as the four-bar not-soar progresses: she repeats the "yeah-eh-ah-ayh" once in each of the first three measures, but then drops the last part of the third articulation, coming back in with only an "eh-ayh" on the downbeat of the fourth measure. Finally, instead of dramatically soaring up to or pausing in anticipation of the downbeat of the chorus, the last half of the fourth bar gently swells into the "aaaaaand" of the chorus's first line. "We Can't Stop" uses the soar to smooth out rather than intensify *individual* or micro-level drama.[138] This smoothed-out soar is how the song *musically* expresses or accomplishes the shift in perspective from the "I" to the biopolitical "we."

"We Can't Stop" adapts to the exhaustion of the soar by finding something different to intensify. In this song, it's not the rhythm or timbre that intensifies, but the *perspective* that does. The move from the "I" to the "We" is an intensification *in* perspective itself. Emphasizing the population over the individual, "We Can't Stop" connects post-maximalist aesthetics to biopolitics.

In a biopolitically equalized population, good girls are encouraged to make a lot of gaga noise so that they have something to resiliently bounce back from. At the same time, a biopolitically equalized population frames black women and black femininity as irreparably noisy, because that is reason to quarantine them as exception. In "We Can't Stop," as with many of the other songs and performances related to her *Bangerz* album, Miley meets the former expectation by appropriating the latter kind of noise, generating individual noise by co-opting ratchet aesthetics such as twerking, fashion, and even black women's embodied aesthetic labor itself (i.e., in the form of backup dancers).[139] (As Heidi R. Lewis explains, before "ratchet" became a quasi-derogatory term for "women that are unintelligent, loud, classless, tacky, and hypersexual," it "meant getting excited, partying, 'going hard'.") Miley appropriates the excessiveness MRWaSP associates with ratchetness as proof of her *own* excess.[140] It's how she shows she's resiliently intensifying herself, pushing herself to and past her own limits. Miley uses this noise to fold herself into the "we" — it's her way of participating in the gaga party we're all having.

This party, is as Chris Taylor observed, actually the work of human capital production and real subsumption. "We Can't Stop" isn't about the pleasures individual or collective autonomy, he argues. Instead, it expresses the crushing banality of the human capital grind. Partying isn't fun because it's work; and it's not just work, but "hyperemployment," the unending transformation of leisure and rest time into sites of surplus-value production. Part of Miley's job in "We Can't Stop" is to expropriate surplus value from ratchet black femininity: investing it in *herself*, she's turning black women's bodies and bodily expression into *her* gaga spectacle. Miley can turn ratchetness into nonstop gaga capitalization only if black women, the black women she imitates and instrumentalizes, are excluded from this "we" (they may be able to participate as instruments, as service workers, but not as members). This means that black women don't benefit or profit from their own work; they can't enter the party because they don't have enough human capital to make the cover charge. Miley's investments in black femininity produce actual black women as exception. Thus, because she mellows the soar in a way that produces black femininity and black women as exception, a similarly-positioned black woman can't mellow the soar as a way of demonstrating her inclusion in the biopolitical "we."

This is why Miley's laid back (or, as Taylor suggests, pathetically sad) aesthetic registers differently with pop audiences than Rihanna's melancholy does. "We Can't Stop" *sounds* very similar to Rihanna's work on *Unapologetic*. Like "We Can't Stop," Rihanna's "Diamonds" is musically flat and has a muted soar. This is likely because it was written by the same duo, Rock City, that wrote Rihanna's "Pour It Up." (In fact, "We Can't Stop" was originally written *for Rihanna*, but because Rihanna already had a hit with "Diamonds," the duo gave the song to Miley instead.[141]) "We Can't Stop" may be painfully dull, but for all their commentary on the song's relaxed, Benadryl-tempered vibe, critics never chide Miley for being insufficiently resilient, or for not writing a banger. Because "We Can't Stop"'s dullness is not seen as the result of insufficient resilience, it is not an example of melancholy. Instead, it reads as a sublimation of the soar into collective consciousness. We don't hear a melancholic "me," but a properly-balanced "we."

Because Rihanna is black, she can't leverage blackness to achieve the same shift in perspective that Miley does. Rihanna's muted resilience is not seen as evidence of a shift in perspective, of her successful assimilation to the group. Instead, her muted resilience is treated as evidence of her *individual* failure to assimilate. It is read as an individual failure because, as I argued in chapter four, this investment doesn't produce blackness (e.g., in the figure of Chris Brown) as exception. Both Miley and Rihanna invest in blackness; but, because Miley's investments in ratchet blackness augment her MRWaSP human capital (she was seen as edgy and transgressive, perhaps immaturely so, but she wasn't seen as 'post-ethics'), they count as resilience. Rihanna's investments in blackness do not augment her MRWaSP human capital, so they read as melancholic. Even though "We Can't Stop" and "Diamonds" sound very, very similar, they *work* very, very differently.

We should be suspicious of gaga feminism's resilient maximalism. We should be equally suspicious of Miley feminism's biopolitical minimalism. They are all culturally racist feminisms that give women a narrow path to agency and empowerment—a path that produces (some kinds of) blackness as exception. We should be similarly suspicious of aesthetic shifts away from individual transgression and towards collective participation—this "we" may just be the voice of the biopolitical population, the corporate "we."

Neoliberalism will always adapt—that's its schtck, after all: it says it can adapt to incorporate and neutralize anything. Neoliberalism is, in other words, *resilient*. But it is not all-encompassing, and it is not infinitely flexible. There are plenty of already-existing alternatives currently in practice, and there must be points of diminishing returns (why else must background conditions be so carefully managed?). In this book I've tried to locate some of these points in pop music, in MRWaSP, and in feminist and anti-racist practice.

For those of us tasked with the labor of resilience, the question is this: how do we turn resilience against itself, investing in (rather than producing) exceptions and making this kind of life more viable so that MRWaSP itself dies off?

Notes

1   Barrow, Dan. "A Plague of Soars" (2013).

2   Lucas, George. *Star Wars Episode IV: A New Hope.* (1977).

3   Listening to these EDM songs is more than just a rehearsal of skills we'll use later—this listening actively generates the kinds of surplus value the market craves most. In neoliberal capitalism, leisure and pleasure are themselves fully integrated into the means of production. Leisure is labor, in the sense that it produces surplus value, and thus profits, for capital. For example, when I stream or share music online, I generate data that streaming and social media companies then re-sell at a profit. Resilient EDM-pop songs are "industrial music" in its original sense—music used to goad workers into laboring more efficiently and enthusiastically. In his book on the history of industrial music, S. Alexander Reed explains: "In the early twentieth century, 'industrial music' meant the music played for or performed by workers to facilitate their labor...This was a functional music, not consumed as art but disseminated to streamline workers' efficiency, decrease their emotion, increase reliability, and promote unity among them" (19). Reed, S. Alexander. *Assimilate.* Oxford: Oxford University Press 2013.

4   Jhally, Sut. "Bell Hooks: Cultural Criticism & Transformation (1997).

5   See James, Robin. "Loving the Alien" (2012). See also James, Robin. "Neoliberal Noise: Attali, Foucault, and the Biopolitics of Uncool" (2014).

6   Or, as Foucault puts it, biopower is "the right to foster life or disallow it to the point of death" (HSv1 138).

7   Of course, this market is free in name only. As Foucault explains in *Birth of Biopolitics,* "competition as an essential economic logic will only appear and produce its effects under certain conditions which have to be carefully and

artificially constructed. This means that pure competition is not a primitive given. It can only be the result of lengthy efforts and, in truth, pure competition is never attained" (120). Superficial deregulation and free choice is possible only because the background conditions are carefully managed.

8   "A normalizing society is the historical outcome of a technology of power centered on life" (HSv1 144).

9   As philosopher Shannon Winnubst argues, "human capital becomes the barometer for all of life's activities...medical care, public health and hygiene, and even migration all become matters for careful calculation of 'investments we have made at the level of man himself'" (84).

10   On stochastic resonance, see Rouvais-Nicolis, Catherine and Nicolis, Gregoire. "Stochastic Resonance" (2007).

11   See Longinger, H. *Fundamentals of Statistics*.

12   It "promote[s] their claims to be non-racist by using the presence of these [non-white] individuals as cultural symbols to distract many of us" so that what is an "overt racial mission...can be couched as an ostensible hunt for justice" (Sheth 2013).

13   See Puar, Jasbir. *Terrorist Assemblages*. (2007).

14   This idea that the sine wave distributes race is my take on Jared Sexton's claim, via Paul Gilroy, that "'with the body figured an epiphenomenon of coded information...The skin may no longer be privileged as the threshold of identity. There are good reasons to suppose that the line between inside and outside falls elsewhere.' This other threshold of identity, this newly privileged 'elsewhere' that how houses the persistent dividing line, is located *within* the body " (Sexton 234; citing Gilroy 196; emphasis mine). As a feedback process, resilience locates the work of racialization and gendering within the individual body (as fortitude, strength, health), and within the body politic, the

population.

15 This image of mutually-intensifying feedback loops is different than the image of the traffic intersection, which informs feminist concepts of intersectionality, and, in some ways, from Puar's image of assemblages. It is more temporal than just spatial (as the traffic intersection is), and more algorithmic than Cartesian. The image of feedback loops also foregrounds the ways that the interplay of signals can produce new tones (harmonics), and modulate existing tones (feedback, noise, cancelling out, etc.).

16 See Marx, Karl. *Capital, Volume 1*. (1978).

17 See Freud, Sigmund. "Mourning and Melancholia" (2007).

18 Melancholy isn't dialectically related to resilience, either. Melancholy isn't the determinate negation of resilience because the difference isn't logical so much as it is contextual—the difference between melancholy and resilience depends on situational features like who, where, and with what it is performed.

19 See Williams, Alex and Srnicek, Nick. "#ACCELERATE MANIFESTO for an Accelerationist Politics" (2013).

20 On charter schools, see Wells, Amy Stuart, Slaton, Julie, and Scott, Janelle. "Defining Democracy in the Neoliberal Age: Charter School Reform and Educational Consumption" (2002). On cap and trade, see: Jones, Mitch. "The Financialization of Nature" (2013). On the ACA see: Gaffney, A.W. "The Neoliberal Turn in American Health Care" (2014).

21 Voyou Desouevre identified "the dubstep drop" and "the Guetta soar" as two hallmarks of contemporary EDM pop in their blog entry from 9 December 2012

22 See McClary, Susan. "What Was Tonality?" (2001).

23 In the early-mid 20th century, avant-garde European and American composers developed ways of organizing musical works that didn't rely on tonal harmony. Arnold Schoenberg's free atonality and 12-tone serialism, Pierre

Boulez's total serialism, John Cage's aleatory methods, Steve Reich's process music, Karlheintz Stockhausen's electroacoustic experimentation, and Pierre Schaeffer's *musique concrete* are all examples of *post-tonal* music. Because "post-tonal" refers to this 20th century modernist avant-garde, I'm using the term "extra-tonal" to describe EDM-pop's relationship to tonality.

24 "Family resemblance" is philosopher Ludwig Wittgenstein's theory for explaining how particular instances (or tokens) are related to one another, and to a general, overarching term (or type). For Wittgenstein, family resemblance is not an essential, foundational common feature, but "a complicated network of similarities, overlapping and criss-crossing" (*PI* 66)."

25 Popdust's Barry Walters calls this "The Greatest Keychange of All"

26 I'm referencing the official video posted to Jay-Z's "jayz" account on YouTube.

27 As I explain in more detail in *The New Inquiry*, LMFAO's "Party Rock Anthem" uses rhythmic intensification (in the drum machines and vocals) and timbral intensification (in the instrumental synths) to build its main soar in the song's break.

28 We only actually see Guetta during the most intense moments of soaring. This begs the question of his whiteness and its location at the "peak" of the soar. Does living life to the fullest mean participating in whiteness/white privilege?

29 In "Titanium," the soar happens in the second repetition of the last line of the chorus (the song's title). In "She Wolf," it happens in the last two iterations of the last line of the chorus.

30 Here, the soar happens in the last two repetitions of "just one last time"; the last repetition is a particularly distilled example of the Guetta soar, and the timbral swoosh features

more prominently here than in other versions.

31 Several dubstep artists explicitly highlight the role of the physical and physiological force of sound frequencies. The Bug argues that "The sheer physicality of this music is astounding...the dubstep scene's core players; they're obsessed by frequencies and the impact of sonic force, obsessed by the potential for literally moving people through sound, not through hype.'" (O'Connell) Similarly, Juju claims that "You don't hear that 50 Hz kicking you right in the face anymore. That's what brought me to dubstep, which kicks you in the face on every track." (Keast)

32 The drop happens about 3:10 and 3:58 in the official video on Swift's VEVO channel.

33 The video reinforces the "maturity" and gravity of this drop: the boys who were harassing the ice cream man and making small-scale explosions early in the video are now full-fledged gangsters with bombs and assault weapons.

34 This is what I take to be Dan Barrow's point in his commentary on my "Loving the Alien"

35 In the U.S., the busy signal is combination of tones at 480 Hz (a rather sharp A) and 620 Hz (about a D#) that alternate on and off at about 120bpm. It sounds like two voices stuttering on their respective pitches.

36 Music software can easily break audio signal down into its component parts and isolate various timbral dimensions— this is what effects or patches do. However, it is now common to manipulate these effects and patches with a gestural interface like a track pad or a tablet computer. What used to require some relatively specialized knowledge about synthesizer programming and operation now requires little more than basic computer literacy.

37 Musicians have always manipulated timbre. However, timbre has often been something controlled *implicitly*, through the material properties of the instrument (the type

and quality of materials from which an instrument is constructed) or the instrumentalist's body (embouchure, breath support and control), and not *explicitly* as a matter of instrument operation. In other words: timbre is not something produced by pressing keys, covering holes, pressing down, bowing, or plucking strings, or hitting an object. OR: timbre is not part of the propositional content of traditional musical notation. So, timbre was important, but it was not one of the central, explicit, propositionally-formulateable elements of a composition. Synthesizers make timbre propositionally-formulateable: "set decay at 8," for example.

38 Cognitive capitalism, an idea developed most notably by Yann Moulier Boutang, is a political economy geared to produce *affect* (e.g., brands rather than things).

39 Because parts are not integrated into an overarching whole, composited works exemplify the "pseudo-individuality" that Theodor Adorno famously attributes to jazz. See Adorno, Theodor W. "On Popular Music" (2002).

40 For example, the last four modules (FBCA) can be parsed two ways: (1) either F, A, and D are interchangeable (the second F subs for A, and A for D in an ABCD super-module), or (2) the ABC order can be scrambled into BCA. It is difficult to decide between these two options because the song only gives us one full repetition of any sort of pattern (ABCDEF), a slim basis on which to judge conformity or deviation.

41 Unlike industrial mass production, which emphasizes uniformity of product, neoliberal production techniques, such as compositing, treat commutability of conditions as a *means* to increasingly diverse products.

42 Most of the specific practices and general aesthetic features in EDM-pop have been around for decades, e.g., in hip hop, techno, and jungle. So why *now*? Why did EDM-pop break

the US only in the last few years? There are a lot of factors involved: advances in consumer-grade music technology, the culture industry's interest in promoting musical practices and aesthetics that open up new channels of surplus-value extraction, etc. All of them are necessary, none sufficient. Neoliberalism, however, is a particularly important co-requisite. The methods and techniques that generate musical pleasure in EDM-pop are the same ones that neoliberal hegemony demands listeners to extract surplus value from ourselves, our "human capital." That's one important reason why these neoliberal logics of intensity, optimization, and noise-farming now make intuitive or "common" sense to large chunks of the pop music listening public. Listeners can use their implicit understanding of social structures to interpret and find pleasure in EDM-pop songs. *EDM-pop sounds like what entrepreneurial subjectivity, big data, finance capital, and the globalized service economy feel like.* From this perspective, EDM-pop finally broke the States because neoliberalism was embedded deeply enough in the everyday lives of middle-class Americans that mainstream pop audiences felt like it spoke to or about them. It would be interesting to see if and how ethnographic data bears this hypothesis out.

43   See Foucault, Michel. *The Birth of Biopolitics*. (2008).

44   As philosopher Jason Read argues, "Classical liberalism makes exchange the general matrix of society...just as relations in the marketplace can be understood as an exchange of certain freedoms for a set of rights and liberties" (27).

45   For more on Schenkerian analysis, see Forte, Alan and Gilbert, Stephen. *Introduction to Schenkerian Analysis*. (1982).

46   The idea of collective investment in a population is what makes free competition different than a Hobbesean pre-social war of all against all. In the former case, the social

group coheres because of individual competition; in the latter case, there is no macro-level group, and individuals are fighting for themselves more than they are competing against one another.

47 As Steven Shaviro puts it, "transgression today is entirely normative... Far from being subversive or oppositional, transgression is the actual motor of capitalist expansion today: the way that it renews itself in orgies of "creative destruction"." ("AA")

48 "Zeno's paradox" describes a tension between the logical and material possibility of compounding halves. Take a definite length of space—say, a meter—or quantity of substance—say, a pint of beer—and you are going to tackle this one half at a time. You will never cross the whole space in one single bound or shotgun the pint in one guplp, but only proceed forward or drink *half* of the quantity you have in front of you. So, you divide the meter or pint in half, and walk or drink one of the halves. Then, you take half of the remaining 50cm or 8oz, and halve that: 25cm or 4oz. You drink half, and divide the remainder in half: 12.5cm or 2 oz. Logically, this division can go on infinitely; materially, at some point, the remaining space or beer will be imperceptible—you won't be able to see the remaining "half."

49 See Adorno, Theodore "On Popular Music." (2002).

50 Lester Spence's "Staring in the Darkness" makes this argument in more detail.

51 A version of this chapter was published in the *Journal of Popular Music Studies* Trans/Queer Special Issue.

52 As philosopher Shannon Winnubst explains, "sexuality is the heart and lifeblood of biopolitics" (Winnubst, 79) because it, in conjunction with race, is one of the main instruments through which neoliberalism "fosters" or "disallows" life (Foucault HSv1 138). For more on sexuality's relationship to race and racialization, see Stoler,

Ann Laura. *Race and the Education of Desire*. (1995). See also, McWhorter, LaDelle. *Racism & Sexual Oppression in Anglo-America*. (2009). See Also Puar, Jasbir. *Terrorist Assemblages*. (2007).

53   Jeffery Nealon characterizes classical liberalism as a logic of "expansion and assimilation" that proceeds by "conquering or assimilating new territory" (81). In this model, difference is resolved back into the underlying whole. Moreover, conquest is teleological: one progresses through difference back to assimilation (the point of the *Odyssey*, for example, is not the battle of Troy, but Odyssesus' return home).

54   "Arche" is the ancient Greek word for an underlying principle that gives a thing order and coherence. An-arche, in this sense, is the lack of underlying ordering principles.

55   This teleological narrative structure (home—journey—back home) is characteristic of Enlightenment though in general, as Theordor Adorn & Max Horkheimer argue in *Dialectic of Enlightenment*. It is also a way to understand tonal harmony, as Susan McClary argues in *Feminine Endings*. McClary explicitly compares tonality to *The Odyssey*, arguing that tonal songs, like Ulysses, all must wander through foreign lands/keys, but ultimately aim to get back "home."

56   The Sex Pistols' "Johnny B. Goode/Roadrunner" track is an (the?) exception; shit does break down and get fucked up here, as Rotten stumbles through two tracks whose words claims to forget. It is also worth considering The Slits' "So Tough" more carefully in this light. This track was supposedly written about Sid Vicious, a mocking jab at his "radical" macho posturing. "So Tough" might be an insightful feminist critique of negativity-as-macho-posturing.

57   As musically conservative as it was, the song *was* widely regarded as shocking and radical. On the one hand, the other aspects of the song—the lyrics, the band's visual

appearance, their performance practices, album art and other related media—were more unconventional and disruptive than the music itself was. On the other hand, the song's musical minimalism could be interpreted as a post-modern challenge to the modernist aesthetics of prog and glam rock, as well as the modernist ethos that grounded then-mainstream constructions of white heteromasculinity. "Progressive" avant-gardeism was an ideal for both artistic practice and white masculine subjectivity: great art, like great men, was revolutionary—it disrupted convention and charted new, innovative courses. In this context, "God Save's" minimal musical aesthetics would appear as regressions to a more primitive state, a shocking departure from prog/glam decadence. However, the Pistols' superficial rejection of the norm actually reinforces it. They're not rejecting white heteromasculinity, but a specific proggy, glammy articulation of it. The Pistols are still generally interpreted as radical, disruptive, innovative, and avant-garde precisely *because* they challenged then-accepted notions of what constituted avant-garde practice. From this perspective, the Pistols, like generations of hipsters before and after them, disidentified with then-mainstream white masculinity as a means to establish elite status in white heteropatriarchy. Despite the outward appearance of radicality, these race/gender/sexual politics are not very disturbing at all. Halberstam addresses some of the limitations of traditional punk masculinity in *The Queer Art of Failure*, and also in the "What's That Smell?" chapter of *In A Queer Time And Place*. See also Willis, Ellen. *Beginning to See the Light*. (2012).

58   According to Edelman, queer death "works to reduce the empire of meaning to the static of an electric buzz...Such an absolutely inhuman and meaningless language could only sound to human ears like the permanent whine of white

noise, like the random signals we monitor with radio telescopes trained on space, or perhaps like the electronically engineered sound with which Hitchcock ends *The Birds"* (*Edelman*, 153).

59   Reproductive futurity is "blin[d]" to "its own 'automatic reiteration' of the logic that always tops our ideological charts," i.e., to its own compulsion to repeat and re-install itself. (Edelman, 142). "Why marvel that reproductive futurism repeats what it poses as passing beyond?...To 'know the world's the same': though purporting to be wed to the value of difference in heterosexual combination and exchange."

60   See Halberstam, Judith. *In A Queer Time and Place.* (2005).

61   I need to clarify that I'm not arguing that what these scholars identify as "queer" and "black" strategies are in actual fact identical. Each set of performance traditions have their own histories, that sometimes overlap, and sometimes don't. However, from the dominant perspective, a perspective from which each performance tradition is generally unintelligible, they both appear to be unintelligible in apparently similar ways and for apparently similar reasons.

62   Though this is not the place to develop this claim, I should at least note that Edelman's psychoanalytic framework also orients his critique to classical liberalism. Freudian and Lacanian concepts of "death" are very different from biopolitical/neoliberal conceptions of "death."

63   Though fronted by white West Berliner Alec Empire, women and people of color have key roles in the band: Hanin Elias, a Syrian-raised female vocalist and instrumentalist, and as was Afro-German Carl Crack founded the band with Empire; Japanese-American noise artist Nic Endo joined in 1996 and continues her involvement with the band, and African-American MC CX KiDTRONiK has worked with the

band since 2010.

64 As Foucault explains, in neoliberalism "it is no longer a matter of bringing death into play in the field of sovereignty, but of distributing the living in the domain of value and utility. Such a power has to qualify, measure, appraise, and hierarchize, rather than display itself in its murderous splendor; it does not have to draw the line that separates the enemies of the sovereign from his obedient subjects; it effects distributions around the norm" (144).

65 The track was officially released in 1995, on an album titled *1995*, but it was recorded in 1993; the version on *1995* was recorded at a Glasgow concert in 1993.

66 Ronald Bogue attributes this "modularity" to death metal generally. Digital hardcore is often considered a close relative of death metal, grindcore, and other hardcore metal genres. Moreover, this modularity is a key feature of what Lev Manovich calls "The Language of New Medi." See Bogue, Ronald. *Deleuze's Wake*. (2004). and Manovich, Lev. *The Language of New Media*. (2001).

67 This distinction could also be expressed in terms of humanism: the classically liberal subject is a humanist one—wholeness, authenticity, and self-presence are fundamental assumptions. Neoliberal structures of subjectivity do not require wholeness, authenticity, and self-presence—they may accommodate, even require, opposite assumptions. (The "entrepreneurial subject" easily accommodates posthuman forms of corporeal and cognitive enhancement, for example.) For more on the subject of neoliberalism, see Read, Jason. "A Genealogy of Homo Economicus" (2009).

68 According to Foucault, neoliberalism uses "bio-power to designate what brought life and its mechanisms into the realm of explicit *calculations* and made knowledge-power an agent of transformation of human life" (143; emphasis mine). These calculations were both literal (statistics, big

data, biofeedback) and abstract.

69 As Steven Shaviro notes, neoliberalism demands subjects live in the moment: nobody can make future plans because they have to be ready to respond to last-minute, "just-in-time" demands. (*PCA*)

70 Anthropologist Angela Jancius notes a shift from the "Wall" to "unemployment" as technologies of social stratification. Reporting her fieldwork in Leipzig, she explains: "Pastor Wolf opened the discussion by telling us that the 40th anniversary of the Berlin Wall's construction (Tag des Mauerbaus) had brought an appropriate symbolism to the forum. In 1961, a physical wall had been built, dividing the country. He hoped that post-re-unification Germany would not also become a society that built walls separating people — walls, such as the symbolic one created by unemployment." Here, a "unemployment" functions like the Wall once did—to separate the "successful" members of global liberal democratic capitalist society from the erstwhile failures. "Unemployment" became a racializing technology. Though it was (and is) still the case that "whiteness functions as the implicit precondition for inclusion in the national citizenry within the German context" (Weheliye 166), with MRWaSP whiteness moves from being a strictly phenotypical category to a more complex, overtly intersectional or 'assembled' one. "Unemployment" marks class distinctions among whites, separating viable white elites from those poor and working-class whites who must also be left to die (they are, so to speak, queerly white, not white *enough* or not white in the right ways). German national identity is still normatively white; however, neoliberal whiteness claims to be "tolerant" and "inclusive" of (some) racial Others, so those who fail to be tolerant and inclusive are not fully white, because they lack full access to the benefits of whiteness.

71 "Redshirt" describes a character whose sole function is to die or be killed. The term comes from the original *Star Trek* TV series, in which extras wearing red uniform shirts were often killed as a way to advance the plot.

72 See Agamben, Giorgio. *Homo Sacer: Sovereign Power and Bare Life.* (1998).

73 Though the political effects of this shift to biopolitical MRWaSP were amplified by 9/11 and the subsequent Great Recession, ATR's *1995* suggests that biopolitical death was already put to work, even if in nascent form, in the mid-1990s. They may have been particularly attuned to these developments for several reasons. First, bandmembers Cark Crack, an Afro-German, and Hanin Elias, a woman, had first-hand experiences of racism, nationalism, and sexism. Second, ATR widely appropriated from underground and avant-garde artists of color; the musical techniques and aesthetics they appropriated could contain knowledge and critiques of contemporary race/gender/sexual politics.

74 "The lived experience of ambient insecurity" (Horning), precarity is the condition of being barely able to keep up with all the demands made of you, so that you stay just in the black but never have anything left to "put aside" for an emergency or to "invest" in bettering your situation.

75 For more on Deleuze's concept of "control society" see Gilles Deleuze, "Postscript on the Societies of Control". (1992). It is important to theorize ATR with and through Deleuze's work because the band directly and intentionally interacted with it. Empire released a number of solo recordings with record label Mille Plateaux, for example.

76 Whether or not ATR *explicitly* intended this interpretation is not my concern. Artworks, unlike other forms of communication and cultural production, are *expected* to suggest and support interpretations beyond the one(s) explicitly intended by the artists who created them. Because my

argument is about the work (the songs) and not about the band, it is sufficient, for my purposes in this article, that the works themselves provide grounds for my interpretations. The historical question about the band's intentions is a different project, probably best left to someone with more training and interest in purely historical work than I have.

77 This is largely because, as Tricia Rose argues, "in this process of techno-black cultural syncretism, technological instruments and black cultural priorities are revised and expanded. In a simultaneous exchange, rap music has made its mark on advanced technology, and technology has profoundly changed the sound of black music" (Rose, 96). Late 20th-century recording and production technology was influenced by the black musical and cultural priorities embodied in hip hop. Companies wanted to make equipment that hip hop artists and producers would use.

78 As Empire explains in his AV Club interview, "…And that was when we founded Atari Teenage Riot. That was in the beginning of 1992, when there were a lot of attacks from the Neo-Nazi movement on foreigners and immigrants and stuff.

79 The performance principle is, according to Marcuse, "the violent and exploitative productivity which made man into an instrument of labor" (199).

80 As Winnubst argues, "Despite ongoing lip-service to the sacred cows of a Protestant Work Ethic and utility, we respond to their interpellation as a faint nostalgic call, heeding rather the *kinetic circuit of interests*, in whatever guise they may don: compulsive work-outs at the gym; latest hip trends of diet or fashion; quick new fixes for enhanced mental stimulation, whether organic, synthetic, or virtual; and, of course, savvy market transactions, no matter the object or market of exchange…Unbounded pleasure is the distinguishing promise of neoliberalism, no longer

something ot be feared, avoided, moderated, or domesticated" (91; emphasis mine).

81 Both in their emphasis on uncompromising order and their
co-opting of the logic of intensity, ATR's practice of "into the
death" resembles (and perhaps can be seen to anticipate)
the political ideology currently called "accelerationism."
This resemblance does not go very far beyond the surface.
Whereas accelerationism advocates practices that create "*a
positive feedback loop* of infrastructural, ideological, social
and economic transformation, generating a new complex
hegemony, a new post-capitalist technosocial platform"
(manifesto section 19; emphasis mine), ATR's musical
practices create *negative* feedback loops—mastery
undercuts itself.

82 This is not surprising, because in the same way "Delete
Yourself" is based around the Pistols' "God Save" riff, this
song takes the main guitar riff from death metal band
Thanatos's "Bodily Dismemberment."

83 The copy of the liner notes posted on discogs.com lists them
as using a Roland TR-909 drum machine.

84 "What death metal musicians seek in this volume is a music
of intensities, a continuum of sensation (percepts/affects)
that converts the lived body into a dedifferentiated sonic
body without organs" (Bogue 88).

85 Even though we both agree that death is not nothingness or
negation, but "zero intensity," Bogue and I have different
concepts of this null point. He understands death as "the
catatonic body's zero intensity...an ecstatic, disorganized
body of fluxes and flows" (105). For Bogue, zero-intensity
means dissolution and disorganization. In my view, death is
always highly regulated and managed—it is the bare life
that biopolitics has an interest in managing, even if
indirectly. So, for me, zero-intensity is a carefully produced
effect. This effect fundamentally relational—it seems like

zero-intensity compared to what, in a specific regime, counts as high intensity. So "death" has no inherent or necessary content or form; anything can be made to count as zero intensity. Our differences can probably be attributed to our different source texts: him, Deleuze and death metal, me, Foucault and digital hardcore.

86 The queerness of rigidity and hyperattentive discipline in neoliberalism seems like a productive lens through which to examine the associations between industrial/EBM masculinities in 1980s/90s bands like Nitzer Ebb and DAF, and masculinities in queer subcultures.

87 Over/underdrive is a different model of excess than Munoz's very modernist concept of ecstasy. Munoz is significantly indebted to the Frankfurt School—Bloch and Marcuse are central to his work. His concept of "ecstatic" utopian negativity is somewhat comparable to Marcuse's notion of the aesthetic dimension or Adorno's theory of autonomous art: a practice is queerly utopian insofar as it stands outside of the everyday normal lifeworld. "Queerness," he argues, "is essentially about the *rejection* of a here and now and an insistence on potentiality or concrete possibility for another world" (Munoz 1; emphasis mine). As, perhaps, my reliance of Foucault instead of Marcuse indicates, I'm trying to push past modernist frameworks and think with and against neoliberalism in its own terms: not counter-modernisms, but queerly racialized biopolitics. In "Into the Death," excess doesn't negate or reject, but *overdrives normal, everyday life-and-death reality*. Its aesthetic dimension isn't outside or beyond political reality, but an *intensified* version of it. Excess doesn't get tossed out or rejected, but recycled. So, ecstasy wouldn't function as ek-stasis, but as feedback or distortion. If art resisted industrial modernity by being (heteronomously) autonomous from it, it contests biopolitical neoliberalism by fully participating in it, warping and

bending its circuits of intensification.

88 Foucault argues that, in neoliberalism, death was "disqualify[ed]" and "carefully evaded" (SMBD 138) because "death is power's limit, the moment that escapes it; death becomes the most secret aspect of existence, the most 'private.'" (SMBD 138).

89 As Foucault argues, with the advent of biopolitics, "the randomness of death...passed into knowledge's field of control and power's sphere of intervention" (SMBD 142).

90 It's doubtful that ATR's work actually realizes these race/gender/sexual politics. Their "riot sounds" tend to fuel a love-and-theft hipstersim. However, I do think the concept or practice of bent circuits is a productive means for theorizing counter-hegemonic race/gender/sexual politics. It's not the bending itself that makes this practice critical and counter-hegemonic—like ATR's largely white, straight, cis-male fanbase, or neoliberal feminist Sherly Sandberg, one can "lean in" to the circuits of power so that they bend in ways that amplify one's role in privilege.

91 The interpretation I offer here is very different than their general reception, which easily subsumed their work in a hetero-white-boy avant-gardeist rockism. In the same way that the queer elements of classical punk often got resig-nified as part of subcultural straight white masculinity (Nyong'o 2008), the potentially queer elements of ATR's *1995* were commonly interpreted by their largely white, hetero, male fanbase as means of performing their identities as radical, avant-garde white straight men. Though the band was superficially inclusive of women and men of color, and the music was even theoretically queer, these elements were tolerated as part of the performance of a post-feminist, post-racial neoliberal subject, who is still homonormative, white, and masculine. From this perspective, ATR's fanbase interpreted their music as part of

the multi-racial white supremacist patriarchal project I described earlier.

92 Empire cites both influences in his AV Club interview.

93 As Tavia Nyong'o explains, "1970s punk represents the moment at which those specifically male homosexual associations [the relationship between john and hustler, rough trade] lose their exclusivity and punk becomes a role and an affect accessible to people within a range of gendered embodiments who deploy punk for a variety of erotic, aesthetic, and political purposes" (110).

94 Homonationalisim is, as Puar defines it, a "brand of homosexuality [that] operates as a regulatory script not only of normative gayness, queerness, or homosexuality, but also of the racial and national norms that reinforce these sexual subjects" (TA 2). More simply, it is "homonormative nationalism" (TA 38) or "national[ist] homosexuality" (TA 2).

95 In a 2008 appearance at a Wall Street Journal event, Emmanuel said, in his role as White House Chief of Staff: "You never want a serious crisis to go to waste. And what I mean by that is it's an opportunity to do things that you think you could not do before."

96 "The male figure cannot bear the burden of sexual objectification...hence the split between spectacle and narrative supports the man's role as the active one forwarding the story, making things happen" (Mulvey 838).

97 "The foundations of intersecting oppressions become grounded in interdependent concepts of binary thinking, oppositional difference, objectification, and social hierarchy" (PHC 71).

98 In a deregulatory environment, "it is necessary then...not to intervene on the mechanisms of the market economy, but on the conditions of the market" (Foucault BoB 138).

99 The male gaze instrumentalizes femininity in constructing a regulatory order. Jacques Derrida's *Spurs: Nietzsche's Styles*

instrumentalizes femininity in deconstructing the regulatory order of "the metaphysics of presence."

100 As an emergent, dynamic process, compositional processes also resemble agential realist notions of "phenomena."

101 As Shaviro argues, "the editing methods and formal devices of digital video and film belong directly to the computing-and-information technology infrastructure of contemporary neoliberal finance" (PCA 3).

102 Finding pleasure overwhelming sensory experiences does sound, at least at first, a lot like Kant's concept of the (mathematical or dynamical) sublime. In *The Critique of Judgment*, Kant discusses the proper aesthetic response to perceptions of things so large and/or so powerful that they threaten to overwhelm us, like the concept of infinity or the Matterhorn. Sublimity is the affective or aesthetic response to the knowledge that one's *reason* is capable of containing and controlling these perceptions: the experience of thinking infinity may blow my mind, but my capacity for rational thought allows me to condense it into the *concept* of infinity, which I can master. In Kant, the threat comes from the *content* of the perception, and the pleasure from knowledge of one's inherent, authentic self (I *am* a rational being). In resilience discourse, the *perceptual, physiological experience itself* (not the content of the perception) is what's threatening, and pleasure comes from the experience or performance of overcoming (not from the knowledge that one is already capable of mastery). In other words, Kant's theory assumes an already-constituted subject, complete with self-presence, interiority, and authenticity, whereas resilience discourse produces a post-authentic subject sans interiority (or exteriority, insofar as the two are mutually constitutive). See Battersby, Christine. "Stages on Kant's Way: Aesthetics, Morality, and the Gendered Sublime" (1995)

103 She defines this "shock doctrine" as "waiting for a major crisis, then selling off pieces of the state to private players while citizens were still reeling from the shock, then quickly making the "reforms" permanent (Klein 6).

104 As Shaviro argues: "flexibility, versatility and resourcefulness...are forced upon all of us—by the very conditions of neoliberal globalization. If you don't adapt to these conditions, you simply won't survive" (PCA 58)

105 For more on the metonymical function of "intersectionality" to reference women of color and especially black women, see Puar, Jasbir, "I'd Rather Be A Cyborg Than A Goddess" (2011).

106 For more on the perception of Twitter as "wild" and disconnected from meatspace social relations, see Boesel, Whitney Erin. "New Myspace: Bringing (Re)Gentrification Back" (2012).

107 As Mulvey explains, "as soon as the fetishistic representation of the female image threatens to break the spell of illusion, the erotic image on screen appears directly (without mediation) to the spectator" (844).

108 Though both videos include the black female performer's acknowledgement of the male gaze, one important point of contrast between my analysis of "Video Phone" and Shaviro's reading of Grace Jones's "Corporate Cannibal" in PCA is the presence, in the former, and absence, in the latter, of resilience discourse. While Jones, like Beyonce, is "self consciously performative" and "frustrates the desire of the male voyeur, precisely by dropping the pretense of being unaware of it" (Shaviro PCA 57), Jones uses this awareness to negate the male gaze; Beyonce, on the other hand, uses that awareness to sublimate the male gaze into resilience.

109 Or, as Shaviro puts it, "aura does not come from the performer himself, so much as from the *production process* in the course of which he is transfigured" (Shaviro PCA 86n59).

110 To the extent that we live in a "digital and post-cinematic 'media ecology' (Fuller 2005), in which all activity is under surveillance from video cameras and microphones, and in return video screens and speakers, moving images and synthesized sounds, are dispersed pretty much everywhere" (Shaviro, 8), it is not just undesirable, but damn near impossible to avoid some sort of surveillance. As Shaviro suggests, this surveillance network parallels, if not constitutes "reality" itself.

111 At the time the video was made, baggy white Ts and low-slung jeans were common fashion signifiers of urban working-class black masculinity. On "saggy" pants, see Neal, Mark Anthony. "Coming Apart at the Seams" (2010). Neal argues that "The issue of "sagging" or the practice of young African-American men wearing their trousers well below their waists, has functioned like a social panic in some municipalities, where local officials have sought to pass ordinances banning sagging pants, as the style is thought, by some, to be evidence of Black male criminality." Similarly, plain white t-shirts are also associated with black male gang members. For example, Pennsylvaina State Senator Anthony Williams tried to ban white tshirts, and many nightclubs ban white tshirts as a purported security measure

112 Bradley writes, "The (hyper)masculinization of Beyonce's voice in this track signifies her attempt to situate herself not only in hip hop's masculine discourse but *southern*hip hop and its renderings of the south as a similarly masculine space. The sonic intonations of chopped and screwed give Beyonce a pass to dabble in 'ratchet-speak,' sonically alluding to images of "baby hair and dookie braids.' We hear ratchet rather than see it."

113 See, for example, bell hooks's *Outlaw Culture.* (2006)

114 For an example from non-black media, see Kai Wright's

article "Turning Hustlers into Entrepreneurs" in The American Prospect, republished in Utne Reader. The mainstream black media also tends to distinguish these terms along class lines. For example, see Errol I. Mars's profile of Russell Simmons on BlackEntreprenerProfile.com. Hip hop media also tends to use "hustle" to refer to less-than-legal forms of entrepreneurship. See Mark Anthony Jenkin's 2009 profile of Snoop Dogg in *The Source*.

115 On the Robo-Diva figure in Beyonce's work see James, Robin. "Robo-Diva R&B" (2008).

116 "The K Foundation Burn A Million Quid" is a film of a 1995 performance art by The KLF/K Foundation. In this piece, the group burns a million British pounds, the profits of their music act(s) The KLF and the Timelords.

117 For more on Weezy's Afrofuturism on *Tha Carter III*, see Weiner, Jonah. "Lil Wayne and the Afronaut Invasion" in *Slate*. and Chris Norris "Weezy Phone Home" in *Rolling Stone*.

118 The song offers an example of talking back. Here, Beyonce asks to speak to her interlocutor's boss. This question challenges its addressee's assumption that the speaker is Beyonce's equal; Beyonce is the addressee's superior, and ought to speak to or with her equal, the addressee's boss.

119 In this way, Robo-Diva parallels what Steve Shaviro identifies, in *Post Cinematic Affect*, as Grace Jones's existence as pure signal: "Jones embodies capital unbound, precisely because she has become a pure electronic pulse" (PCA 31). Though there are differences between Beyonce's and Jones's performances in their respective videos, my reading of "Diva" is indebted to his work on Jones. The underlying question, here, is why Jones's and Beyonce's works adopt such similar strategies. Why is "embod[ying] capital," in the form of algorithms and electronic signals, a contemporary black feminist strategy? The idea of resilience discourse

helps us answer that question, at least in part. Neoliberalism turns us into either human capital or "the exception," and Beyonce, like Jones, are attempting to embody capital in ways that complicate and/or sabotage its production of blackness as "exception."

120 As Williams and Srnicek put it, "the left must take advantage of every technological and scientific advance made possible by capitalist society. We declare that quantification is not an evil to be eliminated, but a tool to be used in the most effective manner possible. Economic modeling is — simply put — a necessity for making intelligible a complex world. The 2008 financial crisis reveals the risks of blindly accepting mathematical models on faith, yet this is a problem of illegitimate authority not of mathematics itself. The tools to be found in social network analysis, agent-based modeling, big data analytics, and non-equilibrium economic models, are necessary cognitive mediators for understanding complex systems like the modern economy. The accelerationist left must become literate in these technical fields."

121 "We declare that only a Promethean politics of maximal mastery over society and its environment is capable of either dealing with global problems or achieving victory over capital" (Williams & Srnicek).

122 I use the term "goth" to distinguish the late-20th century music genre from "gothic," the 19th century literary genre.

123 See "Lady Gaga Returns with 8 New Songs on 'The Fame Monster'.

124 Vanilla Ice's early 1990s track "Ice Ice Baby" samples the bassline from Queen and David Bowie's single "Under Pressure." However, Vanilla Ice (Robert Van Winkle) has claimed in several instances that the bass loop in his track is in fact *not* the bassline from "Under Pressure" because his bassline has an extra note. See Stillman, Kevin "Word to

your mother". (2006).

125 On 8/13/13 at 6:48pm S. Alexander Reed (@industrial_book) tweeted: "So does @ladygaga's vocal on "Applause" resemble @petermurphyinfo or is it just me? (Hint: It is not just me; they really do.)"

126 Quoted in Hutton, Jen. "Gaga and the Gaze" (2010). My thanks to Doug Tesnow for pointing me to this article.

127 Originally this was in a video of an interview available on YouTube here: https://www.youtube.com/watch?v=xgdubZabTdo . Though it was available in November 2010, by June 2014 the link was dead. To see the link in its original context, see my blog post from Dec 2010 here: http://its-her-factory.blogspot.com/2012/12/rihannas-unapolo-getic-shadow-feminism.html

128 Thus, it shouldn't be surprising that the attributes Halberstam ascribes to gaga feminism sound a lot like the characteristics of neoliberal capitalism. For example, just as neoliberal subjects need to be flexible and adaptable, gaga feminism's "wisdom lies in the unexpected and unantici-pated" (27). It's an aleatory feminism for a deregulated world. This flexible, improvisatory subjectivity that can capitalize on any and every feature of every moment of a "reality [that] is being rescripted, reshot, [and] reimagined" (GF 29) is what allows us to constantly push ourselves to and balance upon the "edge of glory.").

129 For Halberstam's theory of failure, see Halberstam, Judith. *The Queer Art of Failure*. (2011).

130 This section appeared, in preliminary form, in *The New Inquiry*. My thanks to Rob Horning for his fabulous editorial work, which really helped me refine my thinking on several of the points I make in my reading of *Unapologetic*. James, Robin. "Melancholic Damage" (2013).

131 This is perhaps why depression has received such attention

as a clinical psychological problem—depression and its detached disinvestment in the world is a genuine threat to neoliberal structures of subjectivity and sociality.

132 On the racialization of the term "welfare queen" and the stereotype that welfare recipients are mainly black women, see Sparks, Halloway. "Teens, Queens, and Model Mothers: Race, Gender, and the Discourse of Welfare Reform" (2003). See also Chapter 4 of Patricial Hill-Collins's "Black Feminist Thought," cited earlier in Chapter 3 of this book. For an example of such an ecard, see this one, by Jackie 1058546.

133 On their website, they describe their mission as: "The Icarus Project envisions a new culture and language that resonates with our actual experiences of 'mental illness' rather than trying to fit our lives into a conventional framework...Participation in The Icarus Project helps us overcome alienation and tap into the true potential that lies between brilliance and madness. The Icarus Project is a collaborative, participatory adventure fueled by inspiration and mutual aid. We bring the Icarus vision to reality through an Icarus national staff collective and a grassroots network of autonomous local support groups and Campus Icarus groups across the US and beyond."

134 With these investments, we must be silent partners. We invest the resources, the human, social, and capital people need, but we don't run the business. We leave the day-to-day, on the ground operations to the people who know what they're doing. Or, as Beauvoir puts it, "All that an external action can propose is to put the oppressed in the presence of his freedom: then he will decide positively and freely" (87). So, while these projects should be directed by the people they serve, they need to be funded by those of us whom MRWaSP otherwise vests with the resources to do so.

135 See Federicia, Silvia, "The reproduction of labor-power in the global economy, Marxist Theory and the unfinished

feminist revolution". (2010). See also England, Paula. "Emerging Theories of Care Work". (2005).

136 Moreover, I think the "notion that there is a neutral external vantage point from which one can begin the work of critical assessment" (135) is, as Raley puts it, a "fantasy." We are deeply, deeply embedded in neoliberal practices, ideologies, and material conditions. It would be pure bad faith for me—or, well, for anyone in the Global North—to claim that I'm somehow outside MRWaSP, an objective, "neutral" observer of white supremacist patriarchy.

137 It's a spurious cycle because there's no underlying linearity, as in the diurnal cycle from daylight to dark, which marks the progress from one day to the next, or the regress back in time to last night or the day before yesterday. Time is intensificatory, not linearly progressive. The lyrics illustrate this. They cap off a line about partying through the night until the sun rises with an extra "alright." Adding the "alright" to "sunlight," this line of lyrics tops off an already rhyming couplet with a bonus rhyme. It compounds the rhyme. And this compounding shifts the meaning of the line—it performs the new meaning that it also functionally executes. The lyrics treat "night" and "sunlight" not as a pair of alternating concepts (that can be used to mark time), but as a trio of rhyming sounds. The meaning of "night, "sunlight," and "alright" isn't their verbal content, but their poetic form (i.e., the rhyme). The presence of each word intensfies the affective and sonic force of all three members of the trio. By compounding the rhyme the lyrics perform the shift from linear to intensificatory time. In other words, time isn't a line, it's Zeno's paradox; not pro- or re-gress, but involution.

138 This post-maximalist style of intensification is also evident in fashion. Normcore, a fashion trend that emerged in 2014, can be understood as a response to the normalization and mainstreaming of transgression; when everyone's edgy, the

most avant-guard thing to do is to conform, e.g., to middle-American, middle-market "mom" or "dad" style. It is one of several recent fashion trends, such as pastel goth and soft grunge, that intensify edginess by pushing hardcore aesthetics past the point of diminishing returns, transforming it into something soft and smooth. (The term "normcore" is credited to the art collective K-Hole; it appears in their "Youth Mode" web publication)

139 See Cottom, Tressie McMillan. "When Your (Brown) Body Is A (White) Wonderland". (2013).

140 Britney Cooper explains, "Ratchet acts are meant to be so over-the-top and outrageous that they catch your attention and exceed the bounds of acceptable saying." (Cooper)

141 In an interview with *Vibe Vixen*, Rock City member Timothy Thomas says: "We originally wrote ["We Can't Stop"] for Rihanna and we wounded up giving it to Miley," Timothy reveals. "We felt like this could be somebody's first single. We knew it wasn't going to be Rihanna's because at the time she already had "Diamonds." We didn't know who to give it to and Mike WILL was like 'I'm in with Miley. I want to play it for her because I think this will be dope for her.' We said okay let's do.:"

Bibliography

1991: The Year Punk Broke. Prod. We Got Power Productions and Sonic Life. Dir. Dave Markey. Perf. Sonic Youth, Nirvana, Dinosaur Jr, Babes in Toyland, Gumball, The Ramones. Tara Films, 1993. DVD.

"About Us." *The Icarus Project.* Web. 06 June 2014.

Adorno, Theodor W. "On Popular Music." *Essays on Music.* Ed. Richard D. Leppert. Trans. Susan H. Gillespie. Berkeley, CA: U of California, 2002. 437-69. Print.

Agamben, Giorgio. *Homo Sacer: Sovereign Power and Bare Life.* Trans. Daniel Heller-Roazen. Stanford, CA: Stanford UP, 1998. Print.

Ahmed, Sara. *The Promise of Happiness.* Durham: Duke UP, 2010. Print.

Alcoff, Linda. *Visible Identities: Race, Gender, and the Self.* New York: Oxford UP, 2005. Print.

Appiah, Kwame Anthony. "Is the Post- in Postmodernism the Post- in Postcolonial?" *Critical Inquiry* 17.2 (1991): 336-57. Web.

Atari Teenage Riot. *1995.* Atari Teenage Riot. Alec Empire and David Harrow, 1995. CD.

Atari Teenage Riot. "1995." *Discogs.* Web. 30 Oct. 2012.

Barrow, Daneil. "Girls Go Wild in the Social Factory: Spring Breakers, Sound, Neoliberalism." Politics of Contemporary Music. United Kingdom, University of Warwick. 26 Apr. 2014. Web. 26 June 2014.

Barrow, Daniel. "A Plague Of Soars - Warps In The Fabric Of Pop." *The Quietus.* 13 Apr. 2013. Web. 17 June 2014.

Battersby, Christine. "Stages on Kant's Way: Aesthetics, Morality, and the Gendered Sublime." *Feminism and Tradition in Aesthetics.* Ed. Peggy Zeglin. Brand and Carolyn Korsmeyer. University Park, PA: Pennsylvania State UP, 1995. 88-114. Print.

Beauvoir, Simone De. *The Ethics of Ambiguity.* Trans. Bernard

Frechtman. Secaucus, NJ: Citadel, 1997. Print.

Beyonce, and Lady Gaga. *Video Phone*. Beyonce. Columbia Records, 2009. CD.

Beyonce. "Video Phone Ft. Lady Gaga." *YouTube*. YouTube, 17 Nov. 2009. Web. 30 June 2014.

Biletzki, Anat. "Ludwig Wittgenstein." *Stanford Encyclopedia of Philosophy*. Stanford University, 08 Nov. 2002. Web. 23 Jan. 2013.

Boesel, Whitney Erin. "New Myspace: Bringing (Re)Gentrification Back." *Cyborgology*. 27 Sept. 2012. Web. 30 June 2014.

Bogost, Ian. "Hyperemployment, or the Exhausting Work of the Technology User." *The Atlantic*. Atlantic Media Company, 08 Nov. 2013. Web. 13 June 2014.

Bogue, Ronald. *Deleuze's Wake: Tributes and Tributaries*. Albany: State U of New York, 2004. Print.

Boutang, Yann Moulier. *Cognitive Capitalism*. Cambridge, UK: Polity, 2011. Print.

Bradley, Regina. "I Been On." Web log post. *Red Clay Scholar*. Mar. 2013. Web. 24 Mar. 2014.

Briehan, Tom. "Atari Teenage Riot: Is This Hyperreal?" *Pitchfork*. 7 July 2011. Web.

Browne, David. "Trilling Songbirds Clip Their Wings." *The New York Times*. The New York Times, 24 Dec. 2010. Web. 14 Jan. 2013.

Calvin Harris. *Sweet Nothing*. Calvin Harris, 2012. MP3.

Caramanica, Jon. "Rihanna, Icy Hot and Steely-Strong." *The New York Times*. The New York Times, 20 Nov. 2012. Web. 01 July 2014.

Carter, Sean, and Alicia Keys. "Empire State of Mind." *YouTube*. 30 Oct. 2009. Web. 14 Jan. 2013.

Clark, Martin. "Grime / Dubstep." *Pitchfork*. Pitchfork, 23 May 2007. Web.

Clarkson, Kelly. *Since U Been Gone*. Kelly Clarkson. RCA, 2004.

CD.

Clarkson, Kelly. *Stronger*. Kelly Clarkson. RCA, 2011. CD.

Collins, Patricia Hill. *Black Feminist Thought: Knowledge, Consciousness, and the Politics of Empowerment*. New York: Routledge, 2008. Print.

Cooper, Britney. "(Un)Clutching My Mother's Pearls, or Ratchetness and the Residue of Respectability." *The Crunk Feminist Collective*. 31 Dec. 2012. Web. 16 June 2014.

Cottom, Tressie McMillan. "The Logic of Stupid Poor People." *Tressiemc*. 29 Oct. 2013. Web. 01 July 2014.

Cottom, Tressie McMillan. "When Your (Brown) Body Is a (White) Wonderland." *Tressiemc*. 27 Aug. 2013. Web. 16 June 2014.

Cruz, Taio. *Hangover*. Taio Cruz. Island Records, 2011. CD.

Dean, Jodi. "Drive as the Structure of Biopolitics: Economy, Sovereignty, and Capture." *Krisis* 2 (2010): 2-15. Web.

Deleuze, Gilles, and Félix Guattari. *A Thousand Plateaus: Capitalism and Schizophrenia*. Trans. Brian Massumi. Minneapolis: U of Minnesota, 1987. Print.

Deleuze, Gilles. "Postscript on the Societies of Control." *October* 59.Winter (1992): 3-7. Web.

Depeche Mode. *Construction Time Again*. Depeche Mode. Mute, 1983. Vinyl recording.

Depeche Mode. *Some Great Reward*. Depeche Mode. Mute, 1984. Vinyl recording.

Depeche Mode. *Strangelove*. Depeche Mode. Mute, 1987. Vinyl recording.

Derrida, Jacques. *Spurs: Nietzsche's Styles*. Trans. Barbara Harlow. Chicago: U of Chicago, 1981. Print.

Desouevre, Voyou. "OMG Is like Rihanna like OK like." Web log post. *Dangerous & Lazy*. 9 Dec. 2012. Web. 26 Dec. 2012.

Diamonds. Dir. Anthony Mandler. Perf. Rihanna. 2012. Web.

Dilts, Andrew. "From Entrepreneur of the Self to Care of the Self"." *Foucault Studies* 12 (2011): 130-46. Web.

Du Pleiss, Michael. "Goth Damage and Melancholia." *Goth: Undead Subculture.* Ed. Lauren M. E. Goodlad and Michael Bibby. Durham: Duke UP, 2007. 155-70. Print.

Dybwad, Barb. "Lady Gaga's "Bad Romance" Takes Over #1 Most Viewed Video on YouTube." *Mashable.* 14 Apr. 2010. Web. 30 June 2014.

Edelman, Lee. *No Future: Queer Theory and the Death Drive.* Durham: Duke UP, 2004. Print.

Emanuel, Rahm. "Rahm Emanuel on the Opportunities of Crisis." *YouTube.* Wall Street Journal, 19 Nov. 2008. Web. 30 June 2014.

England, Paula. "Emerging Theories of Care Work." *Annual Review of Sociology* 31.1 (2005): 381-99. Web.

Fanon, Frantz. *Black Skin, White Masks.* Trans. Richard Philcox. Grove, 2008. Print.

Federicia, Silvia. "The Reproduction of Labor-power in the Global Economy, Marxist Theory and the Unfinished Feminist Revolution." *Caring Labor an Archive.* 25 Oct. 2010. Web. 09 June 2014.

Fisher, Mark. "Exiting the Vampire Castle." *The North Star.* 22 Nov. 2013. Web. 30 June 2014.

Flo Rida. "I Cry." *YouTube.* WILD ONES - WMG, 28 Sept. 2012. Web. 03 Aug. 2014.

Forte, Allen, and Steven E. Gilbert. *Introduction to Schenkerian Analysis.* New York: Norton, 1982. Print.

Foucault, Michel. *The Birth of Biopolitics Lectures at the College De France, 1978-1979.* Trans. Graham Burchell. New York: Palgrave Macmillan, 2008. Print.

Foucault, Michel. *The History of Sexuality.* Trans. Robert Hurley. Vol. 1. London: Penguin, 1990. Print.

Foucault, Michel. *Society Must Be Defended: Lectures at the Collège De France, 1975-76.* Trans. David Macey. New York: Picador, 2003. Print.

Fraser, Nancy. "From Discipline to Flexibilization? Rereading

Foucault in the Shadow of Globalization." *Constellations* 10.2 (2003): 160-71. Web.

Freud, Sigmund. "Mourning and Melancholia." *The Standard Edition of the Complete Psychological Works of Sigmund Freud.* Ed. James Strachey. Vol. 14. London: Hogarth, 2007. 243-58. Print.

Gabbatt, Adam. "Occupy Wall Street Activists Buy $15m of Americans' Personal Debt." *Theguardian.com.* Guardian News and Media, 12 Nov. 2013. Web. 09 June 2014.

Gaffney, A.W. "The Neoliberal Turn in American Health Care." *Jacobin.* 15 Apr. 2014. Web. 23 June 2014.

Gangnam Style. Dir. Cho Soo-hyun. Perf. Psy. *YouTube.* YG Entertainment Inc., 15 July 2012. Web. 25 June 2014.

Ganz, Caryn. "Rihanna, 'Unapologetic' (Def Jam)." *SPIN.* 28 Nov. 2012. Web. 01 July 2014.

Godfrey, Sarah. "Why Have so Many D.C. Area Nightclubs Banned White T-shirts?" *TBD.* 11 Oct. 2010. Web. 30 June 2014.

Goldberg, Michelle. "Feminism's Toxic Twitter Wars." *The Nation.* The Nation, 29 Jan. 2014. Web. 30 June 2014.

Goodwin, Andrew. "Sample and Hold." Ed. Andrew Goodwin. *On Record: Rock, Pop, and the Written Word.* Ed. Simon Frith. London: Routledge, 1990. Print.

Gracie, Bianca. "Miley Cyrus' "We Can't Stop": Review Revue." *Idolator.* 3 June 2013. Web. 13 June 2014.

Greenburg, Zack O'Malley. *Empire State of Mind: How Jay-Z Went from Street Corner to Corner Office.* New York: Portfolio/Penguin, 2011. Print.

Guetta, David. *Play Hard.* David Guetta Feat. Ne-Yo & Akon. Parlophone, 2013. CD.

Hadfield, James. "Atari Teenage Riot: The Interview." *Time Out Tokyo.* 14 Nov. 2011. Web. 30 June 2014.

Halberstam, Judith. *Gaga Feminism: Sex, Gender, and the End of Normal.* Boston: Beacon, 2012. Print.

Halberstam, Judith. *In a Queer Time and Place: Transgender Bodies, Subcultural Lives.* New York: New York UP, 2005. Print.

Halberstam, Judith. *The Queer Art of Failure*. Durham: Duke UP, 2011. Print.

Halberstam, Judith. "What's That Smell?" *In a Queer Time and Place: Transgender Bodies, Subcultural Lives*. New York: New York UP, 2005. Print.

Hanson, Todd. "Atari Teenage Riot." *The A.V. Club*. 23 July 1997. Web. 03 Aug. 2014.

Harris, Calvin, and Example. *We'll Be Coming Back*. Calvin Harris. Columbia Records, 2012. MP3.

Harris, Calvin, and Example. "We'll Be Coming Back (Official Video) (Ultra Music)." *YouTube*. Ultra Music, 20 July 2012. Web. 02 Jan. 2013.

Harvey, David. "Neoliberalism as Creative Destruction." *The ANNALS of the American Academy of Political and Social Science* 610.1 (2007): 21-44. Web.

Hooks, Bell. *Outlaw Culture: Resisting Representations*. New York: Routledge, 2006. Print.

Hopper, Jessica. "Rihanna: Unapologetic." *Pitchfork*. 26 Nov. 2012. Web. 01 July 2014.

Horkheimer, Max, and Theodor W. Adorno. *Dialectic of Enlightenment*. Trans. Edmund Jephcott. Stanford: Stanford UP, 2002. Print.

Horning, Rob. "Google Alert for the Soul." *The New Inquiry*. 12 Apr. 2013. Web. 30 June 2014.

Horning, Rob. "Precarity and "affective Resistance"." *The New Inquiry*. 14 Feb. 2012. Web. 15 July 2013.

Hutton, Jen. "Gaga and the Gaze." *Chicago Art Magazine*. 02 July 2010. Web. 30 June 2014.

Jackie 1058546. *Mommy Is Living the American Dream. No Job, Get My Nails Done, Hair Done, Go out to Eat, Buy New Clothes, & Act Fabulous. Thank You Welfare System!* Digital image. *Someecards*. Web. 02 June 2014.

Jackson, Michael. *Smooth Criminal*. Michael Jackson. Warner Brothers, 1988. Vinyl recording.

James, Robin. "From "No Future" to "Delete Yourself (You Have No Chance to Win)": Death, Queerness, and the Sound of Neoliberalism." *Journal of Popular Music Studies* 25.4 (2013): 504-36. Web.

James, Robin. "Loving the Alien." *The New Inquiry*. 22 Oct. 2012. Web. 17 June 2014.

James, Robin. "Melancholic Damage." *The New Inquiry*. 30 May 2013. Web. 30 June 2014.

James, Robin. "Neoliberal Noise: Attali, Foucault, and the Biopolitics of Uncool." *Culture Theory and Critique* 55.2 (2014): 138-58. Web.

James, Robin. "Rihanna's Unapologetic Shadow Feminism, Part 2." Web log post. *It's Her Factory*. 23 Dec. 2012. Web.

James, Robin. ""Robo-Diva R&B": Aesthetics, Politics, and Black Female Robots in Contemporary Popular Music." *Journal of Popular Music Studies* 20.4 (2008): 402-23. Web.

Jancius, Angela. "Unemployment, Deindustrialization, and 'community Economy' in Eastern Germany." *Ethnos* 71.2 (2006): 213-32. Web.

Jenkins, Mark Anthony. "The Hustle." *Source* Winter 2010: 64-69. Print.

Jhally, Sut. "Bell Hooks: Cultural Criticism & Transformation." Media Education Foundaton, 1997. Web. 17 June 2014.

Jolie, Angelina. "My Medical Choice." *The New York Times*. The New York Times, 13 May 2013. Web. 30 June 2014.

Jones, Lisa. *Bulletproof Diva*. Norwell, MA: Anchor, 1997. Print.

Jones, Mitch. "The Financialization of Nature; Or, Neoliberal Environmentalism at Work." *Democratic Socialists of America*. 21 Apr. 2013. Web. 23 June 2014.

The K Foundation Burn A Million Quid. Dir. Gimpo. Perf. The K Foundation. K Foundation Inc., 1995. Videocassette.

Keast, Darren. "Dawn of Dubstep." *SF Weekly*. 15 Nov. 2006. Web. 25 June 2014.

Ke$ha. *Tik Tok*. Ke$ha. Conway Recordings, 2009. CD.

K-Hole. "YOUTH MODE: A Report on Freedom." *K-HOLE*. Web. 13 June 2014.

Klein, Naomi. *Shock Doctrine: The Rise of Disaster Capitalism.* London: Picador, 2008. Print.

Lady Gaga, and Beyonce. *Telephone.* Lady Gaga Feat. Beyonce. Interscope, 2009. CD.

Lady Gaga. *Dance in the Dark.* Lady Gaga. Interscope, 2009. CD.

Lady Gaga. *Monster.* Lady Gaga. Interscope, 2009. CD.

Lady Gaga. *Paparazzi.* Lady Gaga. Interscope, 2009. CD.

Lady Gaga. "Paparazzi." *YouTube.* 25 Nov. 2009. Web. 15 Nov. 2010.

"Lady Gaga Returns With 8 New Songs on 'The Fame Monster'" *PRNewswire.* Web. 28 Nov. 2010.

Lady Gaga. "Telephone Ft. Beyonce." *YouTube.* 11 Mar. 2011. Web. 15 Nov. 2010.

Latour, Bruno. "Steps Toward The Writing Of A Compositionist Manifesto." *New Literary History* 41 (2010): 471-90. Web.

Lewis, Heidi R. "Exhuming the Ratchet Before It's Buried." *The Feminist Wire.* 7 Jan. 2013. Web. 16 June 2014.

Longinger, H. "Signal and Noise." *Fundamentals of Statistics.* Web. 18 June 2014.

Ludacris, Usher, and David Guetta. "Rest Of My Life." *YouTube.* The Island Def Jam Music Group, 11 Nov. 2012. Web. 14 Jan. 2013.

Macpherson, Alex. "Rihanna Unapologetic." *FACT Magazine.* 23 Nov. 2012. Web. 01 July 2014.

Manovich, Lev. *The Language of New Media.* Cambridge, MA: MIT, 2001. Print.

Marcus, Lilit. "Pennsylvania State Senator Trying to Ban White T-Shirts." *The Gloss.* 29 June 2010. Web. 30 June 2014.

Marcuse, Herbert. *Eros & Civilization.* Beacon, 1974. Print.

Mars, Errol I. "Russell Simmons." *Black Entrepreneur Profile.* Web. 30 June 2014.

Martin, Prada Juan. "Economies of Affectivity." *Multitudes.* Web.

26 June 2014.

Marx, Karl, and Friedrich Engels. "Capital Volume 1." *The Marx-Engels Reader*. Ed. Robert Tucker. New York: W. W. Norton, 1978. Print.

Matusavage, Philip. "Rihanna - Unapologetic." *MusicOMH*. 19 Nov. 2012. Web. 01 July 2014.

McClary, Susan. *Feminine Endings: Music, Gender, and Sexuality*. Minneapolis: U of Minnesota, 1991. Print.

McClary, Susan. "What Was Tonality?" *Conventional Wisdom*. Berkeley: U of California, 2001. 63-108. Print.

Mulvey, Laura. "Visual Pleasure and Narrative Cinema." *Film Theory and Criticism: Introductory Readings*. Comp. Leo Braudy and Marshall Cohen. New York: Oxford UP, 1999. 833-44. Print.

Muñoz, José Esteban. *Cruising Utopia: The Then and There of Queer Futurity*. New York: New York UP, 2009. Print.

Neal, Mark Anthony. "Coming Apart at the Seams: Black Masculinity and the Performance of Obama-Era Respectability." Web log post. *New Black Man*. 07 Apr. 2010. Web. 30 June 2014.

Nealon, Jeffrey T. "Empire of the Intensities: A Random Walk Down Las Vegas Boulevard." *Parallax* 8.1 (2002): 78-91. Web.

Neocleous, Mark. "Resisting Resilience." *Radical Philosophy*. Mar.-Apr. 2013. Web. 17 June 2014.

"NEW SURVEY: Should Welfare Recipients Have Limitations on Where They Can Spend the Money?" *TPNN*. 22 Mar. 2014. Web. 01 July 2014.

Ne-Yo. *Miss Independent*. Ne-Yo. Def Jam, 2008. CD.

Niven, Alex. "Welcome To The New Age: 2014 & The New Utopian Pop." *The Quietus*. 14 Jan. 2014. Web. 11 June 2014.

Norris, Chris. "Weezy Phone Home: Is Lil Wayne Hip-Hop's Alien or Simply the Greatest?" *Rolling Stone*. 03 Feb. 2010. Web. 26 Mar. 2014.

North, Anna. "The Rewards Of Being White, Male And A Rule

Breaker." *BuzzFeed*. 08 Mar. 2013. Web. 01 July 2014.

Nyong'o, Tavia. "Do You Want Queer Theory (or Do You Want the Truth)? Intersections of Punk and Queer in the 1970s." *Radical History Review* 2008.100 (2008): 103-19. Web.

O'Connell, Sharon. "Dubstep." *Time Out London*. 04 Oct. 2006. Web. 25 June 2014.

Park, Suey, and David J. Leonard. "In Defense of Twitter Feminism." *Model View Culture*. 03 Feb. 2014. Web. 04 Aug. 2014.

Pennington, April. "Urban Legends." *Entrepreneur*. 1 May 2014. Web. 30 June 2014.

Platon, Adelle. "Vixen Exclusive: Songwriting Duo Rock City Say Miley Cyrus' 'We Can't Stop' Was Meant For Rihanna." *Vibe Vixen*. 08 June 2013. Web. 13 June 2014.

Pour It Up. Perf. Rihanna. Island Def Jam, 2013. Web.

Psy. *Gangnam Style*. Psy. Schoolboy/Universal Republic Records, 2012. MP3.

Puar, Jasbir. "'I Would Rather Be a Cyborg than a Goddess' Intersectionality, Assemblage, and Affective Politics." *European Institute for Progressive Cultural Policies* (2011). Web. 30 June 2014.

Puar, Jasbir K. *Terrorist Assemblages: Homonationalism in Queer times*. Durham: Duke UP, 2007. Print.

Public Enenmy. *Bring the Noise*. Public Enemy. Def Jam/Columbia, 1988. CD.

Raley, Rita. "Dataveillance and Counterveillance." *"Raw Data" Is an Oxymoron*. Ed. Lisa Gitelman. Cambridge, MA: MIT, 2013. 121-46. Print.

Randall, Robert. "Rihanna's 'Unapologetic' Shines Light on past Drama." *Los Angeles Times*. Los Angeles Times, 16 Nov. 2012. Web. 01 July 2014.

Read, Jason. "A Genealogy of Homo Oeconomicus: Neoliberalism and the Production of Subjectivity." *Foucault Studies* 6 (2009): 25-36. Print.

"Redshirt (character)." *Wikipedia*. Wikimedia Foundation, 28 July 2014. Web.

Reed, S. Alexander. *Assimilate: A Critical History of Industrial Music*. Oxford UP, 2013. Print.

Reed, S. Alexander (@Industrial_Book). "So does @ladygaga's vocal on "Applause" resemble @petermurphyinfo or is it just me? (Hint: It is not just me; they really do.)" 13 August 2013, Tweet.

Reich, Steve. "Music as a Gradual Process." *Writings on Music, 1965-2000*. Ed. Paul Hillier. Oxford: Oxford UP, 2002. 34-35. Print.

Rihanna. *Where Have You Been All My Life*. Rihanna. Def Jam, 2011. CD.

Roberts, Randall. "First Take: Taylor Swift Accents New Single with Hint of Dubstep." *Los Angeles Times*. Los Angeles Times, 09 Oct. 2012. Web. 02 Jan. 2013.

Robinson, Zandria. "What's More Special Than Gold?" *New South Negress*. Web. 30 June 2014.

"Rolling Jubilee." *Rolling Jubilee*. Web. 09 June 2014.

Rose, Tricia. *Black Noise: Rap Music and Black Culture in Contemporary America*. Hanover, NH: U of New England, 1994. Print.

Rouvais-Nicolis, Catherine, and Nicolis Gregoire. "Stochastic Resonance." *Scholarpedia*. 2007. Web. 18 June 2014.

Sandberg, Sheryl. *Lean In: Women, Work, and the Will to Lead*. Knopf, 2013. Print.

Sartre, Jean-Paul. *Being and Nothingness*. Trans. Hazel E. Barnes. New York: Washington Square, 1993. Print.

Sex Pistols. *God save the Queen*. The Sex Pistols. Virgin Records, 1977. CD.

The Sex Pistols. *Johnny B. Goode/Roadrunner*. The Sex Pistols. Virgin Records, 1979. Vinyl recording.

Sexton, Jared. *Amalgamation Schemes: Antiblackness and the Critique of Multiracialism*. Minneapolis: U of Minnesota, 2008. Print.

Shaviro, Steven. "Accelerationist Aesthetics: Necessary Inefficiency in Times of Real Subsumption." *E-flux*. June 2013. Web. 25 June 2014.

Shaviro, Steven. *Post-Cinematic Affect*. Winchester, UK: Zero, 2010. Print.

Shepard, Susan Elizabeth, Aeysha A. Siddiqi, and Sarah Nicole Prickett. "Rihanna On My Mind: Chatting About the "Pour It Up" Video." *The Hairpin*. 22 Mar. 2014. Web. 01 July 2014.

Sheth, Falguni A. *Toward a Political Philosophy of Race*. Albany: SUNY, 2009. Print.

Sheth, Falguni. "The Irony of MLK Day 2013: A Renewed Invitation into White Supremacy." *Translation Exercises*. 21 Jan. 2013. Web. 20 June 2014.

Silver, Nate. *The Signal and the Noise: Why so Many Predictions Fail—but Some Don't*. New York: Penguin, 2012. Print.

Skrillex, and Nero, orchs. By Monsta. *Monsta "Holdin' On" Remix*. Skrillex and Nero. OWSLA/Polydor, 2012. MP3.

Skrillex, and Sirah. "Bangarang." *YouTube*. Warner Music Group, 16 Feb. 2012. Web. 25 June 2014.

Skrillex. *Bangerang*. Skrillex. Atlantic Records, 2012. MP3.

Skrillex. *First of the Year*. Skrillex. Big Beat, 2011. MP3.

Skrillex. *Scary Monsters and Nice Sprites*. Skrillex. Rec. 22 Oct. 2010. Big Beat/Mou5trap, 2010. CD.

The Slits. *So Tough*. The Slits. Island Records, 1979. Vinyl recording.

Snead, James A. "On Repetition in Black Culture." *Black American Literature Forum* Black Textual Strategies, Volume 1: Theory 15.4, (1981): 146-54. Web.

Spade, Dean, and Craig Willse. "Marriage Will Never Set Us Free." *Organizing Upgrade*. Organizing Upgrade, 06 Sept. 2013. Web. 25 June 2014.

Sparks, Halloway. "Teens, Queens, and Model Mothers: Race, Gender, and the Discourse of Welfare Reform." *Race and the Politics of Welfare Reform*. Ed. Sanford Schram, Joe Soss, and

Richard C. Fording. Ann Arbor: U of Michigan, 2003. 171-95. Print.

Spence, Lester K. *Stare in the Darkness: The Limits of Hip-hop and Black Politics*. Minneapolis: U of Minnesota, 2011. Print.

Spivak, Gayatri Chakravorty. *A Critique of Postcolonial Reason: Toward a History of the Vanishing Present*. Cambridge, MA: Harvard UP, 1999. Print.

Star Wars Episode IV: A New Hope. Dir. George Lucas. 20th Century Fox, 1977.

Stillman, Kevin. "Word to Your Mother." *Iowa State Daily*. 27 Feb. 2006. Web.

Stoler, Ann Laura. *Race and the Education of Desire: Foucault's History of Sexuality and the Colonial Order of Things*. Durham: Duke UP, 1995. Print.

Swift, Taylor. *I Knew You Were Trouble*. Taylor Swift. Big Machine, 2012. CD.

Swift, Taylor. "I Knew You Were Trouble." *YouTube*. Vevo, 14 Dec. 2012. Web. 2 Jan. 2013.

Swift, Taylor. *We Are Never Ever Getting Back Together*. Taylor Swift. Big Machine, 2012. CD.

Taylor, Chris. "And Then Theory Wept: Precarity Talk and Miley's Sadness." *Of C.L.R. James*. 15 Jan. 2014. Web. 13 June 2014.

Thanatos. *Bodily Dismemberment*. Thanatos. Shark Records, 1990. Vinyl recording.

Tiqqun. *Preliminary Materials for a Theory of the Young-Girl*. Trans. Ariana Reines. Cambridge, MA: MIT, 2012. Print.

"TODAY's 'Love Your Selfie' Series Explores Our Body Image Obsessions." *TODAY*. 20 Feb. 2014. Web. 01 July 2014.

Walters, Barry. "The Greatest Key Change of All – Popdust." *Popdust*. 13 Feb. 2012. Web. 14 Jan. 2013.

Webbie. *Independent*. Webbie. Trill/Asylum/Atlantic Records, 2008. CD.

Weheliye, Alexander G. *Phonographies: Grooves in Sonic Afro-modernity*. Durham: Duke UP, 2005. Print.

Weiner, Jonah. "Lil Wayne, Tha Carter III, and the Afronaut Invasion." *Slate*. 20 June 2008. Web. 18 Nov. 2012.

Wells, A. S., J. Slayton, and J. Scott. "Defining Democracy in the Neoliberal Age: Charter School Reform and Educational Consumption." *American Educational Research Journal* 39.2 (2002): 337-61. Web.

Whitefield-Madrano, Autumn. "We Shall Overcome: The Problem With the Body-Love Therapeutic Narrative." *The Beheld - Beauty, and What It Means*. 5 Sept. 2012. Web. 30 June 2014.

Williams, Alex, and Nick Srnicek. "#ACCELERATE MANIFESTO for an Accelerationist Politics." *Critical Legal Thinking* (2013). 14 May 2013. Web. 20 June 2014.

Willis, Ellen. *Beginning to See the Light*. Minneapolis: U of Minnesota, 2012. Print.

Winnubst, Shannon. "The Queer Thing about Neoliberal Pleasure: A Foucauldian Warning." *Foucault Studies* 14 (2012): 79-97. Web. 14 June 2014.

Wittgenstein, Ludwig. Philosophical Investigations. Trans. G.E.M. Anscombe. Pearson. 1973. Print.

Wiz Khalifa. *Work Hard, Play Hard*. Wiz Khalifa. Atlantic/Rostrum, 2012. CD.

Wright, Kai. "Turning Hustlers into Entrepreneurs." *Utne*. May-June 2010. Web. 30 June 2014.

Young, Iris Marion. *On Female Body Experience: "Throwing like a Girl" and Other Essays*. New York: Oxford UP, 2005. Print.

Contemporary culture has eliminated both the concept of the public and the figure of the intellectual. Former public spaces – both physical and cultural – are now either derelict or colonized by advertising. A cretinous anti-intellectualism presides, cheerled by expensively educated hacks in the pay of multinational corporations who reassure their bored readers that there is no need to rouse themselves from their interpassive stupor. The informal censorship internalized and propagated by the cultural workers of late capitalism generates a banal conformity that the propaganda chiefs of Stalinism could only ever have dreamt of imposing. Zer0 Books knows that another kind of discourse – intellectual without being academic, popular without being populist – is not only possible: it is already flourishing, in the regions beyond the striplit malls of so-called mass media and the neurotically bureaucratic halls of the academy. Zer0 is committed to the idea of publishing as a making public of the intellectual. It is convinced that in the unthinking, blandly consensual culture in which we live, critical and engaged theoretical reflection is more important than ever before.